The Which? Guide to Managing Stress

About the author

Mark Greener has worked as a pharmacologist in the fields of research and academia, and is now a medical journalist. Mark has contributed to both consumer and specialist publications, including *Health Which?*. He has written widely on the subjects of drugs, nutrition, health and the pharmaceutical industry for medical, nursing and consumer magazines, and is the health editor for *Pharmaceutical Times* and consultant editor on *Pharmaceutical Visions*. For Which? Books he has written *Which? Way to Manage Your Time – and Your Life* and *The Which? Guide to Managing Asthma*.

Acknowledgements

The author and publisher would like to thank the following for their helpful comments on the manuscript: Dr Kathryn Abel, Dr Harry Brown and Dr Judy Shakespeare.

The Which? Guide to Managing Stress

Mark Greener

CONSUMERS' ASSOCIATION

Which? Books are commissioned and researched by Consumers'
Association and published by Which? Ltd, 2 Marylebone Road,
London NW1 4DF
Email address: books@which.net

Distributed by The Penguin Group:
Penguin Books Ltd, 80 Strand, London WC2R 0RL

First edition August 1996
Second edition April 2002

Copyright © 1996, 2002 Which? Ltd

British Library Cataloguing in Publication Data
A catalogue record for this book is available from the British Library

ISBN 0 85202 926 8

For a full list of Which? books, please call 0800 252100, access
our website at www.which.net, or write to Which? Books,
PO Box 44, Hertford SG14 1SH.

Editorial and production: Joanna Bregosz, Mary Sunderland
Original cover concept by Sarah Harmer

Typeset by Saxon Graphics Ltd, Derby
Printed and bound in England by Clays Ltd, Bungay, Suffolk

Contents

Introduction

Stress is inescapable. Rich or poor, man or woman, young or old, everyone suffers from it to some extent. Indeed, stress per se isn't all bad. Without a certain degree of stress you wouldn't bother getting out of bed in the morning. Dealing successfully with a difficult, stressful problem leaves you with a sense of achievement. However, excessive stress can affect people in very different ways. As this guide explains, the factors that trigger our stress-related symptoms vary wildly. Some of us stay cheerful in the face of adversity that leaves others mentally or physically broken. Others suffer disproportionately from seemingly trivial life events. Excessive stress leaves some people cross and tense. In others, it has a more serious legacy, causing or worsening numerous physical illnesses, including irritable bowel syndrome, heart disease and some cancers.

Certainly, excessive stress can have serious consequences. For example, in *The Hound of the Baskervilles*, Sherlock Holmes is called in following the death of Lord Baskerville from a heart attack induced by stress. And this 'Baskerville effect' seems to be a clinical reality. A study published in the Netherlands in 2000 found that the risk of death due to coronary heart disease and stroke rose by more than 50 per cent on the day the national football team was eliminated from the 1996 European championship. The authors estimated that about 14 'extra' men died from cardiovascular disease on the day of the match. Late in 2002, researchers from Birmingham and Bristol confirmed the link between stress associated with important sporting events and heart disease, finding that the risk of being admitted to hospital with a heart attack in men aged 15 to 64 rose by 25 per cent on 30 June 1998, when England lost to Argentina in a penalty shoot-out, and over the next two days.

But it isn't only the body that suffers the ravages of excessive stress. In susceptible people, excessive stress can trigger psychological symptoms such as depression, clinical anxiety and insomnia. These conditions need treating promptly before they begin to devastate the sufferer's ability to lead a normal life. With the appropriate therapy, most patients with psychological problems can recover and regain a sense of optimism and tranquillity – this guide explains the treatment options.

Society as a whole suffers from the consequences of stress. For example, stress contributes to alcoholism, smoking and drug abuse, which impose enormous economic and social burdens over and above the tragedy of the lives these addictions destroy. Furthermore, in late 2002 the Health and Safety Commission (HSC) reported that in 2001-02, 40.2 million working days were lost due to work-related illness and injury, with stress, anxiety and depression accounting for 13.4 million days. Over this period, the HSC estimated that there were 265,000 new cases of stress.

Indeed, surveys suggest that a quarter of the workforce regard their occupation as the leading cause of stress in their life. Changes at work, such as employers imposing increasing demands, a long-hours culture and growing job insecurity, have increased our per-ception of occupational stress. People in poorly paid roles with little responsibility are more likely to suffer – a different pattern from the classic 'executive' stress of high-flyers with more control over their lives. Nevertheless, people often attribute their stress to the work-place, when the true cause lies elsewhere. For example, stress may have been triggered by other life events – or could arise from the way a person handles a situation he or she finds difficult. Under pressure many of us fall back on inappropriate coping strategies that do not help us to deal successfully with our problems in the long run. This book looks at ways to determine the causes of your stress, and also shows how to maximise your personal effectiveness and efficiency when facing life's challenges. The difference between the two qual-ities is critical: effectiveness means producing a desired change, while efficiency is attaining an end with maximum productivity and the least wasted effort. Accomplishing both allows you to control your circumstances, rather than the other way around. This sense of control is perhaps the single most important strategy to tackle stress.

Against this background, managing excessive stress is essential – for ourselves, our families and society at large. This book will help you stay on top of stress, rather than letting it control you. Although stress means different things to different people, some common strategies and guidelines will put you back in charge of your life and circumstances. In turn, this will go a long way to alleviating your stress-related symptoms. So over the course of this book, we will explore the nature of stress and identify the triggers in your life. We will examine useful strategies – from meditation and time management to psychoanalysis – that can bolster your innate stress defences. At the end, and if you take some of the steps outlined, you should be better placed to tackle the stress that is an inevitable part of life.

How to use this book

Managing stress is a voyage of self-discovery. You need to understand the factors that cause you stress and develop a personal plan to combat it, as well as discover the best way to implement the changes. By tackling the causes of your stress, you will learn more about yourself. You will have a clearer idea of where you are going and how you are going to get there. Manage your stress, and you will manage your life more effectively.

This book explains what stress is, and how it affects different people. It makes suggestions that will help you beat stress and stay at the peak of your mental and physical powers. Not all of these will be appropriate for you – so take what you find useful and experiment.

- **Chapter 1** describes the nature of stress and explains its biological basis.
- **Chapter 2** reveals how our personalities play a large role in determining our reactions to the events around us – from daily hassles to major disasters – and, therefore, our susceptibility to excessive stress. Each of us draws on a number of innate and learned strategies to counter the effects of stress. However, as will become clear, not all these stress defences are appropriate. Indeed, many common defences are counterproductive and maintain or worsen stress instead of countering it.
- **Chapter 3** shows you how to develop an individualised plan to identify – and tackle effectively – the most pressing causes of excessive stress in your life. It outlines the techniques of 'assertive coping', and offers some problem-solving approaches to put you back in control.
- **Chapter 4** examines the challenges people face at different times in their lives. This should help you identify the key issues

affecting you and your family, and help you develop suitable assertive coping techniques.

- **Chapters 5 to 9** explain how stress can cause or exacerbate several common physical and psychological illnesses. They provide information that will empower you to develop suitable techniques to cope with your health problems.
- **Chapter 10** provides a directory of stress-beating strategies that can bolster your defences against the trials and tribulations of everyday life as well as more significant life events. Many strategies also offer effective first aid for generalised stress.

Throughout this book we refer to recent scientific studies, quoting key authors and researchers where appropriate. The relevant publications are listed in the Bibliography on pages 259–73. Further reading suggestions are made at the end of most chapters.

---

* An asterisk next to the name of an organisation in the text indicates that the address and telephone number will be found in this section.

Part 1

Living with stress

Chapter 1

What is stress?

Stress dominates modern life. For example, marital difficulties, work problems and family conflicts – all important stress triggers – are common topics for coffee-time conversations and daytime TV chat shows. Indeed, numerous strands of evidence show just how much we live in an 'Age of Anxiety'.

- Work-related stress affects 20 per cent of employees (approximately five million British people), accounts for some 6.5 million lost working days and costs employers around £370 million annually, Tearle reported in 2002. Indeed, the disability arising from stress might be as great as that caused by accidents at work or common diseases such as raised blood pressure, diabetes and arthritis, according to a paper by Kalia.
- The World Health Organization estimates that mental disease, including stress-related disorders, will become the second commonest cause of disability by 2020.
- Our desire to alleviate the mental and physical symptoms arising from excessive stress has created a multi-million-pound industry encompassing practitioners from counsellors and psychotherapists to consultants employed by major companies, and alternative and complementary healers using everything from herbs to acupuncture to colour therapy.
- A 'lack of control' – which as we'll see is a key factor in stress – 'has leaked into our personal lives', according to Dunant and Porter. In addition, many of us haven't developed the capacity to tolerate the effects of events or people that are outside our control.

As all these examples suggest, stress – although it has common features and symptoms – means different things to different people.

Nevertheless, some common strategies can help you to restore a sense of control which, in turn, will alleviate your stress-related symptoms. This guide will explore the nature of stress and help you to identify the triggers in your life. We'll take a salutary look at the mental and physical consequences of excessive stress and examine strategies that can equip you better to cope with the stressful situations that life can throw your way.

Stress can be good for you

Ironically, stress isn't all bad. Without a certain degree of stress we wouldn't bother getting out of bed in the morning. Successfully dealing with a difficult, stressful problem leaves you with a sense of achievement. Stress heightens the enjoyment of some sports. Indeed, a certain amount of stress may even be beneficial.

Anxiety – a nagging fear or worry that something awful is about to happen – is a common stress symptom. However, the nagging worry isn't linked to anything specific. In contrast, fear itself – which is the same general emotion as anxiety – has a specific cause. Fear breeds caution and keeps us out of danger. Our ancestors were less likely to pick a fight with a warrior tribe that they feared. Even today, a healthy fear of being mugged keeps you vigilant – and so you are less likely to be attacked. But when fear reaches intensity out of proportion to its cause, it becomes a phobia. So if you fear being mugged while walking through an inner-city area late at night, it's probably a normal reaction. If you are too terrified to leave your suburban house you have developed a phobia.

In other words, when we talk about 'stress' we really mean a point in our lives when our defence mechanisms become over-stretched. As a result, we can no longer cope effectively with the problems, trials and tribulations facing us. We can become over-whelmed by even a seemingly minor crisis. However, we vary markedly in our ability to cope with stress – although our reserves are often deeper than we believe. For example, the frustration of being in a traffic jam or slow-moving bank queue can trigger stress. Yet disabled people often remain cheerful and live full and fulfilling lives despite the frustrations imposed by severe physical disabilities. Keeping our problems in perspective can help counter stress.

When the going gets tough

So why do the symptoms of stress emerge? Stress symptoms indicate excessive arousal. By arousal, psychologists mean that your body is ready to act because you face a real, imagined or suspected threat. You're in a 'heightened' physiological state – your cardiovascular and respiratory systems, for example, are prepared for action, such as to fight or run away. Whether the threat is a looming deadline, a mugger or a hungry sabre-toothed tiger, the physiological reaction is essentially the same. (Although the extent of the activation differs depending on the situation.)

In other words, modern life's trials and tribulations activate a physiological reaction that evolved to help us survive against nature's teeth and claws. As the pressure exerted by these trials and tribulations increases, your arousal rises and your performance improves. So the increased arousal allows you to rise to the occasion and perform at the peak of your abilities. For example, many actors rely on performance anxiety (a form of stress) to shine on stage. On the other hand, if the performance anxiety becomes excessive, actors may develop stage fright, which can paralyse them and stop them performing.

The right amount of arousal – an amount of stress that you can cope with – can be good for your performance and general well-being. Too little arousal leads to boredom and apathy as well as undermining concentration, while over-arousal undermines your performance (you can have too much of a good thing). You feel 'stressed out' when the demands placed on you outstrip your resources, strengths, time or your innate ability to cope. So contending with a sufficiently large number of stressful life events will induce stress symptoms in most people. In others, because they're already weakened from facing several other stressful events, or because they do not respond with appropriate defences, an event that most people would take in their stride can induce severe symptoms.

Doctors describe this relationship between arousal and performance as the 'n'-shaped curve (see picture overleaf). Your performance gradually improves with increasing arousal, until you're at your peak. After this point, increased arousal leads to a declining performance, until you can no longer cope.

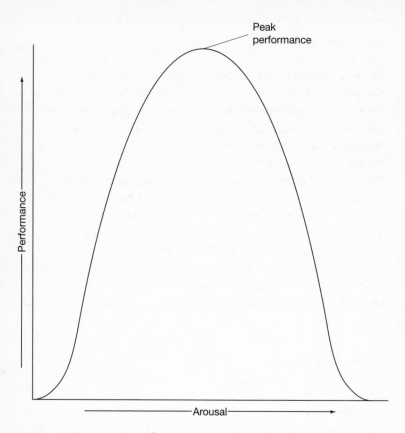

The 'n'-shaped curve showing the relationship between performance and arousal

Quiz: Are you stressed?

How many of these stress symptoms do you suffer in a typical day, and how often?

- headaches
- muscle tension; stiff neck
- feeling isolated
- changed eating habits
- palpitations; rapid heartbeat
- feeling scared
- sleep disturbances; insomnia

Don't crash into burnout

When you start to experience marked stress symptoms, you should rest. Instead, many of us begin burning the candle at both ends in an attempt to compensate for our perceived or actual poor performance, or our fear of perfoming badly. This uses up what's left of your mental and physical reserves and your performance declines further. So you push yourself harder and harder – and feel worse and worse. The body's stress warnings become more intense and more frequent. Your concentration may flag even further. So you work longer and longer hours trying to catch up. Soon you're teetering on the edge of burnout, which Felton defines as 'the exhaustion of physical or emotional strength as a result of prolonged stress or frustration'. Eventually, the smallest additional problem triggers a breakdown. Our quiz overleaf helps you determine how close you are to burnout.

- crying for no reason
- fatigue
- breathing problems
- grinding teeth
- feeling of impending doom
- pallor
- inability to forget problems
- diarrhoea; constipation
- feeling excessively pressurised
- feeling nervous or anxious
- feeling irritable or angry
- feeling jumpy; racing, apprehensive thoughts
- procrastination; worry about making the wrong decision
- increased smoking or drinking
- being brusque, rude or sarcastic
- sexual problems; impotence
- losing interest in your hobbies or job
- poor concentration
- a 'lump' in your throat
- cold hands or feet; excessive sweating; a 'cold sweat'

- weak knees; dizziness; feeling faint
- excessively sensitive to outside stimuli
- muscle twitches and tics
- preoccupied with misfortune
- 'butterflies' in the stomach; nausea; dyspepsia (indigestion).

Keep a record of how often you suffer from these symptoms over four or five days. Everyone suffers from these symptoms from time to time. However, the more symptoms you have and the more often, the more likely you are to be stressed out. Some of these symptoms might also indicate that you suffer from overt depression or clinical anxiety (see Chapter 7). If so, you should seek medical attention. (We'll look at the difference between clinical conditions, such as depression and anxiety, and 'simple' stress in Chapter 7.)

Quiz: Are you on the brink of burnout?

At the end of each day for a typical week, answer these questions. The more times you answer yes, the closer you are to the brink of burnout.

- Did you feel tired all day? Yes / No
- Did you look forward to going to work today? Yes / No
- Has the day's work left you emotionally drained? Yes / No
- Did you feel that you controlled your time well today? Yes / No
- Did you find it difficult to concentrate? Yes / No
- Did you bring work-related problems home with you? Yes / No
- Do you feel confident about the future? Yes / No
- Did you lose your temper over a minor incident today? Yes / No
- Did you set yourself realistic goals? Yes / No
- Were you able to laugh at yourself? Yes / No
- Did you feel that you have a strong support system? Yes / No
- Did you have more responsibility than you can handle comfortably? Yes / No
- If asked to meet an unrealistic deadline, could you say no? Yes / No
- Did you have trouble making decisions? Yes / No
- Were you satisfied with the day's work? Yes / No
- Are you having trouble relaxing at the end of the day? Yes / No
- Did you have difficulty getting to sleep last night? Yes / No

- Did you feel well organised today?   Yes / No
- In general, do you feel pessimistic?   Yes / No
- In general, do you feel in control of your life?   Yes / No

Adapted from *Family Practice Management*, March 1997

The fight-or-flight reflex

Essentially, our level of arousal increases when we face a real, imagined or suspected threat. Initially, our body responds to that threat – the stress trigger or stressor – through a cascade of biological changes, known as the fight-or-flight reflex or, less commonly, the alarm reaction.

Our 'involuntary' or 'autonomic' nervous system controls the fight-or-flight reflex. The autonomic nervous system keeps us breathing and our hearts beating while we sleep. Normally, we cannot consciously control autonomic nervous system activity. This contrasts with the voluntary nervous system, which is under our conscious control. It is easy to decide to pick up a pen (using your voluntary nervous system). It is harder to slow a rapid heartbeat by controlling your autonomic system before giving a presentation. Nevertheless, yoga, meditation, biofeedback and a variety of other techniques might allow some practitioners to exert a limited control over their autonomic nervous system. We'll examine some of these techniques in more detail later in the book (see Chapter 10).

Biologists divide the autonomic nervous system into two groups of nerves – the sympathetic and parasympathetic – that have opposite actions. For example, sympathetic and parasympathetic nerves increase and slow the heartbeat respectively. The balance between the activity of the sympathetic and parasympathetic systems determines our level of arousal. If sympathetic nervous activity dominates, your level of arousal rises. If this arousal is beyond your ability to cope, you feel stressed.

So when you face a stressor or danger, sympathetic nervous system activity rapidly increases. As a result:

- your adrenal glands – which lie on the top of your kidneys – secrete more adrenaline, cortisol and other hormones into your blood. The combination of increased sympathetic activity and the hormonal surge from the adrenal glands diverts your body's resources from your internal organs – such as your stomach – to your muscles

- your body expects you to use your muscles either to fight or run away. So the amount of glucose and fats circulating in your blood increases to provide the energy you will need
- your breathing becomes deeper and more rapid to increase oxygen supply to your muscles
- blood drains from the skin – which is why we go pale when scared. Your heartbeat becomes stronger and more rapid. Blood pressure rises
- the nervous and hormonal actions described above trigger changes in our bowel movements. That's why stress can cause nausea, diarrhoea and contributes to many cases of irritable bowel syndrome (see Chapter 6)
- salivary glands reduce their output, producing a dry mouth, while sweat glands increase production, resulting in a 'cold sweat'
- muscles surrounding hair follicles in the skin contract, causing goose bumps, and the pupils dilate, creating a wide-eyed look. Hearing also becomes more acute
- stress triggers the release of small proteins – known as endorphins – in the brain and from the adrenal and pituitary glands. Endorphins have some of the same action as opiates – such as morphine and heroin. In other words, the endorphins reduce pain and can create a 'high' – which might be one reason why some people become hooked on dangerous pastimes, such as parachuting, or why many people find white knuckle rides exhilarating
- blood clots more quickly, which helps limit the damage from an injury.

The fight-or-flight reflex evolved to get us out of danger quickly and with the least damage possible. We could then rest and refresh our reserves. Psychologists describe our biological response to a threat as the general adaptation syndrome, first described in Selye's landmark publication *The Stress of Life* in 1956.

- **The alarm phase** – the 'fright' or 'alarm'. After an initial shock, your body switches into the fight-or-flight reflex.

- **The resistance or adaptation phase** You take action to try to deal with the stressor. If you succeed, your body rapidly returns to the pre-alarm state. If you fail, however, you can remain in this phase for a prolonged period of time.
- **The exhaustion phase** As the name suggests, if the stressor continues your resources can be depleted. In the classic general adaptation syndrome theory, continued exhaustion predisposes to disease and death.

This response was a life-saver when a rival tribe on the warpath threatened our ancestors. Unfortunately, the fight-or-flight reflex doesn't distinguish between barbarian hordes and a nagging, critical boss – or indeed the internal critical voice in your unconscious (for advice on dealing with a difficult boss, see pages 96–97). Your body is still ready to fight – or flee the office. However, our veneer of civilisation prevents us from doing either. As a result, the fight-or-flight reflex remains activated for long periods, and we rarely rest or replenish our physical, emotional and mental reserves. All too often this heralds exhaustion. So this book largely deals with the resistance or adaptation phase, exploring ways to bolster your resistance as well as to help you adapt more effectively and efficiently. Obviously, we need to aim to avoid the exhaustion phase.

Mental states and stress

Nevertheless, we're not solely at the mercy of our nervous system. Our mental state profoundly influences how we view the level of arousal and the emotions that emerge as a result. (Psychologists describe this as the 'arousal interpretation' theory of emotions.)

A study in the early 1960s graphically illustrated the importance of mental factors in determining stress responses. Lazarus and colleagues showed volunteers a film depicting, in graphic detail, the Stone Age circumcision rites that form part of Native Australian initiation. The films were accompanied by different commentaries. One reassured the viewer that the circumcision didn't hurt particularly. Another commented dispassionately. The two commentaries mimic two important stress defences – denial and intellectualisation respectively (see page 38) – and considerably reduced viewers' psychological stress compared to simply showing the film.

Based on this and other studies, Lazarus and colleagues formulated the cognitive stress theory. According to this model, we first appraise the stressor. We decide whether it can cause us harm or loss, whether it presents a threat (a clear and present danger) or a challenge (a competitive situation). We then mentally decide whether our resources and options can meet the threat or challenge and deal with the associated emotions. This means we can decide to attack or escape. Alternatively, we can become passive, which in severe cases can lead to learned helplessness, which we'll return to below (see page 34). We might re-evaluate some stressors and decide that they weren't a problem after all.

Our view of the stressor combined with our level of arousal influences whether we feel stressed out. The so-called 'arousal interpretation' theory helps express why we feel differently about the same levels of arousal at different times or in different circumstances. For example, the stress of a penalty shoot-out and a problem at work might cause the same level of arousal. However, our mental perception of each event is markedly different. So while a person may not regard the shoot-out as stressful, the problem at work can cause the same person considerable stress.

What triggers stress?

Almost any event can trigger stress – given the appropriate circumstances. Some stress triggers are obvious – for example redundancy, bereavement, divorce, suffering from an incurable illness or moving house. A minor hassle for one person may trigger a breakdown in someone reeling from the stress of divorce and the death of a parent. Nevertheless, as a general rule the greater number of stressful events we endure, the more likely it is that we will suffer physical or psychological symptoms as a result.

Against this background, the 'life stress scale' (see page 24) assigns a value to certain stressful life events – including pleasurable activities such as marriage and Christmas. Even holidays, the very time when we should relax, can cause considerable stress – especially if the resort doesn't live up to its billing in the brochure. The emotional baggage we carry with us on holiday magnifies any stress. After all, holidays are supposed to be an escape from stress.

As a general rule, your risk of suffering a stress-related illness depends on your score during the last year. Half the people with scores exceeding 200 develop health problems. For those with totals over 300, this increases to almost 80 per cent. However, it is important to realise that the figures on the scale might not apply to everyone. For example, the stress of taking out a mortgage depends on your financial circumstances. Moreover, *Stress & Health Among the Elderly* cites the example of a middle-aged woman who, during a study examining the psychological impact of life events, stated that the death of her husband was a positive experience. The researchers assumed it was an error – until they checked. The woman was a devout Catholic whose husband died after a long struggle with painful rectal cancer. The woman said that he'd gone to a better place, he wasn't suffering and eventually she'd join him. Nevertheless, the scale offers a general indication of your likelihood of suffering stress-related problems.

The value of control

Many of the stressors in the table overleaf fall into six broad situations:

- **conflicting motives** e.g. looking after a family as well as working outside the home
- **internal conflict** e.g. working for a company you feel behaves unethically
- **unusual events** e.g. arriving in a new job or a new town and not knowing what to expect
- **unpredictable events** e.g. exam results, appraisal or company take-over
- **loss** e.g. redundancy or the death of a spouse
- **frustration** e.g. not being awarded the promotion you deserve, or being stuck in a traffic jam and missing an appointment.

These six situations also share a common theme: we no longer feel in control. Indeed, feeling that you're no longer in control is a central contributor to stress. For instance, at work the combination of pressure and little latitude to take decisions is, as we'll see, a major contributor to stress. A feeling of being in control also seems to be

The life stress scale			
Event	Score	Event	Score
death of a spouse	100	change in responsibilities at work	29
divorce	73	a child leaves home	29
marital separation	65	trouble with in-laws	29
jail term	63	outstanding personal achievement	28
death of a close relative	63	partner starts or stops employment	26
personal injury or illness	53	begin or end school, college or university	26
marriage	50	change in living conditions	25
being fired	47	revision of personal habits	24
marital reconciliation	45	trouble with boss	23
retirement	45	change in work conditions or hours	20
change in relative's health	44	moving home	20
pregnancy	40	changing schools	20
sexual problems	39	changing religious habits	19
new family member	39	changing social activities	18
business readjustment	39	taking out a small mortgage or loan	17
change in finances	38	change in sleeping habits	16
death of a close friend	37	change in number of family reunions	15
changing to a new type of job	36	vacation	13
change in number of marital arguments	35	change in eating habits	13
taking out a large mortgage or loan	31	Christmas	12
mortgage foreclosure	30	minor law-breaking	11

the critical difference between people who try to tackle their problems and those who feel helpless (though the need to feel always in control can be pathological and may lead to frustration, conflicted relationships and destructive patterns, and cause stress). Clearly, then, regaining control is a valuable way to bolster your stress defences.

However, people differ in the extent to which they feel they can control their life and environment even when facing broadly similar problems. Psychologists characterise the difference in terms of whether the person has an internal or external 'locus of control'.

People with internal loci of control believe that they attain a given outcome – a satisfying relationship, a rewarding occupation, a fulfilling life, for example – through their own actions. People with external loci of control believe the exact opposite: outcome depends mainly on luck or the actions of others. So if your 'locus of control' is internal you feel in command of your situation. If it is external, you feel the situation controls you.

Obviously, people with internal loci of control find it easier to adapt and find solutions to their problems than those with external loci. Indeed, Kahana reported that an internal locus of control partly protected holocaust survivors from depression, anxiety and other psychological problems.

And the loci influence your attitude towards potentially stressful environments, such as work. For instance, Jain and colleagues found that nurses with external loci of control reported less job satisfaction than those with internal loci. Fortunately, the loci aren't fixed. Too many stressful events can externalise an internal locus (as happens in learned helplessness, for example – see page 34). And you can use various strategies to internalise an external locus.

Your ability to take decisions at work is, clearly, closely allied to your locus of control. A study by Dudek and collaborators that enrolled 160 police officers found that feelings of personal control, job satisfaction and personal accomplishment all protected against stress. Emotional exhaustion, not surprisingly, exacerbated stress. This is just one recent example from a plethora of scientific studies showing that demanding jobs in which people have little 'decision latitude' – or leeway to exert control over their occupation – lead to unacceptable stress levels.

Executive stress is fashionable – probably because it is extremely profitable for stress management consultants and those marketing stress solutions. However, while senior executives work hard and face considerable pressure, they control their working life to a much greater extent than their subordinates. Furthermore, an executive's workload tends to be more varied and interesting than that of those lower down the company's hierarchy. Boredom markedly increases stress levels. Seniority also brings financial rewards that allow senior executives to make the most of their leisure time – an important way to bolster their stress defences. And, of course, they can afford the often-expensive stress solutions.

However, as a general rule, a company's most stressed-out employees tend to be those who work long hours, in repetitive jobs, with little control over their working life: production-line workers, check-out assistants and people performing routine clerical work, for example. Of course, these people tend to be poorly paid (financial pressure contributes to stress in its own right as well as limiting the employees' opportunities to bolster their stress defences). This sort of work is more likely to cause chronic stress than varied, demanding jobs – although of course an interesting job with a lot of responsibility can also be stressful.

This exemplifies the important difference between 'stress' and 'pressure'. A deadline for a report places you under pressure – a level of arousal that is more than normal, but something you can cope with. Stress, however, involves factors that are beyond your control. Many people thrive under pressure. No one thrives under chronic stress.

'There's never enough time'

Trying to do more and more in less and less time is another common cause of stress. Indeed, a survey by the Institute of Directors in 1999 found that most of the 5,000 managers interviewed felt that they laboured under time pressure. Eighty per cent cited tight deadlines as the main reason why they worked long hours. More than half those interviewed said that they needed to work long hours to have the opportunity for strategic thinking. The National Work Life Forum reported in May 2000 that half of fathers now spend less than five minutes with their children each day. And a 1998 survey of senior managers found that 38 per cent had refused promotion because of the detrimental effect on their life outside work.

To make matters worse, some employers exploit their workers' fear of redundancy. Our parents and grandparents often counted on job security as the foundation of their life. Those days are effectively gone.

Furthermore, stress at work is no longer a male prerogative. Increasingly, women work outside the home. Twenty years ago, only 40 per cent of families had mothers and fathers who both worked outside the home. Today, that proportion is 60 per cent. Many working mothers feel pressurised into being 'superwomen'. They want – or need – a career. But they also want to be good mothers and homemakers. Trying to fulfil these two demanding, and sometimes conflicting, roles leaves some women tired, tense and stressed. They have little time to develop the interests that could protect them from the ravages of stress. Using some of the time management techniques outlined later in the book and in *Which? Way to Manage Your Time – and Your Life* (also available from Which? Books*) might help.

Working mothers highlight another common cause of stress: trying to bridge the gap between reality and expectation. No one can – or should try to be – the perfect partner, parent, housekeeper, lover and breadwinner rolled into one. No job or marriage is perfect. Yet the media often portrays unattainable visions of the perfect marriage and lifestyle. Few, if any of us, attain this ideal. Moreover, we often bring unattainable expectations to a new job or relationship. The gap between our expectations and the reality commonly causes stress.

The next two chapters look at how we respond to stress as individuals, and the differing effects it can have on people of different ages. In Chapter 3, we'll explore some of the ways in which you can use assertive coping techniques to begin to regain control of your life and bolster your defences against stress. It's not an easy process. Despite what the hucksters and charlatans might have you believe, there is no quick fix to the mental, emotional and physical trauma arising from excessive stress. But just as people recover from depression and other mental illnesses, you can beat stress. You can emerge from the turmoil to enjoy new-found serenity.

Benjamin Franklin commented that nothing is inevitable except death and taxes. Today, in this age of anxiety we can add stress to his list. But as countless men and women worldwide show, unlike death and taxes, we can conquer – or at least tame – stress. The remainder of this book shows you how.

Further reading

Dunant, S. and Porter. R. 1996. *The Age of Anxiety*. Virago Press
Eysenck, M. (ed). 1998. *Psychology: An Integrated Approach*. Prentice Hall
Greener, M. 2000. *Which? Way to Manage Your Time – and Your Life*. Which? Books

Chapter 2

How we respond to stress

In many ways, the events that you find stressful and your response to these stressors are as personal as your fingerprints. No two people react to the same stressor in exactly the same way, to exactly the same extent. We differ in, for example, our personal coping strategies, which may be either beneficial or counterproductive. We differ in our attitude towards major life events because of our experiences, upbringing and personality. And an everyday event that most people would take in their stride can induce severe symptoms in people who are already weakened from facing several other stressful experiences, or who do not respond with appropriate defences.

We differ in our susceptibility to clinical psychiatric diseases, such as depression and anxiety. Our bodies have different strengths and weaknesses that influence the severity and type of stress symptoms that we experience. And, as we'll see in the next chapter, different stressors and different coping strategies may arise at different stages in our life. So we might even react differently to the same stressor at different times.

In this chapter, we'll look at some of the other factors that might influence your reactions to stress. Understanding these will help you devise your personalised stress reduction plan using the steps outlined in Chapter 3. So while stress – and our reaction to it – is intensely personal, and while one person's challenge may be the cause of another's breakdown, we can all learn ways to bolster our ability to deal with stress.

Type A and B personalities

One of the most widely discussed personality traits that might be linked to stress and, more controversially, certain diseases was characterised in 1974 when Rosenman and Friedman, two American cardiologists, noted that many of their heart attack patients shared certain characteristics (called neurogenic factors). The patients were impatient, competitive and easily aroused to anger. This observation led to the idea of type A and B personalities (see box below).

Are you a type A or type B personality?	
Type A	**Type B**
very competitive	non-competitive
impatient	unhurried
goal-orientated	relaxed
aggressive	passive
restless, rapid movements	relaxed
doesn't listen	good listener
fast talker	talks at a reasonable speed

As the box shows, type A people tend to be competitive, impatient, aggressive and ambitious. They move rapidly, talk fast and don't listen. They are continually on the go – always doing something, even it doesn't need doing. They never relax. So they often feel tired and fatigued. However, instead of listening to their bodies, they take fatigue as a sign of weakness and push themselves harder. Anger, hostility and aggression are common coping strategies among Type A people. In other words, people with type A personalities seem to have a higher level of arousal. Inevitably, therefore, people with type A traits can expect to suffer the symptoms of stress more readily than those with type B behaviour. Put simply: they get wound up more easily.

Type B personalities are the exact opposites. They are relaxed, calm and non-competitive. They move at a sensible pace and listen to you. Type B people take life as it comes. Their lower level of arousal may offer these people a degree of protection from the effects of severe stress.

Most of us fall between these two extremes and express different traits at different times. We might be very competitive on the squash court but relaxed at work, for example. Nevertheless, identifying whether you're predominately a type A or B person, especially in the situations that you find stressful, might help you to identify some of the factors in your make-up that contribute to stress. We should not suppose that being a type B is always beneficial in every situation. After all, in today's competitive commercial world it may not pay to be too unhurried or relaxed. It's important to recognise that you need a response appropriate to the environment, which doesn't exceed your ability to cope. You need to find the right balance of traits for you. But to reduce your likelihood of suffering stress-related symptoms, in general you should tend towards the type B traits.

Type A and B traits and disease

Over the years, numerous studies have explored whether type A and B traits influence our risk of suffering certain conditions, especially cancer and heart disease. Unfortunately, the evidence is, to say the least, inconclusive. Any effect, if it exists at all, seems to be very small. (Remember we're discussing the effects of personality traits on disease in this section – not the probability of suffering stress symptoms.)

For example, several studies link certain type A character traits such as extroversion and hostility with an increased risk of breast cancer. However, much of the evidence supporting the link is circumstantial. For example, Lillberg and colleagues, who reported results from one of the first epidemiological studies examining personality factors and breast cancer risk – which enrolled almost 12,500 Finnish women – found that type A behaviour and other personality factors do not seem to play 'an important role' in influencing the risk of breast cancer. (Epidemiology is the scientific study of disease patterns in different populations, such as those with or without a certain personality trait.)

Similarly, the role of personality traits in determining the risk of heart disease remains controversial – even though the idea of type A and B personalities originated in cardiology. Certainly, some studies link type A personalities with an increased risk of heart disease. For example, type A traits almost doubled the risk of suffering a heart attack in men and approximately trebled the risk among women in a Japanese study reported by Yoshimasu in 2001. Furthermore, in this study people who had demanding jobs, but few opportunities to take decisions (a combination we'll look at again later) were almost twice as likely to suffer a heart attack. In another study, Cole and collaborators reported that people with the greatest time urgency – a key type A trait – were four times more likely to suffer a heart attack compared to those with a more laid-back approach to time. Other studies paint a very different picture, however. Some failed to find any link between heart disease and personality traits, while one by Catipovic-Veselica and collaborators linked type B behaviour with an increased risk of dying following a heart attack. You shouldn't draw too many conclusions from a handful of studies. The differing results exemplify the confusion in the scientific evidence.

Fortunately, for the last 10 years, scientists have increasingly used a powerful technique called meta-analysis to resolve questions with contradictory or inconsistent evidence. This combines all studies with similar methods and patients that the authors can find, and then uses statistics to reach a conclusion. Using this technique, a German researcher – Myrtek – suggested that a type A personality was not linked to the likelihood of suffering heart disease, although hostility seemed to be associated with an increased risk. However, Myrtek comments that hostility's effect 'is so low that it has . . . no practical meaning for prediction and prevention'.

We'll return to the link between stress and heart disease later. In the meantime, it's more important to focus on diet, smoking and inactivity as causes of heart disease rather than worry about being hostile or your type A personality traits. Certainly, if stress leads you to eat unhealthily and drink excessively, if it causes you to smoke or you don't have time to exercise, it could indirectly cause heart disease. This link seems far more important than the effect exerted by personality, which, if it exists, is very small. Indeed, the small size of any effect might explain why the results of the studies are mixed.

Micro-, mezzo- and macrolevel stressors

Clearly, stress triggers come in many guises. The impact of these varies depending on your personality, experiences, attitudes, values and a plethora of other factors. Moreover, the factors that cause you stress can vary from the global – the threat of war perhaps – to the intensely personal, such as an unresolved issue from your childhood, to the almost mundane, such as traffic jams. What causes you stress depends on your personal circumstances.

Untangling these issues helps you identify and address the factors that cause you stress. One approach would be to write down everything that stresses you out or winds you up. Don't think about this. Simply write it all down. The destruction of the rainforest. Your boss. Your daughter's latest boyfriend. Lack of money to pay for this year's holiday. Whatever. Then break the stressors down into the three categories described below.

- **Microlevel stressors** The slow, steady accumulation of everyday hassles seems to indicate your risk of suffering stress-related illness more accurately than the number of dramatic events you experience. Such everyday stressors as delays on the train, traffic jams and minor family rows are the commonest form of stress. Despite this, the cumulative impact that microlevel stressors can have on your physical and emotional well-being is not as well studied as the impact of mezzolevel events. Nevertheless, it is clear that the build-up of everyday, even seemingly trivial, hassles undoubtedly undermines your physical and mental health. For instance, researchers in the 1970s found that the number of stressful day-to-day events patients experienced predicted their risk of contracting the common cold.
- **Mezzolevel stressors**, or memorable life events such as preg-nancy, divorce and death, are less common but better-studied than microlevel stressors. While persistent mezzolevel stressors tend to have more impact on your physical and psychological health than short-lived events, even one-off events can damage your mental and physical health. For example, in a study by Conroy, 18 out of 19 suicides seemed to follow divorce, death or estrangement in the family.
- **Macrolevel stressors** Although they are generally outside our direct control, sociological, environmental and political issues can cause considerable stress. Some years ago many people felt anxious and stressed about the threat of nuclear war between the superpowers. Similarly, surveys suggest that morale in the

USA fell dramatically after President John F. Kennedy's assassination in 1963. And admissions to mental hospitals rise during recessions in the US economy. It seems that the social, economic and political climate can influence our levels of arousal and, therefore, the risk of developing stress-related symptoms.

After putting your problems into these categories, defined by Chiriboga, the traffic jam you became caught in is revealed as a microlevel stressor. The ongoing problems with your father in-law are a mezzolevel stressor. The economic recession is macrolevel. This approach helps you clarify the issue – and allows you to develop a plan to tackle it. Chapter 3 explains how you can formulate such a plan.

All stressors can be intensely frustrating. Nevertheless, appreciating the differences between these levels can help you determine the extent to which you can do something about your stress triggers. Although they may seem to be outside your sphere of influence, that's not to say you should ignore macrolevel stressors such as iniquitous economic development and environmental destruction. You can work with non-governmental organisations, such as Greenpeace★ or Friends of the Earth,★ to help make a difference. Doing something, even if you are a small part of a wider initiative, helps you feel that you're in as much control as you can be. This helps to counter the anxiety caused by macrolevel stressors.

Adapting to stress

Each of us draws on a number of innate and learned strategies to counter the effects of stress. However, not all these stress defences are appropriate. Indeed, some reactions to stress can make matters worse. For example, in 1967 two researchers, Overmier and Seligman, described a phenomenon called 'learned helplessness'. They trained dogs to jump over a fence to avoid electrical shocks. But if the shocks were uncontrolled and unpredictable – for example, if the shock didn't always stop when the animal jumped the fence – often the animals learned to be helpless. In other words, they did not attempt to avoid the shock even if it was possible.

Some researchers believe that these behavioural changes are analogous to the emotional, motivational and cognitive deficits in some people assailed by considerable stress and depression. For example, people who experience a number of stressful events outside their control – a death in the family, redundancy and suffering a debilitating illness – may come to believe that they can change nothing. As a result, they don't try to amend an adverse situation even when they could. They feel helpless, apathetic and question their abilities. They become assailed by self-doubt. They come to believe that any attempt to alter their circumstances, no matter how hard they try, is futile. So they are less likely to take the necessary steps to resolve their problems, which exacerbates their stress. In many cases, other people bear their anger for them.

Case history: Joe

Joe lost his job as an electrical engineer in a round of redundancies. He began, despite years of experience, to question his abilities. Joe became deeply depressed. He was unable to apply for new engineering jobs that were well within his abilities, start his own business or even mend simple electrical faults around the house.

Stress and mental illness

Stress can be an important and common trigger for psychological symptoms in some patients. It can, in susceptible people, trigger or exacerbate a variety of mental disorders including depression, anxiety and insomnia. It's hard for anyone who hasn't suffered from a serious mental illness to appreciate fully the disability and distress that such conditions bring. In most cases, serious mental illness can be successfully treated. Most people recover to live relatively full and active lives.

Stress isn't the only factor that causes these mental conditions. In particular, in many cases an imbalance in brain chemicals, which may be genetically inherited, seems to predispose certain people to develop some psychiatric illnesses (see Chapter 8). In some people, an accumulation of stressful life events can trigger a severe breakdown, and in a few cases the intense mental torment may drive the person to suicide. Fortunately, appropriate treatment can reduce the risk of suicide in, for example, severely depressed people or those with schizophrenia (see Chapter 8).

Pill popping may not be the answer

Doctors often fail to get to the root of the problems that cause psychiatric symptoms. In severe mental illness, this is under-standable. Doctors need to treat the acute problems, such as the risk of suicide, urgently. However, if stress triggers, for example, a case of 'the blues' rather than severe depression, pills might not be the answer to your symptoms. Rather you need to identify and address the underlying cause. Yet doctors still prescribe drugs for relatively mild psychiatric symptoms. In some cases, doctors might prescribe inappropriately because we can't articulate – or even understand – the cause of our symptoms. This makes it difficult for any doctor in the limited time available in a consul-tation to deal with the stress-causing problems. Prescribing, for instance, a sleeping tablet might help you get some rest. But it's not going to solve the relationship problems or tackle the bullying boss that you lie awake at night worrying about. This book shows you how to identify the true causes behind your stress and deal with the consequences. In many cases, you'll be able to avoid the need for a prescription.

The twilight zone: mental bandages for stress

Fortunately, most people don't fall into the pit of despair charac-terised by learned helplessness or suffer from psychiatric symptoms that need treatment. Nevertheless, we employ a variety of conscious and unconscious defences to help tide us over an emotional or psychological 'rough patch'. Such tactics do not directly confront the cause of our stress. Rather, they alleviate the anxiety triggered by stressful and traumatic events by distorting either reality or our self-perception.

How we shield ourselves from stress

The strategies described below allow you to cope from day to day without tackling the underlying problem. They can act as mental bandages patching you up until you have the resources to deal with the problem. However, allowing these behavioural patterns to become entrenched, and not tackling the cause, leaves you in a psychological twilight zone.

Repression and suppression

Repression is possibly the most powerful coping strategy. Indeed, Freud commented in *Three Essays on the Theory of Sexuality* that 'repression is the cornerstone upon which the edifice of psycho-analysis rests'. Psychoanalytical theory has evolved considerably since then. But Freud's comments underscore the importance of repression.

Repression involves unconsciously banishing thoughts and desires that cause conflict, anxiety and stress from the conscious mind. For example, certain expressions of sexuality might conflict with our religious, social or moral codes. In extreme cases, some people 'resolve' this conflict by totally repressing their sexuality. Likewise, memories associated with guilt, anxiety or trauma can be 'forgotten'. However, the stress-provoking thoughts and desires remain active in the unconscious.

Psychologists believe that repressed thoughts and desires can re-emerge from the subconscious and trigger stress symptoms – although the person is often unaware of the cause of their distress. In other cases, the repressed thoughts and desires re-emerge in dreams, when the person is under the influence of drugs or alcohol, or as irrational ideas. Psychoanalysis, discussed in more detail in Chapter 10, explores a patient's psyche to try to reveal and under-stand these repressed thoughts and desires. This helps the person change his or her behaviour, thereby alleviating stress and tension.

On the surface, suppression seems to be a related defence mech-anism. However, suppression consciously blocks the stressor from becoming the centre of the mental attention. It puts things 'out of mind', but cannot banish them to the repressed unconscious. For example, you can train yourself mentally to push unpleasant thoughts aside, perhaps by focusing on something else. Repression, by contrast, is unconscious. Suppression can be a useful technique to deal with immediate problems. However, if taken to extremes it means that you don't tackle the underlying problem.

Denial

Denial is another powerful coping strategy. People in denial unconsciously avoid accepting the reality of their situation – even when they face overwhelming evidence. A widower might not accept that his wife has died. Many alcoholics deny the damage wrought by their addiction on themselves and their families. Alcoholics Anonymous* and other rehabilitation programmes for addictions succeed because, in part, they encourage people to face their addiction and accept responsibility for its consequences. Similarly, terminally ill patients may deny the truth until they can muster the emotional resources to face reality.

Rationalisation, intellectualisation and cognitive dissonance

Rationalisation attempts to explain away stressful situations. So John, who was turned down for a job, convinced himself it was not all the advert made it out to be. Rationalisation also helps resolve inner conflicts. For example, someone fiddling his employer could rationalise his dishonesty by convincing himself that 'everyone else does it, so why shouldn't I?'

Intellectualisation moves the problem from an emotional to an intellectual level. Remember the study using the film of Native Australian circumcision rites on page 21? The dispassionate, intellectual commentary considerably reduced viewers' psychological stress. Certainly, learning the facts can keep problems in perspective. But over-intellectualisation can deny and repress the valid emotional elements surrounding a problem, such as horror and shock.

Cognitive dissonance is another related strategy. According to this theory, we all have a basic need for consistency in our thoughts, especially when it impacts on our self image. This makes it difficult to hold two opposing views without enduring increased arousal (stress). As a result, we change our behaviour or views to resolve the inconsistency. For example, if someone forces us to do something against our will, we might persuade ourselves that we took the decision on our own. This means we feel better and don't undermine our sense of self.

Sublimation

Sublimation transforms a socially unacceptable trait into a more acceptable form. Many psychologists believe that many works of art result from sublimation – the artist transforms the energy generated by 'primitive' urges into a more socially acceptable form. Similarly, sport may be a sublimation of aggression and dancing a sublimation of sexuality.

Identification

You can attempt to overcome stress by imitating someone you admire. For example, a young woman might identify with her more attractive and socially adept friend and attempt to take on some of her friend's characteristics. In turn, she masks many of her own desirable characteristics. Essentially, identification means you play a role, rather than being your own person. The inner conflict that this can generate can cause considerable stress.

Identification is also, in analytic theory, the first form of our relationship with others. Using this unconscious process, we may take on the emotional attributes and some parts of the characters of parents and teachers. This forms the basis for the internalisation, unconsciously, of the 'conscience' or superego. The superego may, however, be distorted, cruel and persecuting, never satisfied with anything the ego attempts. We may then 'project' this stress on to 'the boss', 'the authorities', 'God' and so on. Psychoanalysis helps you understand and explore these concepts – see Chapter 10.

Reaction formation

People who cope with stress through reaction formation unconsciously behave in a manner opposite to their real thoughts and feelings. Usually, the behaviour is more socially acceptable than the urge. Someone who hates his wife might tell everyone how good their relationship is, for example. Other people may replace aggressive feelings with over-politeness, obsequiousness and stilted behaviour.

Projection

Projection, a primitive unconscious defence, lays the blame for your stress, anxiety and other problems firmly at the feet of someone else.

A woman who consistently accuses her faithful husband of infidelity on business trips may be concealing her own urges, for example. In other words, she wants to be unfaithful but won't admit it. Projection alleviates anxiety by attributing the stress-provoking thoughts and feelings to objects, events or people in the outside world. While this strategy can be effective, projection distorts reality – blaming someone else means that you don't take responsibility for your predicament.

Aggression and displacement

Aggression is another common reaction to stress, even among animals. When scientists placed two rats in a cage and gave one an electric shock, it attacked the other animal. Road rage is an example of stress leading to aggression: a driver reacts violently when another car cuts him or her up. Someone trying to mend a car may throw the spanners down in frustration. A child may throw a jigsaw into the air when he or she cannot get all the pieces to fit. This is 'directed aggression' – the violence is directed against the cause of the frustration.

'Displaced aggression' or displacement uses someone else as the scapegoat for the stressor. You really want to hit your boss, but instead you kick the cat or pick an argument with your wife. Again, this displaced aggression doesn't address the cause of the problem.

Withdrawal

Some people cope with anxiety and stress by retreating into a mental shell and hoping their problems will go away. They narrow their horizons until their lives are within limits they feel they can control. In some ways, withdrawal is a mild form of learned helplessness. A strategic withdrawal can provide a breathing space to re-evaluate our lives, problems and priorities. But, taken to extremes, withdrawal can cut away the social supports that help us deal with stress and may lead to apathy and depression.

Regression

Some people deal with stress and anxiety by reverting to an earlier, less mature stage of their psychological development. After the birth of a new baby, for example, older children who were fairly independent may start bed-wetting or thumb-sucking again.

Other children who regress may have temper tantrums. In some cases, people can become obsessed with recapturing their past glories or interests. Obviously, going back to your roots and a once-loved hobby can help tackle stress. But if the balance is lost, a focus on the past can mean that we don't deal with our problems in the present.

Assertive coping

At the other extreme to learned helplessness, we can employ constructive coping strategies to deal with stressors. Psychologists call these strategies 'assertive coping'. As the brief explanation below shows, these all share a common theme: they're all problem-solving approaches that put us back in control. As such, assertive coping helps us prevail over adversity, be it redundancy, terminal illness or financial problems. Chapter 3 helps you develop an individualised plan to tackle your problems through assertive coping. In it, we explore how you can implement the three broad lines of defence against stress outlined below.

Change your environment

In certain circumstances, you can change your environment to minimise stress. However, the change has to be realistic. People with difficulties at work can change their environment by finding a new job or setting up their own business. But unless you're a very unusual person, assertive coping probably does not include dropping out and becoming a crofter in the Scottish highlands or running a vineyard in France. It might seem a romantic idea and it works for some people. But you need special skills and the right temperament to make such dramatic changes work. Don't be put off if you want to pursue this dream, however. Find the time to acquire the skills (see the suggestions in *Which? Way to Manage Your Time – and Your Life*, from Which? Books*). In the meantime, try to tackle the immediate stressors.

Change your behaviour

Be honest: often you make – or at least contribute to – your own stress. Perhaps you are bored and frustrated at work, so you don't make enough effort and your boss is always on your back. Perhaps you have few friends because you feel uncomfortable in social gatherings. Perhaps drink or drugs are ruining your finances, undermining relationships at home and alienating the people best placed to help you. In these circumstances, changing your behaviour resolves the underlying problem. You might need to try various approaches to boost your self-confidence or seek help for your alcohol or drug abuse. However, the good news is that you can change your behaviour.

Change your response to stress

Sometimes you really are helpless. Perhaps your wife is dying from terminal breast cancer. Perhaps you've reached retirement age and feel at a loose end. Perhaps your mother is severely demented from Alzheimer's disease and no longer recognises you or her grandchildren. In these situations there is little you can do to resolve your predicament. However, changing your response to the stressor might help you cope. For example, find out more about the illness suffered by someone close to you. This helps you feel in control of the disease, rather than feeling that the condition controls you. Identify and acknowledge the things you do – perhaps unknowingly – that make your situation worse. Perhaps you could think more positively, for example using cognitive behavioural therapy, psychoanalysis or counselling (see Chapter 10).

Chapter 3

Towards assertive coping

In Chapter 2, we saw that changing our response to stress can help us effectively manage stress before problematic symptoms or inappropriate behaviours emerge. And we saw that these strategies – which broadly mean changing your environment, behaviour or response – all tackle the underlying problem that causes the stress symptoms or inappropriate behaviour. Assertive coping places us back in control of our lives. In this chapter, we will explore how you can assess your personal circumstances and devise an individualised plan to tackle your problems using these strategies. We will then explore ways to implement and stick to this plan. It is only by taking the decision to take charge of your life and deal with the events, situations and people that cause you distress that you will free yourself from the mental and physical effects of excessive stress.

Do you have a stress-related problem?

Asking whether you really have a stress-related problem might seem a strange question. However, remember that stress is a normal biological response. An appropriate level of stress helps us attain our peak performance. So the occasional sleepless night before a big event, a tinge of anxiety for a couple of days before a major presentation, or a 'normal' amount of depression and grief following a relative's death – however upsetting – are not something that requires help from a GP, psychologist or other healthcare professional. They are all natural and appropriate responses that help you adapt to changing life circumstances.

It is important to keep the problems facing you now in perspective. After all, every life has its ups and downs. Every life has moments of tragedy and moments of elation. We should embrace these varying emotions rather than trying to medicalise or manage them away. That said, too many of us suffer pervasive stress-related symptoms that mean the peaks are too few and far between. The bad times dramatically outnumber the good. In other words, when you suffer insomnia for weeks on end; when you can't shake off the anxiety; or when the depression becomes protracted and particularly intense, you have developed a stress-related problem. And that's when assertive coping can help you to restore the balance.

So how do you know if you've developed a stress-related problem that you need to address? The quizzes throughout the book should offer some insight into the severity of your stress. They'll also help you decide whether that stress has begun to spill over into physical and mental symptoms.

- Turn back to the life stress scale on page 24. How many of these events apply to you? Your risk of developing a stress-related problem reflects the number of major life events you have experienced over the past year. In general, the higher your score, the greater your risk of developing stress-related problems. Think about how each event you've experienced over the last year has affected you. Perhaps write down a couple of sentences summarising your feelings. Is it really a problem? Do you find it winds you up just thinking about it? Does it still cast a shadow over your daily life? Or is it in the past without leaving any legacy? These questions can help you clarify the issues that cause you stress as well as providing an insight into the impact of the problems on your life. The answers might help you prioritise your problems and possibly suggest some solutions. If stress-related symptoms have emerged (or even if they haven't), you can use the strategies in this chapter and the tips in Chapter 10 to tackle the problems before they start to affect your mental or physical health.
- We vary widely in our response to stress, and the effectiveness of our coping strategies differs. We all have genetically determined biological weakness and strengths, which partly determine how we react to stress. The questions on pages 16–18 allow you to work out how many stress-related symptoms you have. The more stress signals you experience, the more serious your stress problem might be.
- Stress can trigger anxiety and depression in susceptible people. Your first priority should be to seek professional help. Severe

depression or intense anxiety will probably need treatment from a doctor, and these conditions can impair your ability to review your life and reduce the causes of your stress. Psychiatrists sometimes use the Hospital Anxiety and Depression Scale (see pages 178–79) to determine if patients suffer from these conditions. Although psychiatric conditions can be difficult to self-diagnose, the scales might help you decide whether you need to consult a GP. They are just a guide, however. If you feel that you suffer unacceptable anxiety or depression you should seek help promptly.

• If you've been pushing yourself too hard, the prolonged stress and frustration might be on the verge of overwhelming your defences. In other words, you're at risk of burnout. Our quiz on pages 18–19 helps you determine how close you are to this point.

Stress can exacerbate or, more rarely, cause a wide variety of mental and physical health problems (see Chapters 6 and 8). If you're worried about your symptoms, talk to your doctor. Tackling any potentially serious mental or physical problem – if you're chronically depressed or have numerous risk factors for heart disease, for example – should be your priority. In the latter case, some of the principles outlined in this chapter could help you make the lifestyle modifications that could, literally, save your life.

Key elements in behavioural change

Coping assertively with stress means, directly or indirectly, changing your patterns of behaviour. (Changing your environment or altering your response to stress will indirectly change your behaviour.) However, this isn't easy. Overcoming stress usually means changing entrenched mental or physical habits. You didn't develop these habits overnight. So you cannot expect to change them overnight. Indeed, many psychologists believe that it takes between three and six months to change a fundamental behaviour or habit.

Psychologists now recognise several elements as being central in any attempt to change your behaviour. Taylor describes these as follows.

Self-monitoring

This involves writing down how often you experience a particular inappropriate reaction or stress-related symptom; what factors led to the reaction or the symptom (the antecedents); and its consequences. So if stress causes you to drink excessively, note down how often you drink, how much, what the triggers were (for instance, hassle at work, problems with your partner), the related feelings (for example, intense anxiety) and the consequences (such as the money spent and the time you needed to take off work). You will be more aware of the impact that the problem has on your current life in terms of emotion, expenditure and time.

You should also keep a note after you make any change, such as reducing your stress-related spending, alcohol consumption, smoking or overeating. This helps you monitor your success. If a particular approach doesn't seem to be working, try something else. For example, stress can trigger compulsive eating. As a result, stress reduction strategies can help reduce the compulsion to eat excessively. Some people find that relaxation (see pages 228–29) works. Others could discover through self-monitoring that this hasn't made a marked difference to their habit. So they could try a different approach – see Chapter 10 – to reduce the stress that drives their compulsive eating.

Goal setting

You set yourself clear, specific and achievable goals that move you from your current behavioural patterns to those you want to attain. Many attempts at reducing the causes of stress fail because the person is too ambitious or because the goals are poorly defined. If stress-related overspending has left you in debt you could, on the spur of the moment, decide that you will not spend any more money on yourself for the next six months and pay off your credit cards. This will take considerable willpower and, as such, you might fail. It might be better to set yourself a budget for each month and stick to it. This could take longer, but you're less likely to fail.

In some cases, you also need to consider your long-, medium- and short-term goals as well as the immediate ones. The long-term goal might be to get your ideal job. So, list your work experience, qualifications and interests. See how these compare to the job description for your ideal employer. Set yourself medium-term goals that take you closer to your ultimate ambition, such as further education, learning a new skill or brushing up a foreign language. The short-term goal is to find out what courses, grants and loans are available. The immediate goal might be visiting the library at lunchtime to read some prospectuses. (In the meantime, feeling your career is going somewhere can also reduce stress levels in your current job.)

Contracting

You agree with yourself that you will meet these personal goals. You can do this mentally. However, writing the contract down gives it a permanence and legitimacy as well as acting as an *aide memoire* if needed. It might seem slightly strange writing a contract to yourself, but psychologists recognise it as a powerful technique for change. Indeed, some clinics use patient–doctor contracts when, for example, treating obesity, alcohol abuse or drug addiction. You could draw up the contract with someone you trust, say your partner. The contract could also include a timescale – for example, you will lose 10kg in three months – and agree that, if you succeed, you will have a weekend away. This association between a specific outcome and a reward is a powerful way to change behaviour.

Shaping

This is the process of attaining your goal in specific steps that you can achieve. You can develop your own plans or, for more intractable issues, follow the stages of change model (see pages 56–63), which offers a framework to help you tackle many stress-related problems.

Self-reinforcement

Essentially, you reward yourself when you reach your goal – even if it's a short-term one. This could mean, for example, renting a video or pampering yourself in the bath. Alternatively, you could put some money aside to buy yourself a treat or pay for a special holiday. This approach helps reinforce the behaviour you want.

Stimulus-control

Once you know what triggers your stress-related behaviour, you can take steps to eliminate the stimulus. For example, if stress causes you to eat too many cakes or chocolates, don't have them in the house. You can also reduce your level of arousal, which will mean that the stimulus doesn't have the same effect. So if stress triggers drinking, you might be able to reduce your alcohol consumption if you're more relaxed. The final chapter in this book offers some tips to help bolster your stress defences.

Modelling or observational learning

You can learn to tackle a problem by following the advice of those who have succeeded in overcoming it. You could find inspiration by talking to friends who have experienced similar problems, or join a support group such as Alcoholics Anonymous★ or Weight Watchers.★ Or try reading around the topic. Autobiographies such as Johnstone's *A Head Full of Blue* or Styron's *Darkness Visible* can be inspirational to people struggling to overcome alcohol abuse or suffering from depression respectively. Both authors recovered from their problems. Many self-help books – such as Milam and Ketcham's *Under The Influence* – also include case histories that describe ways in which other people have coped with the problems. For more details, see the 'Further reading' section at the end of this chapter.

Identifying the problem

You need to identify the underlying cause of your stress before you can tackle it. However, identifying the specific cause of your stress might prove more difficult than it seems. Some of the issues might be subconscious or so entrenched in your daily life that you no longer notice how much they disturb you or unconsciously gratify you. One approach is to write down everything that stresses you out or winds you up. Don't think about this: uncritically brainstorming may allow you to engage with your subconscious issues. Simply write it all down.

You then need to decide how to tackle the problems. It's possible to break them down into different levels of stressors (see pages 32–34). Putting your problems into categories helps clarify the issue – and allows you to develop a plan to tackle each one. For example, if the journey to work causes you stress, take a different route, leave earlier or later, or cycle instead of using public transport. You will probably find that you can't change the macrolevel stressors – such as economic inequality – but assessing your problems this way helps you differentiate between those things you can change and those you can't. In the latter case, you can find ways of changing your reaction to stress, perhaps through meditation (pages 226–28), relaxation (pages 228–30) or one of the other solutions in the final chapter that lower your general level of arousal.

Often we know that something is wrong but we have only a vague idea of why. So we may feel stressed at work, but can't quite put our finger on what's wrong. You could try to clarify the issues by answering the following questions (as with most of the exercises in this book, it's best to write your responses down).

What is the problem?

State the problem in a clear, simple sentence, such as: 'I drink too much every Friday night' or 'I can't meet the monthly sales targets'. If you cannot state the problem in a simple sentence, you may have more than one problem. So try breaking the problem down. You can also home in on the fundamental problem by considering what the problem is *not*. So you might *not* be unhappy with your family life or hobbies. What's left? Your social life? Your job?

Who contributes to the problem?

List all the people who increase your stress levels and those whom you feel comfortable around. This might help you identify the people or situations that contribute to your stress. You need to be wary of projection (see page 40), a common coping strategy and largely unconscious process that involves blaming someone else for your stress, anxiety and other problems. In some cases, other people may, indeed, be the problem. However, frequently we have at least contributed to our difficulties. Perhaps, for example, you are a type A personality (see pages 29–32) and your innate aggressive tendencies mean you clash excessively with a colleague at work that you don't particularly get on with. Type A behaviour might simply increase the tension between you. You can work on these traits and use assertiveness training (see pages 230–31) or transactional analysis (see pages 64–66) to attain your objectives.

Where does the problem occur?

Do you develop your stress symptoms mainly at work, at home or in another environment? Do you overeat or drink too much in response to environmental and emotional 'cues', such as when you are anxious or bored? Understanding where a problem occurs can help uncover some of the reasons *why* it occurs.

When does the problem occur?

Is there a time in the month when your stress-related symptoms tend to peak? Perhaps you suffer from premenstrual syndrome (see pages 163–65). Perhaps it's the week before the pay check comes in. Keeping a diary may help to reveal when a problem occurs. In particular, diaries can help you tackle specific problems. So, if you want to cut down the amount of alcohol you consume, keep a record for a couple of weeks of when, where and how much you drink. Keeping a record helps you define your goals and might reveal ways you can change your habits. Tracking your expenses against your mood helps reveal whether you shop in response to stress. For advice on controlling your personal expenditure, see page 52.

Identifying internal stressors

Identifying the internal conflicts, conflicting motives and frustrations that commonly give rise to stress (see pages 22–27) can prove especially difficult. In many cases, these 'internal stressors' reflect the gulf between our aspirations and how we find ourselves today. For example, looking after a family as well as working outside the home and working for a company you feel behaves unethically can lead to stress. But characterising our aspirations can prove surprisingly difficult. It is important to realise that even realistic or 'ordinary' expectations can be a source of conflict, guilt and envy. A counsellor, psychotherapist or life coach can offer a new perspective that helps you get to the root of your problems (see Chapter 10).

Another approach is to write your own obituary – twice. Read a few obituaries in a quality newspaper and then write your own, firstly the way you would like to be remembered at the end of your life. As a good father? An inspirational leader in your field? Someone who worked hard for others? Now the tough part. Be honest – which can be hard – and write your obituary as it would be today. Compare the two. How do they differ? Those differences could be causing you stress (or inner conflict). So plan a route with long-, medium- and short-term goals that will enable you to move from the second obituary towards the first. Be aware of setting your sights too high, however. Trying to meet an unrealistic ideal can also cause considerable stress.

Writing a 'wish list' helps you home in on some inner stressors. Compile a list of your hopes and desires for the future. It does not matter how silly, trivial or unrealistic some of these wishes are. You can filter out the childish fantasies and obviously unattainable dreams later, preferably after putting the list to one side for a couple of days. Of the wishes that are left, you will probably find that there are some that you can realise quickly. Others might take longer to achieve. You might want to rank these in order of importance (considering the 'opportunity cost' – see pages 53–54 – might help you prioritise). Drawing up a wish list can also highlight areas in your current life that fall far short of your expectations, which might be causing your stress-related symptoms. You might need to put in some work on achieving your long-term goals – but at least you will have worked out what really matters to you.

Using another variation on this theme – suggested by the management consultant Brian Clegg – you imagine that you have won the National Lottery jackpot. Which current activities would you still perform? Which would you drop? What would you do with the money? Unfettered by financial concerns, would you open a bookshop? Run a self-sufficient smallholding? Paint? Again, this may uncover some inner conflicts that are causing stress. You can then define your ultimate ambition and plan some ways to make it happen financially – although this might mean making sacrifices. Even if you are unable or unwilling to make the changes, you can still consider some appropriate ways to fulfil your ambitions, perhaps on a smaller scale than if you became rich suddenly. You can still define the long-, medium-, short-term and immediate goals that take you there.

Finding the answer

As you ponder the answers to the above questions, some solutions might immediately emerge. It might be obvious, for example, that if you drink to bolster your self-confidence you need to build up the ability to relate to others without the alcohol – in which case assertiveness training (see pages 230–31) and transactional analysis (see page 64) might help. If a lack of money in the last week of the month causes arguments and stress, try to budget effectively (see box overleaf).

Effective budgeting

You can apply many of the principles outlined in this chapter in order to budget effectively. Money worries are a common cause of stress. So look at your daily and weekly spending after keeping a money diary for a couple of months and ask yourself if you are happy about how your money has been spent. Look at your direct debits and see if you can cut back on any regular payments. Break your budget into:

- **essential spending** – those things you genuinely have to spend money on, such as your mortgage, bills and food, and
- **desirable purchases** – things you do not strictly *need*, such as that designer outfit or daily latte from the coffee shop.

Consider reducing your essential spending by changing your mortgage lender, or switching insurers and utilities companies. *Rip-off Britain – and How to Beat it* from Which? Books* shows how to cut costs on a wide range of goods and services, while *Which?* magazine* regularly supplies consumers with money-saving advice.

You should also determine which, if any, benefits you're entitled to – contact your local Benefits Agency. Write to your creditors and try to negotiate lower payments, or consider combining all your loans into one payment. These steps will allow you to develop a budget that lets you live within your means as well as save for the future. For example, you might aim to save 5 or 10 per cent of your income after tax. On the food budget you might find you can reduce your expenditure by 25 per cent without too much difficulty, especially if you cook in bulk, avoid prepared meals and takeaways, take a packed lunch to work and entertain at home. You may be able to shave even more off your personal expenditure, especially if your spending habits are driven by stress – although you might need to employ transactional analysis (see pages 64–66) if, for example, you need to talk to your partner in order to tackle his or her stress-related spending habits.

Ironically, money worries can cause stress, which fuels spending. Keep a note of your progress and be prepared to change tactics if a particular strategy doesn't seem to be working.

By following the advice in this chapter, you should have a clearer idea of your goals and aspirations. However, you must be honest about what you can achieve. For example, many people harbour a vague ambition to work for themselves, ideally at home. However, working at home suits only some people. You need to be highly self-motivated, able to spend hours alone and to work without the social and administrative support of a corporate culture. In effect, you are everything from MD to company accountant to the person who makes the tea. Ask yourself whether you could really attain your ambition on a practical and emotional level.

Opportunity costs

Often the answer to your stress-causing problems might mean making sacrifices. So you need to decide whether the reduction in your stress is worth the cost. This means balancing the severity of your stress against the sacrifice you need to make. Perhaps, for example, the constant stress at work and your desire for independence means that you would like to work for yourself. Perhaps you would like to undergo formal psychotherapy (see page 233), which can be time-consuming and expensive. Making such decisions isn't easy when we are constricted by limitations on our time and money. Thinking out the options in terms of the 'opportunity costs' can help you decide where your priorities lie.

Opportunity costs is a concept widely used in economics. It is also useful for everyday decisions. For example, if you plan to make a big purchase without resorting to credit you have to choose between the competing demands on your money. If you decide to buy a new washing machine, you may need to put that weekend away on hold. In other words, the cost of the washing machine isn't just the price on the ticket; the cost is also the opportunity to go on holiday. (As this example suggests, the opportunity costs approach is an effective way of deciding whether your next purchase is really worth the other things you will need to forgo.)

Similarly, if you decide to go to formal psychotherapy twice a week, you might miss the opportunity to spend time with your children or to, say, go to the theatre and out for a meal each month. Only you can decide whether the insights you might gain will be worth the other sacrifices.

Opportunity costs can also help you decide whether you can afford to be self-employed, for example. You may make a profit of £40,000 a year, for example. However, if you could have earned £50,000 with an employer, the opportunity cost of your time is £10,000. It is important to realise that this does not tell you anything about whether the price is worth paying. You might gain emotionally by spending more time with your family or by feeling that you control your own life. Only you can decide whether it is worth losing £10,000 to work for yourself. Nevertheless, considering the opportunity cost is a powerful tool to help you balance your competing priorities, evaluate your life choices and move towards assertive coping.

Define your goals

After analysing your problems and your capability to change, you can define your long-, medium- and short-term as well as your immediate goals. These goals should be specific and attainable: for a man, 'drinking no more than 21 units a week from today' (a short-term goal) rather than 'cutting down on my drinking'. Or for a woman, 'being a size 12 within three months' (a medium-term goal) rather than 'losing weight', for example.

Values come first

Goals need to be consistent with your core values. Any inconsistency might breed internal conflict, trigger conflicting motives or lead to frustration, which can contribute to stress. Consciously or not, your values have helped to shape your decisions throughout your life. But despite their importance, most of us do not examine our values. Rather we accumulate values almost by default through our experiences. Yet our careers, relationships and political views all reflect, to a certain extent, values we have held at one time or another (values can change, depending on our life circumstances).

Defining your values means asking yourself some searching questions. So ask yourself what are the one or two most important philosophies underpinning your life? Perhaps it is living according to ethical or religious principles. Perhaps it is the ideals that govern your relationships with other people. And ask yourself: where would I like these philosophies to take me in five or ten years? How do you want to behave, act and be remembered as parent, partner, employer or employee and so on? What do you want to achieve in each of these domains? This statement of your core values should help you align your behaviour with your beliefs.

In particular, we need to stop performing activities that are inconsistent with our core values – otherwise stress is almost inevitable. For example, you might be a committed environmentalist, but work for a company that considerably pollutes the environment. Values that are consistent and remain core to the way we see ourselves and the way in which we want to live need to be better integrated into our daily lives. This helps bolster your stress defences.

Putting your plan into practice

First, think about committing your core values to paper. As mentioned above, writing something down gives it a permanence and legitimacy it may otherwise lack. A written statement is also something you feel you can control. However, once again you need to be honest. No one will see this except you (unless you want someone else to – but think carefully before sharing it). This statement also offers you a vision of what you want to become.

The next step is to define the smaller steps and goals over the medium term (say over the next three years) that will take you towards this vision. Now consider the shorter term. What do you need to do over the next year? Keep breaking the task down into smaller and smaller steps – for example, what do you need to do this month? This week? Today? In this way, you'll make continual progress towards your ultimate goal. As American management guru James Scarnati comments: 'With vision comes direction, and with direction comes purpose, and with purpose comes commitment'.

As you strive towards your objectives, be aware that trying to live by your core values could lead to conflict – for example, between altruism and self-interest. And take care not to be too attached to your past views. Everyone changes and develops, and putting into practice some of the ideas in this book may involve gradually adopting a new mindset. However, some of your family and colleagues may expect you still to adhere to your older views. If they react to the fact that you are thinking or behaving differently (whether consciously or not), this itself can cause stress. In some cases, you might need to explicitly state your new views and values.

Case history: Jan

Jan, a 40-year-old bank manager, had both vision and commitment. She identified three major problems in her life. First, she was dissatisfied with her career and wanted to spend more time on her hobby as a semi-professional photographer. This internal conflict caused stress. Second, she felt weighed under by her financial commitments – especially a huge mortgage that would not be paid off until a couple of years after she retired. Finally, she wanted to get fit. Her father had died of heart disease a week after his fiftieth birthday. Her health concerns caused her considerable distress.

Jan decided to start with her fitness. She booked lessons at a gym and started jogging. She felt a great sense of achievement as her exercise tolerance rose steadily. Jan felt her career and financial problems were intertwined, so she concentrated on paying off her credit cards and loans one at a time and put her house on the market. She quit her job, and moved to a cheaper part of the country where she now splits her time between photography and helping local businesses with their tax, VAT and finances. Her total income is less – but this is almost balanced by her lower outgoings. Gradually, she is building up the time she spends on her photography.

Jan succeeded by setting herself long-, medium- and short-term goals and implementing a plan to achieve them. If all stress-related problems could be solved easily, we would be able quit smoking, stop drinking or excessively eating overnight. In fact, changing habits is hard. However, the 'stages of change' model offers a framework that allows you to think about the steps you will need to go through before you make any behavioural change, whether large or small.

Stages of change

Psychologists originally developed the 'stages of change' model (also called the transtheoretical model of behaviour change) to help smokers quit. However, it proved a powerful tool for major change, and other researchers have applied the idea to other difficult-to-manage behaviours (see box, page 63).

The stages of change model offers a powerful technique for discovering and learning things for yourself. You can employ it to deal with your stress-causing problems or inappropriate responses to pressure. It offers a framework that, along with the other aspects of behavioural change discussed above, allows you to devise a plan to deal with your problems.

The stages of change model

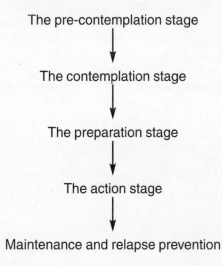

The pre-contemplation stage

↓

The contemplation stage

↓

The preparation stage

↓

The action stage

↓

Maintenance and relapse prevention

We'll look at the different stages in turn, although note that the boundary between the different stages is often blurred. The model applies just as much to making a major change in, say, reducing alcohol consumption, or altering the way you work as it does to quitting smoking. Appreciating where you are on this path as you try to tackle a problem should help you work out how you can move forward.

The pre-contemplation stage

At first, you are not interested in changing – even if it is for your own good. Psychologists call this the pre-contemplation stage, when you are often in denial. Often, however, the denial hides a feeling of disempowerment. In other words, you're not in control. During the pre-contemplation stage many people have, subconsciously at least, an external locus of control (see pages 24–26). Nevertheless, eventually something happens – or the evidence simply becomes overwhelming – and you realise that something has to alter. You have pulled the trigger for change.

Indeed, a trigger precedes every behavioural change, large or small, good or bad. Think back to some habit you changed, whether positively or not. You can probably identify a trigger. In some cases, a particular event prompts you to change. Perhaps stress triggers your excessive drinking or overspending. The trigger to stop might be a fear about the effect on your health or a letter from your bank. Whatever the trigger, once you realise that you have a problem you move into the contemplation stage.

The contemplation stage

The contemplation stage is the first step towards becoming empowered and tackling your stressors or changing the inappropriate behaviour. Ironically, during the contemplation stage you may not really know whether you want to make the change. Often, giving up a behavioural pattern leads to a sense of loss that can be difficult to overcome. Moreover, at this stage, there always appear to be numerous barriers to break through.

For example, heavy drinkers and shopaholics might wonder how they will fill the hours that were previously spent in bars or shopping. Perhaps you fear failure. If your self-confidence is particularly low, the fear of failure may mean that you never take the necessary action to tackle your stress. Indeed, failure can exacerbate the stress, at least in the short term.

So during the contemplation stage you should take a long, hard look at the pros and cons of the change that you are considering. To do this, discover all you can about the stressor or inappropriate behaviour. You may, for example, want to understand the risks associated with smoking and look at the various techniques that can help you quit.

Asking yourself two key questions can help during the contemplation phase. Firstly, ask yourself: 'What would it take for me to change?' This may uncover the factors motivating you to change.

For instance, a smoker realises that a diagnosis of cancer or heart disease would motivate her to quit. However, she knows that it would be too late to take action to preserve her health by the time she gets ill. So she reads some books and articles about the health hazards to encourage herself to take immediate action. Recognising how much money she spends each week on her nicotine addiction might be another motivating factor. In the latter case, noting the expenditure helps her move to the next stage.

Then consider the other side. Ask yourself 'What are the barriers and problems that stop you from making the change?' For example, what currently stops you from giving up smoking? Critically, you need to ask yourself what you get, or used to get, from your current behaviour – despite the fact that it now causes stress. Alcohol, over-eating and excessive spending can offer a short-term release from stress, for example. However destructive the habit has become, we usually started because the habit gave us some pleasure. But now it may have become painful. Focusing on the factors that motivate the change aims to replace the pain with pleasure. So you could use some of the money that you once spent on smoking to pay for something pleasurable for yourself. This switch will spur you towards behavioural change.

Again, in many cases you may not be able quite to put your finger on what is holding you back or presenting the obstacle. So try brain-storming: list *everything* you feel *could* hold you back. Do not make any judgements about these factors at this stage. List everything, no matter how silly it may appear. Then strike out the things you can do nothing about: age, physical illnesses and so on. Next, strike out the factors that are impractical, perhaps for financial reasons. You will then be left with the barriers and obstacles that fall within your control.

Typically, people spend three or four months mentally chewing things over before they decide to prepare to make a life change. However, some people remain at this stage for years. If you have been contemplating a change for several months, you need now to consider whether you really want to move on. Do you subconsciously consider the opportunity cost to be too great, for example? If not you need to begin preparing for change.

The preparation stage

By the time you reach the preparation stage, you will have decided to make the change and will now be taking specific steps towards carrying out a plan, probably within the next few weeks. The preparation stage offers an ideal time to experiment with smaller changes, which give you confidence but are not enough to make a significant difference. You might try to avoid stress-provoking situations as far as possible – for example, drinkers and smokers may try to avoid the environmental cues that, in the past, led to binges or lighting up. This might entail keeping a diary or record of the impact of the changes. Internal cues could be dealt with through relaxation or meditation (see Chapter 10). If you stick to your resolutions, you should see a modest reduction in your inappropriate behaviour or some alleviation of your stress-related symptoms.

The action stage

The small-scale experiments undertaken at the preparation stage give you the confidence to move to the next, bigger step – the action stage. Once you have made inroads with the smaller changes, you can then make bigger alterations – for example, move from reducing your alcohol consumption to staying within the safe limits, or from cutting back on your spending to staying within a budget for good – and take determined action to incorporate the new behaviour into your daily life. You then need to stick with it. Again it is important to monitor your progress and reward yourself when you attain your goals.

Maintenance and relapse prevention

Unfortunately, the power of environmental and external cues means that relapses are common. And stress is a common trigger for relapses. A particularly stressful day can lead to a smoker reaching for the packet or a drinker stopping off for several pints. Some of the relaxation and other techniques in Chapter 10 can lower your general level of arousal. This should mean that you can cope with an increased level of stress before getting to the point where your behaviour becomes inappropriate or you develop stress-related symptoms.

When you relapse, it can be hard to pick yourself up again. However, don't give up. If you do slip up, don't be too hard on yourself. Perform a post-mortem to help prevent further relapses. Look at the reasons why you lapsed. Can you identify any triggers that led to the relapse? Is there anything that you can do to prevent yourself from lapsing again? After several months, these new patterns of behaviour become habitual and your life changes for the better.

Sticking with the programme

As you might expect, change carries an emotional cost. On the life stress scale (see page 24), revising personal habits scores 24 points, two less than starting or leaving school, college or university and one more than trouble with your boss. However, following some simple rules can help.

Find the time

Many of the strategies that you might need to counter stress can be time-consuming. Counselling, exercise and constructive hobbies all eat into your leisure hours, for example. And you need to find time to monitor your progress. So the first step in changing your life is to ensure that you have enough time to put your new life plan into practice. The time management techniques on pages 219–25 and in *Which? Way to Manage your Time – and Your Life* might help.

Tackle one problem at a time

Unless you are lucky, you will find you have more than one problem. Deal with them one or, at most, two at a time. Often people fail to change their lives because they try to do too much, too soon. Ideally you should concentrate on one or two specific areas and not set yourself too high a target. Succeed in these and you will develop the self-confidence to tackle the next item on your list. So do not necessarily start with the biggest, most intractable problem. Tackling the simpler ones first gives you the confidence to make bigger changes.

This may mean breaking larger problems into smaller ones. Nibble away at the edges of a problem and eventually it will disappear. Make smaller changes that you can maintain and fit into your everyday life. As Gael Lindenfield notes in *Assert Yourself*, starting with a 'mini-risk and gradually working towards taking the big chances with your life' is the 'golden rule of assertiveness training'.

Be realistic

Set yourself clear, specific, achievable and realistic goals. Don't waste your life on unattainable dreams. There is no point in wishing to be a striker for Arsenal if you are fat and forty. But playing for a local team might be a reasonable aspiration.

Focus on the present

Focusing on short-term benefits is a much more powerful motivator than some advantages in the dim and distant future.

Few people can motivate themselves to exercise, for example, on the single premise of maintaining good health when they are elderly. If you want to exercise, concentrate on the immediate benefits, such as feeling fitter, looking better or not getting so out-of-breath.

Sort out your options

Stress can lead you to lose your sense of perspective, especially if you have developed one of the inappropriate stress responses such as denial, repression or projection (see pages 37–41). However, you have probably got more options than you think. If you want to change your job, for example, make a list of your experience and interests both inside and outside work. Then think of all the possible ways you can use these skills. Don't evaluate your ideas at this stage. Once you've brainstormed all the ideas, strike out the totally impractical. Then write down the pros and cons of each career change you are contemplating, with relation to specific job descriptions. This should help you find one or two careers that are more in line with your aspirations and values. And, therefore, they will be less likely to lead to chronic stress.

Don't go too fast

Change your life gradually. Attempting to change too fast, too hard, often leads to boom-and-bust. For example, rapidly increasing the amount of exercise you take can lead to injury or exhaustion. Likewise, dieters are more likely to keep the weight off if they lose it gradually rather than during a crash diet.

Keep a sense of balance

If you work out or play computer games to relieve the stress caused by over-working, don't let that activity become your obsession. You will just be swapping one addiction for another, which will in turn cause stress. Don't switch from being a flagrant spendthrift to a miser. Don't spend so much time developing your small business that you spend even less time with your family. Try to keep a sense of balance.

Applying the stages of change model

Scientists have assessed the potential of the stages of change model for tackling a range of problems.

- Suminski and Petosa used the approach to encourage undergraduate students to exercise.
- Shepherd and Shepherd note that some dieticians suggest using the model to help people eat healthier diets.
- Rusch and Corrigan used the model to improve the insight of people with schizophrenia about the disease and their willingness to take their treatment. (Poor adherence with drugs for schizophrenia is a major obstacle to effective treatment.)
- Mauck and colleagues used the model to explore why many women declined treatment for osteoporosis (brittle bone disease) even after they suffered a hip fracture.

These few studies exemplify the model's potential in addressing a range of behavioural problems. Nevertheless, using the model in clinical practice can pose several problems. For example, Shepherd and Shepherd note that the lack of specific behaviours and appropriate targets makes applying the technique to healthy eating difficult.

Littell and Girvin examined 87 studies that used the stages of change model to alter a variety of behaviours. They found that the stages are 'not mutually exclusive' and relatively few people move through the discrete stages. In other words, the stages merge into each other: the contemplation and action stages can overlap, for instance. Nevertheless, the authors add that the model has 'considerable heuristic value': the stages of change model allows you to discover and learn things for yourself.

Transactional analysis

Implementing a new budget to reduce the stress arising from money worries can mean negotiating with your partner. Effectively dealing with problems between members of your family could reduce the pressure placed on your relationships. Learning to say no to an unreasonable demand from your boss can also help reduce stress. However, this means understanding how we interact when we communicate.

If you are aware of your behaviour and that of the people you are in contact with, you will be better placed to identify and manage the causes of your stress – as well as to help implement your plan for reaching your long-term goals. In the 1950s and 1960s, the American psychologist Eric Berne proposed a system called transactional analysis to explain how people interact. This system can help us understand the communications that cause stress or that inhibit us from meeting our goals. The idea is now sometimes used as part of private and NHS counselling, psychotherapy and marital therapy.

Berne suggested examining the way we communicate as one of three behavioural modes: parent, adult or child. In the parent mode, you are either critical or nurturing. You might tell your subordinates at work, for example, that they must do something. This is the oppressive parent mode. However, you can also show your caring side. If a member of staff has a problem, for example, you may show this nurturing side by offering to 'look after it for them'. This is the supportive parent mode.

The adult mode is most obvious when you are speaking to your peers or, in many cases, your partner. In this mode, you take rational, balanced decisions, free of prejudices, obligations or emotions. On the other hand, the child mode (also known as the infant mode) lets your emotions run away with you. You move into this mode when you experience happiness, anger, jealousy or fear. The child mode also embraces curiosity. In very broad terms, the parent encapsulates our values, the adult is rational, while the child encompasses our emotions and creativity. (Note that the child mode is not necessarily the same thing as being childish.)

It's important to note that these terms are used in a different way to normal conversation. They refer to states of mind. So while curiosity is a normal emotion for adults, transactional analysis regards it as a manifestation of our inner child. The analysis looks at normal emotions. We all are caring, jealous and rational at different times. Even an oppressive parent mode might be appropriate in some situations – for example, when managing certain people in particular circumstances or ensuring a child stays safe. The model offers you a framework to consider your emotions and inter-relationships, and enables you to ask yourself if one or more emotions dominate. We should aim to balance our inner parent, adult and child.

We can be in more than one mode at a time. For example, a presentation you give to your peers might be a parent–child transaction. The discussion that follows is in adult–adult mode. However, you may also have something of the child in you throughout because of nerves, anxiety and so on.

Thinking in these terms can help identify and manage some of the causes of our stress. For example, crossed transactions where the participants use different behavioural modes can cause considerable stress. Your partner might want an adult-to-adult or even an adult-to-supportive-parent conversation about a stress-related problem at work. However, if you answer by changing the topic to the problems that are currently causing you stress, you are in the child mode.

Furthermore, people stuck in the dominating or supportive parent state are authoritarian, which can trigger stress among those around them. At best, they are well-intentioned and benign. At worse, they are bullies, and people stuck in the adult mode tend to be cold and calculating. At the other extreme, people stuck in the child mode are often unable to make decisions.

Nevertheless, you can manipulate crossed transactions. Marriage guidance counsellors often use transactional analysis with their clients. They can, for example, help change a child–child discourse, which can cause stress in a relationship, to an adult–adult conversation. You can also use transactional analysis to help you understand and motivate your work colleagues or staff, which may enable you to tackle some of the stressors at work. Note which persona you tend to adopt naturally. When faced with your boss, you may move from adult to child mode, for example. But to negotiate effectively and address the causes of your stress you might have to use adult–adult mode.

Transactional analysis can also help you understand your responses to stressful situations. If you feel humiliated and clench your fists during a difficult telephone conversation, you may be in the child mode. If you always procrastinate, you may also favour the child mode because you are waiting for someone else to take the decision. This hinders your ability to deal with the conversation effectively. Developing decision-making strategies can help bolster your adult mode.

Berne popularised his ideas in a series of books including *Games People Play* and *What do You Say After You Say Hello,* which explain how you can implement transactional analysis in everyday life. Since Berne's death a number of organisations, including the Berne Institute,* have continued to develop transactional analysis and can offer further support.

Watch where you're going

Finally, if you want to tackle stress, you need to watch where you're going. Look at the life ahead of you instead of what's behind. If you want to take control of your life – perhaps the most important thing you can do to tackle stress – you need to focus on today and the future. Unfortunately, when we are stressed we tend to read from our life script, which can lead to inappropriate reactions.

We write our 'life script' in childhood. So it's largely defined around our childish strategies and imagination. As we mature, this life script becomes buried deep in our unconscious, but may emerge at times of stress. For example, bereavement early in life can undermine self-esteem and one's view of the past, present and future. This life script may mean that you selectively remember or re-enact depressing or negative memories that fuel and maintain a pessimistic view of life. 'This inner nature rarely disappears or dies,' writes the psychologist Abraham Maslow. 'It persists underground, unconsciously, even though denied and repressed . . . it speaks softly but it will be heard, even in a distorted form.'

For example, if you received sympathy when you were ill and cried as a child, then you may still react to stress by crying or developing psychosomatic symptoms (aches and pains with no physical cause). However, the reaction will have little relevance to your current situation. Think back to a recent event you found especially stressful. How did you react? Was it a childish response? Or was it a response appropriate to the reality of the situation and that of a balanced adult? Did you experience inappropriate anger? Were you tearful, anxious or embarrassed? Reflecting on the past year and writing down moments that stand out to you, both good and bad, helps you understand your life script.

Our life script can reflect our true values, dreams and ideals. However, we often reject these aspirations as we try to fit into the image of an 'average', 'successful', 'well-adjusted' adult. Indeed, we often regard these childhood dreams as 'dangerous'. As Maslow points out, turning your back on this part of the life script means rejecting much of what is fundamental to our nature, which can only contribute to stress.

You need to strike a balance. Don't waste your time on attempts to capture your glory days. The American philosopher Irving Singer points out in *The Harmony of Nature and Spirit* that we cannot restore 'those cherished goods of the past'. Singer argues that our position today, the opportunities that we can grasp and the challenges that we need to meet, are the way they are *because* we have moved on from the time when we held the 'cherished goods'. 'It was only in response to their loss that we could have acquired the possibilities present to us now,' Singer says. It is only by making the most of these present possibilities that we will bolster our stress defences and live fulfilled lives.

Further reading

Berne, E. 1968. *Games People Play*. Penguin

Berne, E. 1975. *What Do You Say after You Say Hello*. Corgi

Eysenck, M. (ed). 1998. *Psychology: an Integrated Approach*. Prentice Hall

Greener, M. 2000. *Which? Way to Manage Your Time – and Your Life*. Which? Books

Johnstone, N. 2002. *A Head Full of Blue*. Bloomsbury

Lindenfield, G. 1987. *Assert Yourself*. Thorsons

Maslow, A.H. 1999. *Toward a Psychology of Being*. Wiley, 3rd edition

Milam, J.R. and Ketcham, K. 1983. *Under the Influence*. Bantam Books

Singer, I. 1996. *The Harmony of Nature and Spirit*. The Johns Hopkins University Press

Styron, W. 1991. *Darkness Visible*. Jonathan Cape

Part 2

Stress and your health

Chapter 4

The three ages of stress

Stress, as we saw in Chapter 1, is an innate reaction to a challenge or threat. It's a fundamental, and often beneficial, biological response. It's only when stress becomes prolonged and you don't – or can't – give yourself enough time to recuperate that you begin to develop stress-related symptoms. If the threat is serious and protracted enough, sooner or later anyone could develop stress symptoms. As a result, stress-related problems respect neither social standing, sex nor age. Stress symptoms affect the affluent and the poor, men and women, and haunt us from the cradle to the grave.

We face different challenges and threats at different times of our lives. So the causes of our stress symptoms vary, to a certain extent, as we age. Understanding the 'three ages of stress' helps us to appreciate relevant factors behind our – or our loved one's – distress. And it helps us to identify causes and behavioural patterns (such as inappropriate coping strategies) that we can address using problem-solving techniques, assertive coping and a 'stages of change' model – see Chapter 3.

Stress in children and teenagers

Childhood is supposed to be the happiest time of your life. But childhood can also be a testing – and occasionally traumatic – time, and the effects of this distress can last for the rest of the person's life. For most children, the trials and tribulations of childhood don't have any lasting adverse effect. They manage to negotiate the problems, learning and developing as they mature. Nevertheless, stress can have a relatively greater effect on children than adults, who have developed a variety of coping strategies, although not all may be appropriate (see pages 36–42).

We all lay down many of the mental and emotional foundations that support us against the effects of stress during childhood. So parents can help children by providing a healthy emotional environment in which to prepare for the normal milestones, such as starting nursery and school or the arrival of a sibling. Strong foundations, such as effective coping strategies that we learn from our parents, can support us through a lifetime of trials, tribulations and tension. Weak foundations – such as role models who cope with stress by displaced aggression (see page 40) or alcohol abuse – can leave a child emotionally and mentally vulnerable to the effects of stress. A caring and supportive environment helps the child develop as a well-adjusted individual.

The arrival of a new sibling can be a time of considerable stress for parents and children. Children may worry that the parent will love the new baby more than them. They may find the crying difficult to deal with, or worry that the baby will take their toys. It's probably best to be open. Explain that life will be different, but that the new baby won't change the relationship with the existing children. Explain that the older sibling will still have his or her own toys and so on. It is probably worth discussing these issues several months before the baby is due to arrive to ensure that the children have the opportunity to air their concerns and adjust to the change.

Moving on to nursery and school can also be a time of considerable stress. Such transitions mark an important time in the evolution of your relationship with your child, the gradual separation from his or her dependency on parents. Of course, numerous separations will have taken place since the day the umbilical cord was cut. Weaning, crawling and walking all increase babies' independence. The move to school is one of the next steps that end in adolescence.

But certain children seem to be especially prone to developing separation anxiety, such as those who have had little exposure to others in the first few years of life and those who have been cared for by their parents only. Shy children and those experiencing other stresses in life – such as moving house, a different carer or the arrival of a new sibling – may be more likely to show reluctance to leave the parent's company. Try to stay calm and be sympathetic when facing a temper tantrum arising from separation anxiety. Explain that you understand that the child doesn't want you to leave. Reassure him or her that you'll be back soon. And say that you love the child. You could also gradually increase the time you're away from the child at playgroups, shopping or when he or she is playing with a friend.

This acclimatises the child to your absence and helps him or her understand that the separation is temporary.

Some children – perhaps around two per cent – avoid or refuse to attend school. Once known as 'school phobia', this syndrome isn't the same as truancy. Children may fail to attend school for a multitude of reasons and can display a wide variety of behaviours and stress signals (see page 77). But as a rule of thumb, children with school avoidance or refusal tend to stay close to their parents or caregivers. They may be anxious and fearful. Often such children become very upset or ill when forced to attend school.

You need to get any illness checked out by your doctor. If there isn't a medical reason for your child's problem, try to discover if there is a specific issue at school, such as worry about tests, teasing, or bullying (see pages 79–81). In such cases, you should talk to the teacher and devise a plan to resolve the problem. You could ask another family member or a friend to drop the child off at school. And don't make staying at home too pleasant – you could cut down on snacks, limit TV and so on. Some children initially avoid school because of fear of discipline or because they feel inadequate. But they maintain the behaviour because they can relax at home or spend hours on video games and there is no pressure over school work.

Helping the child relax and develop social skills (perhaps by suggesting he or she joins non-school clubs) or drawing up a contract offering a reward if the child behaves can help overcome school refusal. However, in extreme cases of habitual refusal, help from a psychologist, counsellor or GP might help. You need to act quickly, however, before the problem becomes entrenched.

Being in a single-parent family, although increasingly common, can cause children and parents considerable stress. Nevertheless, there is no reason why, despite the difficulties, a single-parent family can't promote a healthy emotional environment that allows children to thrive. Over the years, researchers have identified several factors that seem to increase the likelihood of overcoming the difficulties of being in a single-parent family:

- positive, active coping styles – essentially the assertive coping skills described in Chapter 3
- good family organisation and time management. *Which? Way to Manage your Time – and Your Life* offers numerous suggestions to

help your family life run more smoothly. These can prevent single-parent families from becoming overwhelmed. And it is important to think of yourself. Ensure that you have time for dating, going to the movies, talking with friends and so on, which helps build your resilience to stress

- placing a high value on loyalty and closeness in the family. Try to centre life around the home, encourage consideration for others in the family and try to talk problems over. This approach should help minimise the stress caused by the trials of everyday life
- highlight the good times and play down the bad and stressful moments
- develop supportive social networks. There is an increasing number of clubs and organisations for single-parent families. Your local library should have details.

Together these strategies can help single-parent families feel that they are in control of their destiny.

The physical effect of stress

Stress can affect a child's psychological, emotional and even physical development. For example, according to research reported by Power and Manor, by seven years of age children who experienced certain persistent stress-related complaints – such as frequent and chronic bedwetting (enuresis) – were around 0.8cm shorter than their less stressed peers. By the age of 23 years, the gap between the children who had still suffered from enuresis at 11 years of age and their peers increased to more than 1cm, even after the researchers allowed for other factors that influence height. One centimetre might not sound like much, but it's a manifestation of the child's inner turmoil.

Indeed, doctors now recognise a condition called psychosocial short stature (also called hyperphagic short stature). Children with this condition are shorter than they should be for their age because of chronic stress. The short stature might arise because stress reduces the production of growth hormone. Ironically, most children with psychosocial short stature show excessive hunger (hyperphagia). Many of these children also suffer from mild learning disabilities. Fortunately, Gohlke and co-workers found recently that the growth of almost all children with

The prevalence of psychiatric conditions in children

As the examples in this chapter suggest, children aren't immune from the effects of stress and other psychological problems. Most cope with the support of the family. However, a minority develop more serious complaints such as anxiety and depression. For example, Keller and colleagues reported in the early 1990s that 14 per cent of a group of children suffered from clinical anxiety. (Clinical anxiety has the same relationship to 'nerves' as full-blown depression has to a touch of the blues – for more detail see Chapter 7.)

On average, the anxiety emerged at ten years old, and almost half of the children – 46 per cent – were ill for at least eight years. In another study, Cooper and Goodyer from Addenbrooke's Hospital in Cambridge found that 3.6 per cent of 1,072 girls aged between 11 and 16 years suffered full-blown depression during the month before the study. Six per cent suffered full-blown depression at some time during the last year. Many other girls showed several symptoms typical of depression, but their condition didn't quite meet the formal diagnostic criteria used by doctors. Around 9 and 21 per cent suffered from this 'partial syndrome' over the last month before the study and during the preceding year respectively.

In many cases, anxiety, depression and other psychiatric diseases emerge when stressful life events act against a genetically determined vulnerability. However, many more children suffer stress-related symptoms without manifesting overt clinical anxiety or depression. For more information about the treatment of depression, anxiety and other psychiatric illness in children and adults, see Chapter 7.

psychosocial short stature tends to catch up after they leave the stressful environment.

Psychosocial short stature isn't the only health problem linked to stress in children. For example, Thernlund and co-workers found that children who experience a number of stressful life events over the first two years are almost twice as likely to develop diabetes before their fifteenth birthday as their less stressed peers. Poor behaviour (one symptom of stress) and coming from a dysfunctional or chaotic family seemed to further increase the risk of developing diabetes. Numerous other environmental and genetic factors seem to contribute to the risk that a child will develop diabetes. The link with stress is just one of these, but it seems to trigger the immune system to mount and destroy the cells in the pancreas that produce insulin. And it's another striking example of how stress can contribute to serious medical diseases, an issue we'll return to in Chapter 6.

Overcoming the scars of sexual abuse

Childhood sex abuse can leave a tragic legacy. In the United States, Kendler found that women sexually abused as children are at markedly increased risk – in general, at least threefold – of developing a wide variety of psychiatric disorders. The link was especially strong with bulimia, drug abuse and alcoholism.

Fortunately, severe childhood sexual abuse remains relatively uncommon. In Kendler's study, around 30 per cent of those interviewed reported experiencing some form of childhood sexual abuse, while 8 per cent reported genital intercourse. Most of the psychiatric and substance-use problems in later life arose in those women that endured more serious abuse, such as intercourse.

Sexual abuse is an extreme example of how our childhood experiences can cast a shadow over the remainder of our lives. Fortunately, in later life we can identify, address and manage many of the mental scars left by less-than-ideal childhoods. As we'll see in the next chapter, that means taking responsibility for your life *now and in the future*, rather than lingering on past hurts, however painful. It's not easy. You might need professional help. But it is possible. The thousands of people that survive sexual abuse as children to live fulfilled lives are a testament to the strength of the human spirit.

Stress is inevitable in childhood – as at any other time of our lives. However, for most children, facing stress doesn't lead to symptoms or behavioural problems. Indeed, they learn how to deal effectively with stressful situations – lessons that they can apply in later life. And you can help your child deal with any problems before they become an issue by implementing some of the strategies outlined in this book, talking to him or her and providing a nurturing and safe environment at home.

Does your child suffer from stress?

Stress symptoms in children differ somewhat from those in adults (see box on page 78). The more stress signals that your child exhibits, the more likely he or she is to be grappling with a problem or feeling anxious or worried.

Of course, talking to your child will help uncover the cause of concern. However, you might have to be proactive. Stress can leave children feeling isolated. They might find articulating their feelings difficult, and when they finally manage to tell their parents what is bothering them, they may worry that they'll be told 'don't be so silly' or, worse, to 'grow up'. Remember that what seems trivial to an adult can be a major problem for a child. Indeed, the stress of any life event, good or bad, is magnified among children who have not developed the coping strategies that adults tend to rely on. If you worry that your children are suffering stress-related symptoms, they need you to offer a sympathetic, understanding and non-judgemental ear.

In particular, the death or severe illness of a parent, sibling, grandparent or other close relative can cause children considerable stress – as Emma's case showed (see page 79). Faced with bereavement, children often run the gamut of emotions including sadness, anger, hostility and disbelief. They may become obsessed with death and ask when they, you or another relative will die. It is best to answer the barrage of questions honestly and openly. This helps children express their grief. Bottling up feelings of despair could lead to any number and combination of the stress signals noted on the next page.

If your child's behaviour is beyond your ability to cope and is causing marked social problems, or if the problems drag on, you could consider seeking professional help from your GP, a child psychologist or a psychotherapist. Psychotherapists and child psychologists help children to make sense of events they cannot understand – such as divorce, a parent's death or being taken into care – and enable them to express their anxieties and fears.

Stress signals in children

This list contains a wide variety of behaviours and these will vary depending on the stage in the child's development. For example, suicidal thoughts and talk might be signals in older children, bedwetting and temper tantrums in younger children.

- aggression and bullying others
- antisocial behaviour
- anxiety and phobias
- bedwetting
- changes in appetite
- doing badly at school; school refusal
- eating problems
- excessive disobedience
- excessive obsessions
- inhibitions
- poor self-confidence
- sleeping problems; excessive tiredness
- smoking, alcohol use and drug-taking
- social withdrawal; not having any or very few friends
- suicidal thoughts and talk
- temper tantrums
- truancy and delinquency
- unhappiness
- victimisation by bullies.

Parentline Plus★ offers counselling and support to parents, while Childline★ offers a similar service to children. You can contact your GP or social worker for help. They can refer you to a child guidance clinic or child psychiatrist, and may be able to put you in touch with a psychotherapist or psychologist. The Association of Child Psychotherapists★ can help you find a local practitioner.

Bullying

For decades, many teachers, parents and health professionals ignored bullying – or considered it just a part of growing up. That

Case history: Emma

Emma's father died in an industrial accident. Emma, an intelligent seven-year-old, understood that her father was dead. But she couldn't understand why. She couldn't accept that her father's death was an accident and became convinced that 'someone killed my daddy'. Emma's mother – Rachel – was also grief-stricken and felt isolated. Both sets of grandparents lived at the other end of the country and could visit only occasionally. Because Emma's questions kept reopening Rachel's emotional scars, they usually went unanswered. So Emma became more confused and scared. She stopped eating and refused to go to school. She would sit brooding in her room, then explode in temper tantrums. During a visit, Emma's grandmother persuaded Rachel to seek help from a child psychotherapist. The child psychotherapist helped Emma reveal her confusion and feelings. She understood that no one had killed her father. Emma is eating again and doing well at school.

attitude is, fortunately, changing. Over recent years, it has been increasingly recognised that bullying is both common and can cause considerable distress.

For instance, Wolke and other researchers from the University of Hertfordshire found that around 4 per cent of 1,639 children between six and nine years were direct bullies. Just over 10 per cent both bullied others and were victims. Almost 40 per cent of the children were victims of bullies. Another study – also by Wolke and colleagues – found that 24 per cent of English pupils were victims of bullying every week.

In general, bullying does not seem to be strongly linked to physical health problems. Nevertheless, Wolke and colleagues queried whether bullying might contribute to stress-related conditions, such as repeated sore throats, colds, breathing problems, nausea, a poor appetite and school worries. In Australia, Bond and colleagues found that recurrent bullying increased the risk that a child would develop anxiety and depression while being victimised. The risk was especially marked among girls.

Bullying can lead to either substance abuse or aggression. Kumpulainen and Roine, for example, found that girls who perceived themselves as failing to perform well at school and who had low self-esteem (which can be a result of bullying) at the age of 12 years were more likely to drink heavily three years later. Among boys, the same factors were likely to lead to aggression and interpersonal problems at 15 years of age.

These and many other studies show that bullying is a much more serious problem than simple playground squabbling. While it can seem trivial to an adult, protracted bullying can destroy self-esteem, the victim's confidence and, occasionally, lives. Some people carry a lingering resentment towards the bullies, the school, their parents who failed to help, and authority generally for the rest of their days. In a few cases, the torment is so intense that the child runs away or commits suicide.

If your child is being bullied, you need to tackle the problem. However, children are often reluctant to admit that it is going on. If you suspect anything, try to talk to your child and, if necessary, the school. Once again, offering a sympathetic, understanding and non-judgmental ear often helps.

How to tell if your child is being bullied

Several things might alert you to the possibility that your child is being bullied. Physical signs such as bruising, cuts and grazes can be significant, but your child might not want to reveal these as the result of bullying. So consider if they are inconsistent with the child's explanation, such as getting the wound in the playground. Your child may also come home with more frequent injuries than are likely to arise from average playground accidents. Similarly, bullies might steal or damage property. Again if the child doesn't admit to this, you need to consider if his or her explanation of the lost or damaged property is consistent and believable. Name-calling, saying or writing nasty comments, social exclusion and forcing a child to do something they don't want to can have a psychological rather than physical effect. So watch for the signs of stress outlined above.

Joining clubs outside school might help your child regain his or her self-esteem. If the bullying is especially severe, consider clubs or organisations several miles away. This reduces the risk that someone else from the school might attend, and gives the victim a chance to form new friendships.

Teaching some bullied children to defend themselves with judo, karate, kung fu or boxing can elevate their self-esteem and allow them to confront the physical threat. Even children who hate sport often enjoy the martial arts – and it may never come to giving the bully a bloody nose. The self-confidence fostered by such sports often allows children to face up to the bully without a physical confrontation, and then walk away. Your local library should have details of the local clubs. Do not encourage your children to fight back, unless there is no other option. Losing a fight further reduces children's confidence in themselves – and you.

Children often find expressing disturbing thoughts or feelings very difficult. However, they can phone Childline★ about bullying or any other problem. Kidscape★ offers advice to children and parents on bullying and other issues including sexual abuse.

Coping with teenagers

Living with teenagers can be a time of considerable stress, tension and conflict for the entire family. After all, teenagers struggle with their sexuality, their increasing responsibilities and their growing independence. They might face drug abuse, racial harassment and unemployment (in older teenagers). Teenagers may be bored, confused and insecure. They worry about their appearance. Even acne can cause considerable stress (see box overleaf).

Meanwhile, parents have to come to terms with their children not being children any more, as well as the need to allow their offspring extra freedom. Teenagers' behaviour can seem quite erratic at this life stage. Separation anxiety, or fear of being parted from parents, can re-emerge in adolescence and be difficult for parents as well as teenagers. Parents may also worry that food fads herald anorexia or bulimia (see pages 86–87).

Adolescence is a crucial time in everyone's development, and this section gives just an overview of some of the issues that may arise.

Acne

Almost everyone suffers from a least a few spots some time during their life. But while acne may be almost inevitable it's not trivial. Quite apart from its cosmetic impact, acne can cause marked psychological effects – as Webster comments: 'Acne is not a trivial disease; it can produce cutaneous and emotional scars that last a lifetime'. Layton agrees, noting that even mild or moderate acne can cause considerable mental distress. Mallon and colleagues found that acne patients showed social, psychological and emotional problems that were as marked as those reported by people suffering from asthma, epilepsy, diabetes, back pain or arthritis.

Acne is common. Estimates vary widely, but Smithard and colleagues found that half of children aged between 14 and 16 years had acne; 11 per cent suffered moderate to severe acne. However, less than a third of children with acne sought help from their doctors. Parents should therefore encourage their children to seek help: doctors can choose from a wide range of effective treatments that can prevent physical and psychological scarring.

The advice in this section should help you decide if something is normal and whether you need to intervene. You can also take some steps to build a healthy emotional environment that limits the effect of stress.

- Treat teenagers like adults. That means having a discussion rather than giving a lecture. Nothing winds teenagers up more than having someone preach to them. Well do you like to be preached at? Transactional analysis, discussed in Chapter 3, can help to improve your dialogue with teenagers.
- Answer any questions – especially about sex – openly and honestly.
- Remember that teenagers might hold completely different views from you about drugs, fashion and the environment, for example. You can discuss these, but speaking from knowledge of the facts (rather than prejudice) and respecting your son or

daughter's position can prevent disagreements from becoming conflicts. For example, don't treat vegetarianism or veganism as a food fad. Both are valid and justifiable choices.

- Try to build your teenager's confidence. Being a teenager is hard enough without being constantly criticised for the way you dress and behave – unless the latter is clearly dangerous.

- Respect privacy. So show interest in your son or daughter's activities and friends, but don't pry.

- Set reasonable rules – but don't expect teenagers to obey. Challenging rules is one way teenagers exert their independence. However, some restrictions – for example, a curfew – are especially important. You could try trading-off less important rules provided the teenager sticks to the curfew.

- Try not to overreact. You were a teenager once. Remember how it felt? Remember how your parents reacted? Your records probably irritated your parents as much as your son's or daughter's latest CD. Being awkward or getting a piercing or a tattoo is just a sign of your child's growing independence and part of his or her need to develop his or her own personality.

- Similarly, don't worry about obsessions. In many cases teenagers just grow out of them. You should, perhaps, intervene if the obsession impacts on the child or teenager's ability to lead a normal social life or is compromising their schoolwork. Spending a few hours on a video game is fine. Playing to the exclusion of schoolwork, other hobbies and friends isn't.

- You will be the role model for how your children deal with their teenagers. Aim to be a positive – rather than a negative – influence.

- The perfect parent and the perfect teenager don't exist. So don't blame yourself when you fail to live up to your own standards or when your teenage child fails to meet your expectations.

Examinations

As if the mental, physical and emotional impacts of adolescence are not enough, teenagers have to cope with the stress of sitting exams that might determine the course of the rest of their lives. Most teenagers recognise the importance of exams. They are unlikely to need you to remind them that they need to do well.

You can help most by keeping the family away from the teenager's room or study area and by offering support. Naturally, you want him or her to do well. But you should be realistic, and if the grades aren't what you expect, support your child and offer practical advice. (The case history of Tony's father opposite offers an example of how *not* to behave.) Failing exams can shatter a teenager's confidence. However disappointed you feel, your child probably feels worse.

Indeed, the stress associated with exams can provoke psychiatric symptoms, including anorexia and anxiety. Research carried out by Hodge and colleagues found that teenagers prone to anxiety were especially likely to suffer marked and excessive exam-related stress. Coming from a lower socio-economic background, poor self-confidence, a downbeat view of their academic and verbal performance, and a belief that they would be unable to cope also increased the risk of suffering from stress. There's a common theme to the latter few points: low confidence. So the occasional reminder of your son's or daughter's past successes and offering support should help bolster his or her confidence and, therefore, performance.

Indeed, support can help teenagers overcome considerable adversity. For instance, the inter-relationship between socio-economic status, drug use and examination performance is complex. However, Miller and Plant examined 6,409 teenagers in the UK and found that, broadly, four types of adolescent tended to play truant, and also tended to have an impression that they were doing badly at school. The children were:

- those that came from single-parent families
- those that lacked 'constructive hobbies'
- those suffering from psychiatric conditions.
- those that engaged in an 'aggressive outgoing delinquent lifestyle'.

Almost inevitably, such children tend to do poorly in their exams. Those teenagers who suffered psychiatric symptoms and those following a 'delinquent lifestyle' were also more likely to use alcohol, cigarettes and illegal drugs (although other factors came into play as well). On the other hand, those adolescents with at least one parent who supported them and exerted some control tended to

---

Case history: Tony

Tony passed his 'A' levels – but not well enough. So he lost his place at veterinary school. Instead of trying to help, his father – a vet – made Tony feel guilty about the time and money invested in his private education. He said Tony's mother was ashamed of having a failure for a son. And his father reminded him at every opportunity that Tony could not expect them to bale him out of his now inevitable life on the dole. Then Tony's father did not speak to his son for six weeks. The father's reaction probably says more about the pressure Tony had to endure than any lack of academic ability. In any case, failing exams isn't the end of the world. Exams can be re-sat. Ambitions can be re-appraised. Tony studied animal physiology instead of becoming a vet. He was awarded a doctorate and is now working in a leading university. His father is speaking to him again!

---

do better at school. There's a lesson here for us all – but it's one that Tony's father didn't learn.

Drug abuse

It's a fact of life. Teenagers try drugs – both legal and illegal. Many smokers start in adolescence, for example. Most older adolescents, and some younger teenagers, drink alcohol at least occasionally. Many teenagers flirt with soft drugs, such as cannabis, and harder drugs including ecstasy. Fortunately, few teenagers become addicts. Overall, smoking and drinking pose a much greater health hazard for teenagers.

Most drugs commonly used by teenagers – cannabis, ecstasy, amphetamines and cocaine (not crack) – are far less addictive than either heroin or morphine. Occasional use of these drugs is very unlikely to lead to addiction, although there might be other hazards. So parents need to keep the risks in perspective to allay their anxiety if nothing else. Heroin and morphine are more addictive. In their book *Under the Influence*, Milam and Ketcham comment that after taking heroin and morphine for four weeks, almost 100 and 70 per cent of users respectively become hooked. Critically, it takes four weeks of regular, probably daily, use to become addicted.

While many teenagers take legal and illegal drugs to escape stress, they often make matters worse. Legal and illegal drug use can cause considerable physical and mental harm. Even occasional use can contribute to suicides, violence and accidents. Furthermore, drug abuse fuels poverty, crime, prostitution, homelessness and the spread of sexually transmitted and blood-borne diseases, including AIDS and hepatitis C.

While most drug users do not become addicted, no one can predict who is likely to remain a recreational user. Addiction is complex, and influenced by more than a drug's biological effects. Personality, age and street culture all play a part.

Several behavioural changes could suggest that your child might be abusing drugs. For example, changes at school, such as an unexplained drop in grades, teachers' concerns about unreliability, lack of productivity and bad behaviour can hint at a problem. Remaining in the bedroom for long periods or staying out late without a reasonable explanation, frequent memory lapses, problems with concentration and a loss of interest in hobbies might also be a sign that a person is using drugs. Sudden secretiveness, deception, unusual or peculiar behaviour, being overly defensive or avoiding questions about friends might, in particular, be signals of a drug-abuse problem. However, these traits are also normal parts of adolescence. The key is to watch for marked changes in behaviour and explore the reasons. While drug use might be part of growing up, you need to remain vigilant for the signs of excessive use. Nick Johnstone's book *A Head Full of Blue* offers an insightful and sobering account of what can happen when adolescent drug use – in this case alcohol – spirals out of control, as well as helping us understand why. It's a book all parents should, perhaps, consider reading.

Anorexia and bulimia

Teenagers are usually highly sensitive about their appearance. In a survey performed by Exeter University in 1998, 58 per cent of teenage girls said that their appearance was their biggest concern. Images in magazines, fashions and peer pressure can all contribute to a teenager's poor self-image. Most models whom girls compare themselves to are some 23 per cent lighter than the average woman. (However, it's over-simplistic to consider a fixation with unrealistic role models as the sole cause of eating disorders.)

If teenagers feel that they do not conform to an ideal body image, their self-confidence can suffer. The Exeter survey found that 59 per cent of girls aged between 12 and 13 years who have low self-esteem are watching their weight and are on diets. In some cases, this misplaced body image leads to anorexia or bulimia, which tend to develop between the ages of 15 and 25 years.

The causes of anorexia, bulimia and other eating disorders are complex. We'll look at these and their treatment in Chapter 8.

Suicide

As in the case of adults who take their lives, suicide is the ultimate condemnation of society's care of young people. However, in some ways suicide in young people is a double tragedy: firstly because of the untreated suffering behind the child's action (which may have been missed for years) and secondly the lost potential of a life cut short.

There are signs that deliberate self-harm among adolescents is rising again after declining between the late 1970s and mid-1980s. For example, in 2000 Hawton and colleagues reported that in Oxford the number of adolescents who deliberately hurt themselves – in three-quarters of the attempts using paracetamol overdoses – rose by around 28 per cent in cases admitted over two years in the mid-1980s and mid-1990s (specifically, 1985–86 and 1994–95). The number of repetitive attempts rose by 49 per cent overall. The increase in repetitive attempts was especially marked among males, rising by almost 57 per cent. This is worrying: repetitive attempts often herald 'successful' suicides.

You can watch for risk factors that signal a teenager may be contemplating suicide or deliberate self-harm. Most adolescents who hurt themselves show interpersonal problems, difficulties with studying or employment problems, for example (although, of course, most teenagers with these problems will not harm themselves). In particular, it is important to notice heavy alcohol or drug use, severe withdrawal and marked depression. And you should always take teenagers' threats to kill or hurt themselves seriously, and watch for verbal signs such as 'I won't be a problem for you much longer,' or 'Nothing matters'. The box overleaf outlines some other warning signs.

Warning signs for suicide in teenagers

According to the American Academy of Child and Adolescent Psychiatry (AACAP), these signs could indicate that your teenager has a psychological problem or is considering self-harm:

- different sleeping and eating habits
- withdrawal from friends and family
- abandonment of regular activities and a loss of interest in pleasurable activities
- violence, rebellious behaviour or running away from home
- excessive drug or alcohol use
- no longer caring about personal appearance
- a distinct personality change
- frequent complaints of feeling bored
- difficulty concentrating
- school work or studies start to suffer
- the teenager mentions physical symptoms that are stress-related
- inability to accept either praise or rewards
- saying that he or she is not a good person, feeling 'bad inside'
- having an urge to arrange his or her affairs, for example giving away favourite possessions and throwing away important belongings
- becoming cheerful soon after a bout of depression
- signs of psychosis, such as hallucinations and bizarre thoughts.

The origins of self-harm tendencies may be complex and go back years. Another paper from Oxford, this time by Houston and colleagues, looked at factors contributing to suicide in people aged between 15 and 24 years. They found that around 70 per cent suffered from at least one psychiatric disorder, usually depression. But although 56 per cent suffered from depression, 'very few' were being treated. And while few of the suicides were addicts, most abused drugs and alcohol. Many endured relationship problems and difficulties with the police and judicial system. In most cases, the suicide was the culmination of difficulties that arose in childhood or early adolescence.

Clearly, it's important to ensure that any teenager having an especially rough time is watched carefully for any signs of suicide. You might want to talk your concerns through with a GP, psychiatrist or helpline, such as that run by MIND.* It's especially important to ensure that depression is effectively treated (see Chapter 7).

Stress in adults

Adults face numerous problems that make stress symptoms almost inevitable. In the previous chapter we looked at some ways in which you can discover what's stressing you out and how to deal with it. Below we discuss some of the general difficulties encountered by adults that may cause or exacerbate stress.

We live in an era of rapid sociological and technological evolution, and traditional patterns of employment are changing. In addition, in many cases our expectations – both as consumers of goods and services as well as in our personal lives – continually increase. Ironically, the huge array of choices open to us can be another cause of stress. Choice is supposed to empower us. But walk down a supermarket aisle. Does the choice of breakfast cereals really empower you? Does the choice of cable and satellite television channels really empower you? Or the choice of Internet sites? Even choosing between the competing choices is time-consuming and a potential source of arguments and can, therefore, be stressful.

Furthermore, images of the ideal lifestyle peddled by the media are often unrealistic and bland. So instead of being a source of pleasure or relaxation, the pursuit of these hopes and dreams, accoutrements or status symbols may be banal and ultimately unsatisfying. Modern mainstream media – as David Edwards remarks in his book *Free to be Human* – aims to create 'a buying environment which maximises advertising sales. This requires the careful avoidance of stimulating deeper thought that interferes with the buying mood'.

And this leads us to another common cause of stress: money. An increasing number of people now look to 'retail therapy' in the hope of countering stress. The spend-spend-spend habit is one that is especially difficult to manage, in part because of the advertising industry. In many cases, advertising is designed to create demand, irrespective of whether the product satisfies the consumer's genuine needs or not. This isn't to say that you shouldn't buy anything. Rather you should consider whether it fulfils your genuine needs or whether you're just enticed by the advertising. (Some ways you can control spending are outlined on page 52.)

To make matters worse, credit is easier than ever to obtain. Yet debts need to be repaid. A short-term lift from shopping can become a long-term burden. Indeed, society seems geared towards encouraging us to earn more to spend more to reflect our social status. Inevitably, consumer debt rises to meet this created demand. Yet the growing amount of debt contributes to the stress. We'll look at some solutions to money-related stress on page 237.

Women and stress

The issues described above are common to men and women. However, some stressors differ between the sexes. In part, this is biological – men don't have a hormonal menopause, for example. (Premenstrual syndrome and the menopause are covered in Chapter 6.) Furthermore, women express their distress in different ways to men. As we'll see in Chapter 7, women are more likely to suffer from depression than men. On the other hand, men tend to abuse alcohol and drugs more than women, although these are obviously not hard-and-fast distinctions.

Apart from the biological causes of stress, women need to contend with societal prejudice. The days when women were destined for jobs as receptionists, nurses and secretaries before being married off are long gone. Yet almost 40 years on from the rise of women's liberation, women at work still face considerable and persistent problems. For example, the government's report *Social Inequalities*, published in May 2000, found that women working full-time earn 30 per cent less than men. This applied in both traditionally female jobs, such as hairdressing, and more male-dominated fields, such as engineering and law.

Despite their growing importance in the workplace, there is a general perception among many employers that women, rather than men, are the carers who meet family commitments and so may be less focused on their jobs. A survey by the Institute of Directors, for example, found that 45 per cent of its members regard women of

The mid-life crisis: fact or fiction?

Researchers describe a mid-life crisis as personal turmoil and coping challenges in people aged between 39 and 50 years, triggered by fears and anxieties associated with advancing age. However, Cornell sociologist Elaine Wethington found that more than half of what people considered to be mid-life crises were due to 'stressful life events'. Women were just as likely as men to believe they had had a mid-life crisis. In Wethington's study, most people who said they had had a mid-life crisis described stressful life events that were specific transitions or events, such as a life-threatening illness or job insecurity. These occurences might prove stressful at any time and are not necessarily related to a 'true' mid-life crisis. Only a fifth of those interviewed said their mid-life crisis arose from an awareness that they were ageing and time was passing them by. Numerous studies now show that a mid-life crisis is not inevitable. Indeed, in many cases, it can be a good thing. The experience can help people construct meaning in their lives and enable them to catch up with reality and define where they would like to be. Again, some of the problem-solving, transactional analysis and life-planning strategies outlined in Chapter 3 might help.

childbearing age as a less attractive employment prospect than other groups. This attitude helps to reinforce the 'glass ceiling' still found in many companies. As we've seen, women still tend to earn less than men. They're also offered fewer promotions and tend to focus on specialist support roles – typically human resources – rather than central line management. Management consultants use the term 'glass walls' to describe this narrow career path.

The result, observed Sharon Mavin writing in *Career Development International*, is that 'women's career development does not simply lag behind that of men, but may proceed in a completely different manner'. Mavin notes that the traditional working pattern – education, full-time career and retirement – applies only for men (although it is beginning to break down even here). Tackling institutional sexism isn't easy. However, some of the problem solving, transactional analysis and life-planning strategies outlined in the previous chapter might help.

Have a peaceful pregnancy

Stress seems linked to fertility. Stress contributes to impotence, for example (see pages 158–63). More fundamentally, Jakobovits and Szekeres note that chronic stress can impair oogenesis and spermatogenesis: the formation of eggs and sperm respectively. And once you conceive, pregnancy is inevitably stressful for the mother-to-be and her partner. You worry about the baby being healthy, making it to hospital in time, having a painful or protracted labour, the expense of a new arrival, and whether your figure – or indeed your relationship – will ever be the same again.

Despite these worries, you need to assertively tackle the problems that cause you stress: for the baby's sake as well as your own. In 2002, O'Connor and colleagues from London's Institute of Psychiatry reported that maternal anxiety during pregnancy roughly doubled the risk that the child would develop behavioural and emotional problems by four years of age. Jakobovits and Szekeres warn that extreme stress in pregnancy may trigger miscarriage or premature birth. The assertive coping strategies in Chapter 3 and the specific suggestions below might help. You can use these techniques to brainstorm and solve any particular problems.

Relaxation during pregnancy can prove difficult – especially if you are on edge because you have had previous miscarriages, you are worried about money, or your relationship is under pressure. However, you can take several steps to help yourself have a peaceful pregnancy:

- plan: for example how you will make it to hospital; how you will cope financially
- try to avoid stressful situations: as far as possible avoid arguments at work and home, try to avoid travelling on public transport during the rush hour; work on a flexitime basis if you can or chat with your boss about altering your hours
- consult your GP or a travel clinic before flying, especially if you have had a miscarriage – air travel, apart from any physical effects, can be intensely stressful. Most airlines will not accept you as a passenger after 32 weeks of pregnancy

- learn about your options: everyone worries about their baby being healthy, and although there are no guarantees, a number of blood tests, detailed scans and other screens are available that may put your mind at rest – your midwife will be able to provide details
- devote some time to yourself each day
- exercise – you can swim, walk and exercise in many other ways during pregnancy. Your midwife or doctor can provide guidance on the safest ways to exercise. Some swimming pools and fitness centres run special sessions for pregnant women.

Having a baby is one of the most enjoyable yet stressful times in a woman's (and her partner's) life. And as mentioned above (page 72) it can be stressful for children. As anyone with a new baby can – and given half a chance probably will – tell you, nothing prepares you for the emotional impact and the effect on your lifestyle. For example, leaving work and coping with the relentless demands of a tiny infant can leave some new mothers feeling isolated and frustrated. Some new mothers develop post-natal depression (see page 180). However, many parent and baby clubs and other organisations offer an opportunity to meet new friends.

Inevitably, some new mother and fathers feel irritable, anxious and depressed. Both parents may have to endure sleepless nights. While a tearful few days are a normal part of childbirth, severe depression certainly is not. For more on dealing with depression see Chapter 7.

Stress at work

We spend most of our waking lives working and commuting. For most adults, changing occupational patterns and problems at work are an important, perhaps the most important, cause of stress. While jobs can be a source of satisfaction and fulfilment, they can be a major cause of tension if you do not get on with colleagues, feel unappreciated and over-worked, or are poorly paid. As mentioned in Chapter 1, a company's most stressed-out employees tend to be those who work long hours, for little pay and who have little control over their working life – production-line workers, check-out assistants and people performing routine clerical work, for instance.

In contrast, senior executives work hard, but their workload is varied and brings financial rewards. And affluence seems directly to impact on your health. A large and growing body of evidence suggests that poverty is associated with an increased risk of developing or dying from various diseases including cancer, heart disease and some psychological conditions. If you are struggling to survive on the minimum wage or less, looking after your health may be sidelined by other worries.

The stress-related symptoms experienced by a boss are often less severe than that of his or her subordinates owing to the varying degree of control that people feel they can exert over their work at different levels of the organisation's hierarchy. Two studies reinforce the value of feeling that you are in control as a defence against stress. The first measured levels of cortisol, a stress hormone, in the pilots and co-pilots of Japanese flight crews. The results, published by Kakimoto and colleagues, found that the captains' cortisol levels showed relatively little change, whether they were flying or not. In contrast, the co-pilots' heart rate varied more markedly and the cortisol levels were higher than those of their captains, again whether they were flying or not. The captain is ultimately in control, which may be one reason why the signs of stress (cortisol and heart rate reactivity) were lower than in their co-pilots. Critically, physically being in control wasn't the point. The captains seemed less stressed even when the co-pilots were at the controls. This suggests that it is important to see yourself as being in control overall.

Secondly, Cropley and a team of researchers from St George's Hospital Medical School in London examined the link between job-strain and psychiatric illness among 160 teachers. They split the teachers into two groups: those with high job-strain, which they defined as highly demanding jobs with little control; and those with low job-strain, typified by few demands and a high degree of control. Teachers under high job-strain were more likely than those exposed to low strain to suffer severe anxiety, worry and fatigue. (However, teaching seems to be an inherently stressful occupation. Even the low job-strain group showed more psychological problems than the general population.)

In other research, Tennant summarised the scientific evidence suggesting that specific, acute work-related stress contributes to depression. Persistent 'structural' factors, inherent in the nature of the job, seemed to play an important role in determining whether or not a worker develops psychological illness.

Despite the problems that we may all experience in the workplace, there are several ways to prevent the pressure developing into stress-related symptoms or behavioural problems. Chapter 3 considered some of the ways to put yourself back in control.

Steer clear of workaholism

It is easy to slip into workaholism – many of the changes in the workplace engender a sense of insecurity and many corporate cultures encourage the syndrome, overtly or implicitly. Indeed, almost a third of senior full-time employees in the UK work more than 46 hours a week. Senior managers often work more than 51 hours.

Ironically, being preoccupied with your job and working long hours may not be professionally – or personally – beneficial. A 1999 study by Burke and MacDermid of 530 managers and professionals found that workaholics tended to derive less satisfaction from their careers than other employees. They also believed that they had fewer prospects and were more likely to quit than their colleagues who managed to strike a better balance between work and home. Time-management techniques can help you better balance commitments at work and home – see pages 219–25.

Information overload is another increasingly common cause of stress at work. Over half the 5,000 executives interviewed for a 1999 survey by the Institute of Management said that they suffered from the problem. Many people receive 50, 100 or even more emails a day and feel pressured to supply an immediate reply. In the age of the sound bite, the executive summary and the bullet point, companies increasingly measure success not only in terms of expertise and performance *per se*, but in terms of how quickly you respond. The seemingly increasing pace of modern life is a common cause of stress. Again, time management techniques can help – see pages 219–25 or consult *Which? Way to Manage Your Time – and Your Life*.

Beating bullying bosses

You know the type: the bosses who run you down in front of your staff. The bosses who cancel your holiday at the last minute – not because they need to, but because they can. The bosses who humiliate you after a presentation. (However, you need to ensure that the boss is really unreasonable. You could perceive a boss as a bully because you have not addressed your inadequate performance, for example.) The good news is that you can beat bosses who are genuine bullies. The bad news is that it takes guts – you need to confront your boss. The techniques of transactional analysis (see Chapter 3) and assertiveness training (see Chapter 10) can help.

For example, you can use these techniques if your boss makes an unreasonable demand. You could remind him or her of your other high-priority tasks. Then have a discussion about which task could be sacrificed. If this isn't possible or appropriate, decide which aspects of the work you need to perform and which you can delegate or reassign among your staff. And you can negotiate. Explain, for example, that you cannot work on a particular project immediately but will be able to do so the following week. Alternatively, you could suggest that a more junior member of staff does the work, which you'll review. This will at least buy you some time.

If our boss forces us to do something against our will, we might persuade ourselves that we took the decision in order to feel better about ourself. However, this is dishonest to ourselves and can cause inner conflict. It is important to avoid this trap, described as cognitive dissonance. If someone, especially a bully, feels he or she can victimise you, that person will.

Your boss might be a bully because of 'displaced aggression'. In other words, he or she is stressed about something else but unleashes anger on you instead of tackling the real cause of tension. In such cases, using transactional analysis techniques as described in Chapter 3 and direct confrontation may resolve the issue. Remember that your boss isn't being intentionally aggressive.

To overcome a bullying boss, first accumulate your evidence. Note examples of times you felt bullied. Reflecting on these at home helps you determine whether you really are being bullied or whether you are making excuses for your own shortcomings or other unacknowledged factors – for example, you are not up to the job or are bored and disillusioned (this is known as projection – see page 39). Next arrange a meeting with your boss. Make sure that it is in private – bullies rarely back down in public. Remind him or her of the situations you feel were unacceptable. Tell him or her that you are not prepared to take the abuse any longer. State that if you are going to be dressed down it should be in private, not in front of the rest of the staff. In some cases, bullies may be genuinely unaware that they have caused offence.

This approach can also work in some cases of sexual or racial harassment. What constitutes harmless flirting or banter for some men and women can be deeply offensive and inappropriate for others. Someone might be entirely unaware that they've caused offence. There is no reason why you should take any comments you find unacceptable. If dealing directly with the person doesn't help, you should consider other forms of redress, such as going to your manager or Human Resources department.

Be warned that tackling someone face to face can backfire. It may make matters worse if the bully feels under increased pressure. You then have to decide how far to take things. You could go over the head of your boss – most companies have a complaints or grievance procedure. In some cases – racial and sexual harassment, for example – you might have a recourse to law. You may feel the best option is to look for another job. But whatever you do, don't put up with it bullying. *The Which? Guide to Employment*, available from Which? Books,★ gives useful advice on your legal rights and how to cope with harassment and discrimination in the workplace.

Relocation stress

Increasingly employers demand a mobile workforce, yet relocation can exert a high financial and mental toll. Children are uprooted from schools, friends and clubs. Either you or your partner may have to quit a job. A new job would need a very attractive salary or other package of benefits to compensate. Until you find your way around the social life in your new location, you and your partner can be thrown together, which may cause friction. So it is not surprising that moving house and changing jobs rank highly on the list of life stress events (see page 24). In an attempt to compromise, some people try commuter marriages – working away during the week and coming home at weekends. But such arrangements can undermine relationships with children and between the partners.

Against these stressors, you need to balance the advantages of relocation: improved prospects, a more interesting job, extra money, the opportunity to start over in a new town, better schools and so on.

Make up your mind by listing pros and cons

Deciding whether to relocate is not easy. You might like to divide a piece of paper down the middle and write the advantages of relocating in one column and the disadvantages in the other. These aren't going to be of equal importance. Losing your place on the pub football team is likely to be far less important than improving your child's educational prospects. Nevertheless, it should give you an idea of whether the advantages of relocation outweigh the disadvantages. This approach is a useful technique for evaluating the benefits and disadvantages of other changes.

Life on the dole

On page 35 we saw how when Joe lost his job he descended into the pit of despair characterised by learned helplessness. He was unable to apply for engineering jobs that were well within his abilities, start his own business or even deal with simple household electrical faults. Spending some time on the dole is a fact of life for an increasing number of people, even for experienced, well-qualified people. The days when entering a profession was a passport to a lifetime's employment are gone. For older people, being on the dole carries an undeserved stigma and can be tantamount to an enforced early retirement. While most of us don't descend into Joe's abyss of despair, unemployment is intensely stressful.

Apart from the financial problems, unemployment takes a toll on your health. For example, Avery and colleagues examined the mental and physical health of miners following the pit closure programme in Nottinghamshire during 1992. Based on a postal questionnaire, they estimated that 52 per cent of unemployed miners might suffer from psychological problems. This compared to 46 per cent of those still working in the mining industry and 22 per cent among people employed in other sectors. Moreover, ex-miners and those still in the industry showed a greater degree of physical ill-health than those in other sectors. The relatively high level of physical and psychological ill-health among working miners could reflect the strain of the uncertainty surrounding the pit closures.

Similarly, Claussen and collaborators found that people who were unemployed for more than 12 weeks were between 4 and 10 times more likely to suffer depression, anxiety and physical illness than employed people. Unfortunately, suffering psychological problems reduced the likelihood of finding employment by 70 per cent.

Indeed, Schwefel comments that unemployment might reinforce and exacerbate existing physical disease, as well as being a risk factor for new ailments, both among the unemployed and their relatives. Schwefel adds that unemployed older people and the children of out-of-work people are especially prone to develop physical illness. Depression and alcoholism seem to be the main psychological problems among the unemployed.

Being made redundant can be a shock – even if it's expected. The trauma can be so great that some people follow their normal routine. They get up at the same time, catch the same train, wander the streets and come home at the same time. This can carry on for weeks. Others drink or lie in bed. But the best way to avoid being overwhelmed by redundancy is not to blame yourself for your predicament. You are hardly to blame for the fact that you have been laid off, so remain positive. You can find another job. It may not be easy. It may mean learning new skills. It may mean moving to another part of the country or setting up your own business. But remain positive that you will find a job and try to remain active (see also Chapter 3).

Relationship difficulties

Many adults experience problems with existing relationships. Others find it hard to form relationships with the opposite sex. Counselling can smooth out the rough patches that many couples go through. Reconciliation services and counsellors help both sides to compromise – both partners have to want the partnership to work and be willing to give and take, and modify unreasonable behaviour. Relate* offers counselling throughout the UK for couples and individuals. Transactional analysis, described in Chapter 3, can also help. You may also want to consider specific counselling if, for example, sexual problems, drink or drugs are causing your relationship difficulties.

Divorce

When you get divorced, as with bereavement, you lose a fundamental and central part of your life, so it's not surprising that divorce ranks second only to bereavement on the life stress scale (page 24) and can have a major psychological impact.

Divorce is increasingly part of modern life. If it happens to you, you need to face the reality of your divorce and move on. Deciding that a marriage has failed is difficult. Many people endure years of misery, despair or even violence before coming to that conclusion; others do not separate but become in entrenched in domestic civil war, in which case marriage counselling may help. Usually it is difficult to decide who is at fault when a marriage breaks up. In most cases, neither you nor your partner is really to blame. Nevertheless, the person who leaves the marital home often feels guilty. Both partners may feel rejected and rake over the ashes of the romantic hopes and ideals they held at the start of the marriage. Divorcees tend to mourn their failed marriage. These feelings can drag on for years before the person comes to terms with the end of the marriage. You should try not to feel guilty or hate your ex-partner as this can make it more difficult to rebuild your life after the divorce.

You also need to think about your children. Divorce can have a devastating impact on children, leading to psychological problems, delinquency, poor school performance and the other stress signals noted on page 77. Kirby, for example, comments that divorce and separation seem to be one reason why some adolescents start smoking. Depression and increased rebelliousness following separation also contribute to the decision to begin smoking. However, the positive principles on pages 73–74 should limit the stress for single-parent families. Some of the problem-solving and life-planning strategies outlined in Chapter 3 might also help.

An amicable divorce, where parents manage to be on good terms after the separation and where the partner without day-to-day care of the children – rightly or wrongly usually the father – is involved as much as possible, seems to go some way to ameliorating the stress of divorce on the kids. So make sure contact arrangements are fair and clear. Although the experience of divorce is distressing, most children emerge relatively unscathed, at least compared to other major life traumas. A study performed by Mack, for example, found that children from families that had seen a divorce were more self-confident and less likely to suffer from depression than children whose parent had died. On the other hand, the quality of the parent–child relationship was lower among the children of divorced parents than among those who suffered the tragedy of a parental death.

To minimise any potential problems, children must explore their feelings and understand that the reason their parents don't love each other any more has nothing to do with them. They also need reassurance that they haven't lost the love of either parent. Clearly, children shouldn't become caught in a 'tug-of-love' between the two parents. And they shouldn't be asked to take sides. There rarely are any. Families Need Fathers★ help children maintain a good relationship with both parents.

Loneliness and social isolation

Many people have been lonely for years because they never found Mr or Ms Right, because they were caring for elderly or invalid relatives (see pages 106–108), because they are married to their career or because their partner died. The answer to loneliness is simple to give, but harder to put into practice: get out there and meet people.

Apart from making your social life more varied, meeting people is good for your health. Several studies now suggest that social isolation increases the risk of suffering from several diseases. For instance, Cacioppo and colleagues found that lonely people showed a number of adverse cardiovascular changes compared to those in people with friends. For example, lonely people showed a faster heart rate and their blood pressure increased to a greater extent with advancing age. (Both of these changes seem to increase the chance of suffering a heart attack.) Moreover, lonely people reported poorer sleep quality. Support from family and friends can also help patients live with serious diseases. For example, Serovich and collaborators found that in HIV-positive women, family support countered feelings of loneliness as well as reducing symptoms of stress and depression.

There are ways to combat social isolation. Almost every town now has a singles' club. Your library or local paper may have details, or you can contact the National Federation of Solo Clubs.★ You could also try joining a local club or evening class to pursue a hobby. You'll meet like-minded people, which always makes starting new relationships easier. Divorcees and single parents can also join Gingerbread,★ which has branches nationwide. It's possible to use the Internet as a way to meet people. But learn the rules of chat rooms and Internet dating first. For example, never divulge your address and always meet someone for the first few times in a public place.

If you still find it hard to meet people you could be suffering from social phobia (see pages 193–4) or you could just be intensely shy. Doctors can treat social phobia. If you are shy, enrol on social skills and assertiveness training courses that help you speak to people and overcome the fear of rejection that underlies many people's shyness. Contact your local library or adult education centre for details of local courses.

Stress in elderly people

For the first time in human history, most of us can expect to live to a reasonable 'old' age. A death before our allotted three-score-years-and-ten now seems a tragedy rather than a commonplace. To be sure, our physical and mental functions decline as we get older. We might be able to slow the decline but, nevertheless, ageing sets limits on our aspirations, while, of course, death remains the inevitable ultimate limit. However, as Thomas Cole notes in *The Journey of Life*: 'human freedom and vitality lie in choosing to live well within these limits, even as we struggle against them'. Indeed, he points out that older people may experience 'higher peaks and greater depths' than younger people 'that enrich reality in later life'.

Holding an optimistic view of ageing might even mean that you live longer. Levy and colleagues found that people who regarded ageing in a positive light lived, on average, 7.5 years longer than those with a negative perception of getting older. Partly, the increased longevity seemed to reflect the power of the will to live. However, social stigma can also influence longevity, by undermining patients' positive view of ageing. Despite the demographic evidence that the population will become top-heavy with older people as the century progresses, we live in a society that values youth and beauty. The young often view everyone over the age of 60 years as past it, and ageist beliefs and practices can cause stress and tension. Yet as the box below shows, advancing age need not limit your ingenuity and creative powers.

A mature way of dealing with stress

Many people enjoy their retirement. They are free from the pressures of raising a family and holding down a job, and can devote time to themselves. However, some elderly people can face considerable hardship. Many live in poor housing, while others cannot afford to heat their home adequately. Children grow up and move away, removing an important social support. Retirement may bring financial problems – so planning for a pension well in advance of retirement age is particularly important. Illness begins to limit an elderly person's movement and older people start living in the shadow of their own death and that of relatives and friends. They may have to move into a nursing home or care for a partner declining into the disability of Parkinson's disease or Alzheimer's.

So you might expect stress, anxiety, depression and other stress-related problems to worsen as you get older. This isn't necessarily

---

Time to blossom late in life

There are numerous stories of people beginning the work that made them famous only in middle age or beyond. George Eliot's first published fiction, *Scenes from Clerical Life*, did not appear until she was 38 years old. Ian Fleming began writing his first novel at 43 years of age. That book, *Casino Royale*, started the James Bond industry. Brahms completed his first symphony at the same age. And William de Morgan led a successful career as an Arts-and-Crafts potter until the age of 66. Then he felt depressed, and friends suggested writing as therapy. The resulting novel, *Joseph Vance*, became a best-seller. Over the following 19 years, de Morgan published eight more novels. You don't need to compose a symphony or publish best-selling novels. You can still take up new hobbies well past retirement with considerable success.

the case. Indeed, even though depression and other psychiatric disorders are under-diagnosed and under-treated in elderly people, and sleep problems are common, elderly people may well be better prepared to deal with stress than the younger generation.

Several contributions to Wykle and colleagues' book *Stress & Health Among the Elderly* show that your view of, and reactions to, stress change as you get older. For example:

- elderly people tend to view individual life events – such as bereavement, financial problems and serious illness – as more stressful than younger people. However, older people are less likely to report experiencing stress or stress-related health problems. This could suggest that elderly people are more reluctant to own up to suffering from stress, but our coping style also matures as we get older
- elderly people tend to view stressors as unchangeable. Younger people tend to believe that stressors are problems waiting to be solved. This may reflect difference in the challenges faced at different ages. As we've seen, problems at work are a common cause of stress in younger and middle-aged adults. And you can change jobs or work conditions. Older people tend to be concerned with ill-health – which they are often unable to influence
- younger people are generally more likely to use inappropriate coping strategies – such as projection, denial and regression – that distort reality (see pages 37–41). By middle age you tend to evolve more mature coping styles, such as humour and sublimation (see also pages 37–41)
- younger people use direct confrontation to solve problems. As you age you increasingly use indirect action
- older people also have a lifetime's experience to draw on. For instance, coping with the death of your parents helps you deal, to a certain extent, with the loss of a partner. When it comes to the common stressors, you've generally been there.

However, these are only trends: elderly people may also enter denial, such as the elderly man who still lays a place at the dinner table for his dead wife or the old woman who dismisses a large cancerous tumour on her wrist as 'a touch of arthritis'. Using the techniques in this book should help you further develop your defences against stress and live a full and active retirement.

Moving into a nursing home

Moving into a nursing home is intensely stressful. You are leaving the house you may have lived in for several years and entering a communal home with people you don't know. So you must ensure that your new home satisfies your needs. Being involved in the choice of a suitable home also helps your relatives cope with the change.

However, as Whitlatch and colleagues found in their study of demented people in nursing facilities and their relatives, the family caregiver can also become depressed following the move into a nursing home. A close relationship between the caregiver and the patient as well as a less stressful care home environment increased the likelihood of a good outcome and the probability that both sides would adjust. On the other hand, high levels of stress among residents and caregivers, and the presence of stressors in the nursing home, predicted poor adjustment to the change in circumstances by the patient and the relatives originally caring for them.

So how can you pick a home? Nursing homes must register with the local authority, and Social Services inspect homes at least twice a year. So ask to see the Social Service reports of any home you are considering. Your local authority department might also be able to provide details of local residential care, and the district health authority will have lists of local nursing homes, which may be particularly useful if you're trying to find homes that offer specialist skills – care for people suffering from dementia, for example.

Age Concern★ and Help the Aged★ offer further advice on finding a home. While you are visiting a home look for obvious signs of neglect (see below). The Registered Nursing Homes Association★ is the trade association for nursing-home owners and also gives advice to those seeking a home.

What to look for in a nursing home

Think about the following points when assessing a nursing or retirement home:

- Is the home bright and cheerful?
- Are the members of staff helpful and professional?

- Are there sufficient numbers of staff to cope with the number of residents?
- Are residents active or slumped in chairs staring into space?
- Is the menu appetising? Will it meet any special nutritional needs (religious, ethical and medical)?
- Are the home and gardens pleasant and well maintained?
- Does the home have easy access to public transport, social services and healthcare?
- Is any special equipment available?
- Will the home allow you to decorate and personalise your room with some items of furniture, ornaments or pictures?

You may want to consider drawing up a legal contract between yourself and the owner. This should include when the fees are reviewed. Ask if you (or your relative) can stay in the home for a week or so before taking a final decision. You might have to pay, but there will be a chance to meet the other residents. You need to ask yourself one fundamental question: does this place feel as if it could be a home-from-home?

Caring for an ill relative

Caring for an ill relative places the carer under considerable stress. For example, Blake and Lincoln, from the University of Nottingham, found that 37 per cent of spouses caring for partners who had suffered a stroke showed marked strain (essentially, stress by another name). Not surprisingly, the level of strain was strongly linked to depressed mood. The carers' perceptions of their spouses' ability to independently perform the activities of daily living (washing, dressing, hygiene, etc.) was also strongly linked to their stress levels. Often the patient's needs submerge those of the carer – who may also be suffering from his or her own set of health problems. Not surprisingly, when the ill person finally dies, the gap in the carer's life can be huge.

You can take several steps to help minimise the stress of caring for an ill relative. For example, Mizuno and colleagues used a stress-management programme to help 56 people looking after a demented or disabled relative. The programme included problem-solving techniques (see Chapter 3) and relaxation training (see pages 228–30). Following the programmes, the carers were less depressed, angry, hostile, tense, anxious and confused. They suffered fewer general illnesses, showed enhanced immune functioning and were better able to cope socially. The benefits persisted for two months after the programme ended. By following the advice in this book, you should be able to use similar techniques in all the situations that cause you to feel stressed.

Many people find that learning about the disease they or a relative are suffering from helps to reduce stress. This may reveal new ways you can help the person you're caring for. It also helps you understand the medical reasons for the care you are giving and the patient's behaviour. This is especially important if, for example, the patient becomes aggressive or behaves in a sexually inappropriate manner. It is also worth contacting and co-operating with your local nurses, GPs and specialists. Ask if any specialist services are available. Many areas now run Parkinson's disease clinics and may have nurses trained to deal with incontinence or pressure sores, for example.

Furthermore, support groups have grown up around most chronic diseases and offer practical advice. Your local library should hold lists of local organisations and may have a directory of national organisations. Your GP or consultant may also be able to provide details of the local self-help group. Many people find that sharing their experiences and gaining advice and support from others in a similar situation combats stress.

It's also important to find time for yourself. Try to get out at least once a week. Social Services might be able to arrange residential care that allows you to go on holiday. And remember the simple things. Check, for example, that the patient's hearing aid works and that spectacles have the correct prescription, and consider whether home modifications could make life easier. Some Social Services departments might be willing to help with the cost of this.

SeniorLine★ is Help the Aged's free helpline for senior citizens, their relatives, carers and friends.

Further reading

Cole, T.R. 1992. *The Journey of Life: A Cultural History of Aging in America.* Canto

Donnellan, C. 2001. *Confronting Eating Disorders*. Independence

Edwards, D. 1998. *Free to be Human*. Green Books

Greener, M. 2000 *Which? Way to Manage Your Time – and Your Life*. Which? Books

Johnstone, N. 2002. *A Head Full of Blue*. Bloomsbury

Milam, J.R. and Ketcham, K. 1983. *Under The Influence*. Bantam Books

Wykle, M., Kahana, E., Kowal, J. et al (eds). 1992. *Stress & Health Among The Elderly*. Springer

Chapter 5

Overcoming alcohol and nicotine abuse

Many people smoke or drink to relieve stress. However, you run the risk of addiction to alcohol and nicotine which can cause numerous health problems or even death. This chapter examines the inter-relationship between stress, drinking and smoking and suggests how to cut these substances out of your life or stay within safe limits.

Stress and alcohol

Alcohol abuse is a major medical and societal problem. According to National Statistics, in 2001 over 38 per cent of men aged between 16 and 74 years were 'hazardous drinkers'. Among men between 16 and 24, the proportion of hazardous drinkers reached 53 per cent. Apart from drinking excessively, hazardous drinkers engage in other risky behaviours, such as becoming involved in arguments, injuring themselves or others, or failing to turn up for work because of a hangover. Furthermore, one in nine men – roughly 2.5 million people – is dependent on alcohol. Men are three times more likely than women to be alcohol dependent. For many people, stress is a major contributing factor to these sobering statistics.

Beating problem drinking

In any bar on any night, you will see people attempting to drown their stress in alcohol. For most people, a couple of pints aren't going to do any harm – provided they stay within the healthy drinking guidelines (see overleaf). Indeed, light drinking may help you unwind. But the key word is light. Drinking doesn't drown your problems. Indeed, in many cases, stress feeds on alcohol. So how much can you drink without putting your physical or mental health at risk? How do you know if you are over the limit? And how can you defeat problem drinking?

Safe drinking amounts

Currently, the government recommends drinking no more than 28 units of alcohol a week for men and 21 units for women. A unit is half a pint of normal-strength beer, a glass of wine or a pub measure of spirits. This doesn't mean you can 'spend' your entire weekly allowance each Friday night down the pub. Indeed, the guidelines suggest that you should keep to a daily, rather than weekly, limit. You should also have several drink-free days a week.

Overall, men who drink an average of three to four units a day and women who drink two to three units daily do not face a 'significant health risk'. Consistently drinking over these limits increases your risk of damaging your health. However, these are only guidelines. Individuals' tolerance for alcohol varies widely. For example, these variations partly reflect genetically determined differences in our ability to metabolise alcohol.

Binge drinking – where you occasionally drink well over the safe limit – is dangerous, even if you only do it two or three times a year. Regularly drinking more alcohol than is recommended may be even more hazardous as your body doesn't get the time to recover. You don't even have to get regularly drunk to suffer some of the harmful effects of alcohol.

Have you got an alcohol problem?

For many people, alcoholism conjures up an image of a homeless degenerate swilling super-strength lager. However, alcoholism strikes people from all walks of life and backgrounds. Many people who abuse alcohol hide or deny their problem even to themselves. The first step to recovering from alcohol abuse is to admit that you have a problem.

So how do you determine if you – or a loved one – has an alcohol problem? Doctors recognise certain key features of alcohol dependence. The more of these features that apply to you, the more likely you are to have an alcohol problem.

- **Compulsion** – an irresistible urge to drink. In severe cases, drinking alcohol becomes the most important thing in your life.
- **Withdrawal symptoms** Between 6 and 24 hours after a drinking session, alcohol levels fall and withdrawal symptoms emerge, including tremor ('the shakes'), insomnia, agitation and sometimes fits. Withdrawal symptoms usually peak between 24 and 48 hours of the last drink.
- **A regular drinking pattern** Most people vary their drinking pattern. Alcoholics drink regularly, in part to stave off withdrawal symptoms.
- **Tolerance** As you drink more, you metabolise alcohol more efficiently and your tolerance increases. Alcoholics often seem to be unaffected by amounts of alcohol that would leave a moderate drinker thoroughly drunk.
- **Returning to your old pattern of alcohol consumption** after abstaining for a while.

Delirium tremens

Delirium tremens, the most serious withdrawal symptom, develops between one and five days after the alcoholic stops drinking alcohol. Sufferers shake violently and appear disorientated and agitated. Their heartbeat and respiration rate rise. They may experience epileptic fits and hallucinate. Seeing 'pink elephants' is something of a joke, but the hallucinations brought on by delirium tremens can be terrifying. One alcoholic saw spiders the size of dinner plates crawling over his bedroom. Another felt maggots burrowing under her skin.

Untreated delirium tremens can kill. The dangers of withdrawal mean alcoholics likely to develop delirium tremens are managed in detoxification units. However, increasing numbers of mild-to-moderate withdrawal symptoms are now managed at home with the support of a nurse or GP. This avoids the stigma of needing to go into a detoxification unit.

Many people with a drink problem fall short of being full-blown alcoholics. Nevertheless, you may still have an alcohol problem if you get drunk every Friday night after work. Indeed, you could have a drink problem if:

- you feel you should cut down on your drinking
- you feel guilty about drinking
- people annoy you when they criticise your drinking.

Another way to see if you are at least mildly dependent is to try not to drink for a fortnight. You might be surprised at how difficult this is.

The downward spiral of alcohol abuse

Alcoholism can catch you in a downward spiral. Perhaps you are under stress at work or at home. So you begin to stop off at the pub and drink three pints a night to unwind or give you the Dutch courage to go home. At this level, you are considered a heavy social drinker. When your alcohol consumption increases to around eight units a day you may begin to experience medical, legal, social and employment problems. Around half of people drinking eight units a day manage to control their drinking or stop altogether. However, around a quarter of people drinking at this level develop chronic alcoholism. They may need detoxification and can end up socially isolated, unemployed – or even dead.

Alcohol is a major contributing factor to accidents in the home, at work and on the roads. Alcohol abuse also contributes to an increased risk of suicide. Bradvik and Berglund followed 1,312 alcohol-dependent men for between 28 and 48 years. Just over nine per cent of the men killed themselves over this time. This suicide rate clearly underscores the devastation that alcohol can bring.

What causes excessive drinking?

Many people drink to drown their sorrows. Certainly, having many problems increases the risk of excessive alcohol consumption. However, heavy drinking can cause yet more difficulties. It also exacerbates stress, sleep problems, anxiety and depression. Alcohol abuse traps the drinker in a cycle of increasing stress, as illustrated by Jack's story.

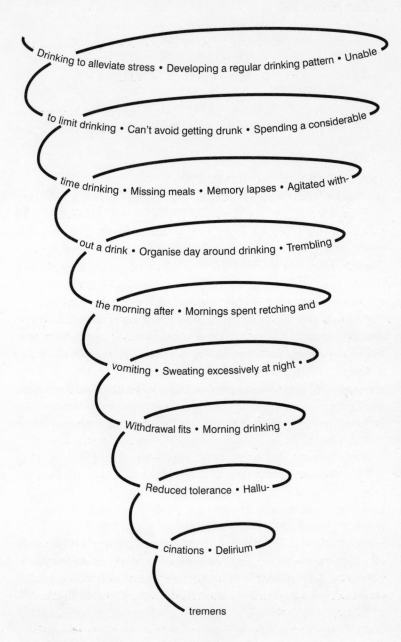

Drinking to alleviate stress • Developing a regular drinking pattern • Unable to limit drinking • Can't avoid getting drunk • Spending a considerable time drinking • Missing meals • Memory lapses • Agitated without a drink • Organise day around drinking • Trembling the morning after • Mornings spent retching and vomiting • Sweating excessively at night • Withdrawal fits • Morning drinking • Reduced tolerance • Hallucinations • Delirium tremens

The downward spiral of alcohol abuse

Case history: Jack

Jack was a salesman for an engineering company facing widespread rationalisation after a hostile takeover. Since joining the firm ten years ago, Jack had become a mainstay of the company. However, he was still recovering from the breakdown of his 14-year marriage six months before. The risk of redundancy left Jack feeling increasingly stressed out, worried and anxious. He started drinking heavily in the pub after work and in hotel bars during sales trips.

Jack then started bringing his drinking home with him. He felt his judgement slip and, once a legend for his punctuality, began missing appointments and taking more time off sick to nurse his increasingly frequent hangovers. Jack's sales figures began to slip. When the rationalisation reached the sales force, Jack was one of the first to be made redundant.

Jack probably wouldn't have been singled out if he hadn't started drinking heavily. Alcohol abuse often undermines performance at work. A reputation as a 'drinker' is not good for your employment prospects – even among professions traditionally thought likely to abuse alcohol such as sales reps, doctors, journalists, publicans and seamen. Neither is a poor sickness record. Alcohol abusers take around two-and-a-half times as many days off work as their colleagues.

Why can't some people control their drinking?

Why is one person able to control his or her drinking, while another under the same amount of stress gets drunk every night? Personality seems to play a part. 'When I had that first drink inside me, I was immune to everything. There was nothing, nothing in the whole wide world, that could touch me,' Nick Johnstone wrote in *A Head Full of Blue*, his evocative memoir of his struggle against, and recovery from, alcohol abuse. Such feelings help drive the compulsion to drink.

In some cases, alcoholism develops in the wake of a stressful life event – such as marital problems, unemployment or bereavement – although not everyone who loses a spouse or a job descends into alcoholism. There seems to be a difference in the brains of alcoholics that predisposes them to alcohol abuse. Alcoholics may be more sensitive to the effects of endorphins – the chemicals in your brain that make you feel euphoric. These 'feel good' chemicals also encourage addictions. As Olive and collaborators noted, alcohol triggers the release of endorphins in a part of the brain called the nucleus accumbens, which is involved in learning and motivation. This release makes drinkers feel good, reinforcing their need to drink and increasing their risk of developing alcoholism. Amphetamine and cocaine also trigger an increase in endorphins in the nucleus accumbens; the similarity between the biological actions of these drugs can help to explain why alcohol is addictive. (Two drugs used to treat alcohol abuse – naltrexone and nalmefene – seem to act by blocking the action of endorphins.) Indeed, it is possible that if alcohol were introduced today it would be considered a Class A drug.

People who abuse alcohol are more likely to suffer from a range of other psychological (mental) health problems than the general population. Burns and Teesson found that overall, around a third of people who either abused alcohol or were dependent also suffered from at least one other psychological health problem over the year before the study. People with alcohol problems were ten times more likely than the general population to abuse drugs. They were also four times more likely to suffer depression and three times more likely to experience an anxiety disorder.

In some cases, patients develop psychological health problems because they drink. In others, they drink to alleviate their mental distress. People with anxiety disorders might drink to alleviate the symptoms of their condition, for example – so social phobia sufferers may use alcohol to help them cope when meeting other people.

Another part of the jigsaw lies in your genes. Alcoholism undoubtedly runs in families. But is this genetic? Or do children learn to drink from their alcoholic parents? Of course, both factors probably contribute to a greater or lesser extent. Children learn, to some degree, their drinking habits from their parents and other role models. However, numerous studies confirm that your alcohol tolerance is, in part, genetically determined. For example, in 2002 Dick and colleagues linked genes on two chromosomes with an increased risk of alcohol-dependency. These genetic factors only predispose you to alcohol abuse, however. You are the one who consciously picks up the glass.

The health risks of excessive drinking

Heavy drinking carries a number of risks – not least a blinding hangover the following morning. The worst hangovers follow drinks such as brandy and bourbon. These contain high levels of chemical substances known as congeners, which give a spirit or wine its distinctive character. Although drinks with a high alcohol content cause most damage, the long-term effect on your health also depends on how much you drink. So you undermine your well-being whether you drink vodka, beer or wine to excess.

Over the years, doctors have linked alcohol to an increased risk of developing a large number of diseases.

Cancer

Alcohol contributes to between two and four per cent of all cases of cancer. The mouth and throat are especially vulnerable. Alcohol consumption has been linked to liver, breast and colorectal cancer. Indeed, even moderate drinking may increase your risk of developing certain cancers. A study in 2002 by Horn-Ross and collaborators found that consuming 20 or more grams of alcohol per day increases a woman's risk of developing breast cancer by 50 per cent. (Two glasses of wine contain roughly 20 grams of alcohol.) Flood and colleagues found that having more than two alcoholic drinks a day increases the risk of colorectal cancer by 16 per cent. In addition, alcohol might enhance the effects of cancer-producing chemicals in tobacco and food.

Liver disease

The liver metabolises alcohol. So, heavy drinking can lead to severe liver diseases, such as cirrhosis. Between 10 and 20 per cent of people who drink heavily develop cirrhosis of the liver. Alcohol kills liver cells. This forms scar tissue that chokes the liver's blood supply. As a result, patients develop symptoms of cirrhosis including jaundice, fever, enlarged spleen, confusion and drowsiness. Before the 1970s, doctors believed alcoholics' poor diets caused cirrhosis. However, most doctors now agree that long-term alcohol abuse directly causes cirrhosis – even if alcoholics eat adequate diets. A further 10 to 35 per cent of heavy drinkers develop hepatitis, an acute inflammation.

Brain damage

We all know that alcohol affects the brain – that's why we drink! Alcohol relaxes, reduces inhibitions and acts as a social lubricant. However, chronic drinking can cause memory loss, seizures and absent-mindedness. It also undermines concentration and co-ordination. In severe cases, alcohol-induced brain damage can mimic dementia. Drinkers who develop 'Korsakoff's syndrome' are unable to remember recent events or learn new information.

Heart disease

The government's 1995 revision of the safe drinking guidelines was partly based on studies showing that 'light to moderate' drinking reduces the risk of heart disease. However, once alcohol consumption exceeds the recommended level, the risk of developing heart disease begins to increase. Excessive drinking exacerbates high blood pressure and damages heart muscle.

It is difficult to explain why moderate alcohol consumption might be beneficial for some aspects of your health. Certainly, people who stay within the recommended limits may be more likely to exercise, eat healthy diets and look after other aspects of their health. Moreover, some red wines contain high levels of chemicals known as flavonoids, which may mop up potentially harmful free radicals – and of course, a few drinks help you relax. Whatever the explanation, it seems that in this case, a little of what you fancy does your heart good.

Strokes

The majority of strokes (ischaemic strokes) are caused by atherosclerosis – a hardening of the arteries. The less common haemorrhagic strokes occur when a blood vessel bursts and blood leaks into the brain. Alcohol abuse seems to increase the risk of both types of stroke.

Doctors first noted the link between heavy drinking and strokes in 1725. Then in the 1970s and 1980s a number of studies suggested that heavy drinking increased the risk of suffering a stroke, especially among irregular drinkers. Moreover, the risk of suffering a haemorrhagic stroke was found to rise steadily with increasing alcohol consumption. Hart and colleagues reported that drinking more than 35 units a week doubled your chance of dying from a stroke, compared with non-drinkers.

Digestive system

Alcohol damages the lining of the gastrointestinal tract. This can lead to stomach ulcers (see pages 144–46) and reduces the amount of vitamins and minerals absorbed by the body. For example, alcoholics may absorb lower amounts of vitamins A, E and D. Vitamin A deficiency impairs night vision. A lack of vitamin D contributes to softening of the bones, which predisposes you to osteoporosis.

Alcoholics commonly develop deficiency in one of the B vitamins called folate (folic acid), which may – in a few cases – make them more likely to develop anaemia. Fernando and Grimsley, for instance, found that 11.1 per cent of alcoholics suffered from folate deficiency. Deficiency in thyamine, another member of the B vitamin family, affects nerve function and might contribute to the cognitive problems in alcoholics mentioned above.

Impotence

Brewers' droop is probably the best-known form of alcohol-induced impotence. Fortunately, it's short-lived. However, while it lasts, impotence can cause considerable anxiety, embarrassment and stress. For advice on treatments see pages 158–63. Chronic alcohol abuse can cause the testes to waste away, and may lead to nerve damage, which can be irreversible. Both can lead to impotence.

Health problems in women

Among women, chronic alcohol abuse can impair the menstrual cycle, contribute to infertility, and speed the onset of the menopause.

As women's bone loss declines rapidly after the menopause, heavy drinkers are more likely to develop osteoporosis – brittle bone disease – which leaves them vulnerable to life-threatening fractures. Several factors increase the risk of developing osteoporosis, including poor vitamin D absorption and hormonal changes. Alcohol also seems to poison cells known as osteoblasts, which lay down new bone. The diet of heavy drinkers exacerbates this decline.

They are also more likely to fall than the general population, thus increasing their risk of fractures. However, bone formation returns to normal within a fortnight of stopping drinking – even among chronic alcoholics.

How to cut down

If you are worried about your drinking, you may be able to reduce your alcohol consumption by following a few simple rules:

- set yourself a limit – and stick to it. Monitor your progress by keeping a drink diary
- quench your thirst with non-alcoholic drinks
- alternate alcoholic and non-alcoholic drinks
- dilute your drink with a mixer
- drink low-alcohol wine and beer
- have drink-free days each week
- you may have to avoid your usual haunts and drinking partners on 'dry' days
- find a hobby or exercise that doesn't involve going down the pub
- drink slowly – you eliminate one unit of alcohol an hour
- don't drink on an empty stomach – food slows the rate at which you absorb alcohol into the blood
- keep a drink diary for a month recording how much and where you drank, the number of drink-free days and the amount of money you spent on alcohol – the latter can be very sobering!

Once you have begun to reduce your alcohol consumption, you need to deal with some of the problems that led you there. The problem-solving approaches and assertive coping techniques outlined in Chapter 3 may help. Organisations such as those on page 120 may also help you control your drinking.

How to get help

If you still cannot cut down your drinking, you may need professional help. In some cases this may mean consulting a doctor. Doctors can now prescribe several drugs to help motivated people reduce their alcohol consumption. For years, disulfiram (Antabuse) was the only direct pharmacological support for people who wanted to stop drinking. When a patient drinks alcohol after taking disulfiram, they suffer an intensely unpleasant reaction – including flushing, throbbing headaches, nausea and vomiting – that can last for several hours. The idea is that this reaction means that the drinker avoids alcohol.

Even the small amounts of alcohol in medicines, toiletries and mouthwashes can induce the disulfiram reaction. Large amounts can cause arrhythmias (disordered heart beats), falls in blood pressure and collapse. Furthermore, disulfiram is associated with several unpleasant side effects. In rare cases, disulfiram can cause psychotic reactions, for example.

More recently three medications have proved to be effective in between 20 and 50 per cent of alcoholics: naltrexone, nalmefene and acamprosate. However, in common with other addiction programmes, drugs for alcoholism are most effective when combined with behavioural treatments. Feeney and colleagues reported that adding acamprosate to cognitive behavioural therapy (CBT) markedly improved abstinence rates. For example, 42 per cent of those treated with a combination of CBT and acamprosate completed the 12-week rehabilitation programme. This compared to a success rate of 32 per cent among those treated with CBT alone. Furthermore, 38 per cent of patients who received CBT and acamprosate abstained from drinking after 12 weeks. This compared to 14 per cent of those treated with CBT alone. At best, only half of people who abuse alcohol respond to one of these treatments alone.

If you, a friend or partner has a drink problem, voluntary organisations such as Alcoholics Anonymous★ may be more approachable and more sympathetic than the local GP. Alcoholics Anonymous and other self-help groups aim to fill the void when someone stops drinking. Moreover, if the stress gets too much, the recovering alcoholic has someone to turn to for advice and support. Al-Anon★ and Alcohol Concern★ can help the families of alcoholics cope, and educate them about ways to help. But even with the support of these groups, stopping drinking is very difficult – especially if the person has abused alcohol for several years. Drinkers need all the help they can get to get off the booze.

Stress and smoking

In the time it's taken you to read this chapter, someone has probably died from lung cancer. Around 94 people die from lung cancer in the UK every day – that's about one every 15 minutes. Indeed, lung cancer is now the commonest cancer in men and the third most common malignancy among women. However, survival rates are poor and it is the biggest cancer killer in the UK, accounting for more than a quarter of all deaths from malignancies. Tragically, most of these deaths could be prevented.

There is no reason for anyone to be unaware of the well-publicised risks of smoking. Smoking causes around 87 per cent of lung cancers as well as a range of other malignancies. Nevertheless, around a quarter of adults still smoke. Many smokers don't believe that they will be unlucky enough to endure smoking-induced heart disease, respiratory problems and cancer – a classic example of denial. The reality is somewhat different.

Around 38,800 people are diagnosed with lung cancer in the UK each year. However, a declining smoking rate means that lung cancer is becoming less common in men. In 1999, 21,130 men died from the disease – a reduction of 39 per cent since 1984. (Indeed, prostate cancer could soon overtake lung malignancies as the commonest cancer in men.) However, as women started smoking in large numbers later than men, deaths from lung cancer in women are still increasing: they rose by four per cent between 1984 and 1999, for example.

As well as causing lung cancer, smoking accounts for around a third of all malignant tumours, including those in the mouth, throat, oesophagus, pancreas, bladder, kidney, cervix and stomach. If that is not enough to put you off, smoking increases your risk of developing heart disease, circulatory problems and non-cancerous lung diseases such as emphysema and bronchitis. Moreover, smokers increasingly find themselves social lepers, banished outside or to a polluted room at work. Smoke-free zones in restaurants and cinemas and smokeless flights and trains are increasingly common.

In smokers' defence it is incredibly difficult to quit, especially if you smoke under stress or because you suffer from depression, anxiety or other mental problems. Lindstrom and colleagues found that immigrants, unmarried people and those with poor education and worse psychological or social conditions were less likely than those living in better circumstances to quit smoking. Macleod and collaborators from the University of Birmingham found that high levels of stress were associated with increased smoking and alcohol consumption.

This intimate link between stress and smoking means that you may have to sort out some of your other problems before you are able to stop smoking. Quitting is hard enough without having to contend with the burden of depression or alcohol withdrawal, but it's worth making the effort. Follow the advice in this book to get on top of your difficulties and formulate a personal action plan. While much of the damage caused to your lungs by smoking is irreversible, you can prevent any further decline. Stopping smoking dramatically reduces the likelihood of developing cancer. Moreover, many of the changes that predispose you to heart disease return to normal a few weeks after you stop smoking (although it takes five years for the risk to drop to that of a non-smoker). This means that it is worth trying to quit no matter how old you are.

A passive killer

If staying healthy – or alive – isn't a good enough reason to quit, think about the harm you are doing to your partner, friends and children. You would not allow a toddler to smoke. The Children's Act banned selling cigarettes to the under-16s as long ago as 1908. But parents still endanger the health of millions of children through passive smoking.

Mounting evidence suggests that passive smoking is more than just unpleasant. It's also dangerous. Kropp and Chang-Claude discovered that passive smoking increases a woman's chance of developing breast cancer by 60 per cent. Radon found that being exposed to tobacco smoke at work for more than eight hours a day was linked to an increased risk of developing chronic bronchitis, as well as roughly doubling the risk of developing asthma and wheezing. Even occasional passive smoking can damage your health. Panagiotakos and co-workers found that being exposed to smoking less than three times per week was associated with a 26 per cent higher risk of developing heart disease. Regular exposure to passive smoke almost doubles the risk. Passive smoking also seems to contribute to cot death. So if you can't quit for the sake of your health, stop for the sake of the people around you.

How to quit

As with many life changes, the first step is to want to quit. Many women stop smoking when they become pregnant. Pregnancy can also provide fathers-to-be with the motivation they need.

It's important to be realistic and recognise how hard it can be to quit. Only between 1.5 and 3 per cent of smokers quit each year, according to Peters and Morgan. Between five and ten per cent of smokers taking inactive placebos in studies of nicotine replacements such as gum or nicotine patches manage to quit for at least a year. So it is also important to remain positive – even if you have a setback. The stages of change model outlined in Chapter 3 can help guide you towards abstinence. And you can take a number of steps to make quitting smoking less stressful.

- Try to identify your smoking triggers. Do you smoke when you're tense? When you're bored? Only after meals? Are you a social smoker? Keep a diary and note when and where you light up, and how you feel when you smoke. Once you've identified your smoking triggers you may be able to avoid them.
- Don't cut down. Give up. There isn't a safe level of regular smoking. In any case, nicotine is so addictive that few heavy smokers are able to cut down to a small number of cigarettes a day for any time. Each puff of each cigarette reinforces your addiction.
- Switching to low-tar cigarettes is better than nothing, but you'll be healthier still giving up. However, many people who switch to low nicotine cigarettes end up smoking more.
- Get other health problems, such as depression and anxiety, treated. Chapter 7 offers some suggestions that might help.
- If you smoke to relieve anxiety or stress, try other ways to relax. Sedative smokers are especially likely to benefit from relaxation.
- Often smokers feel irritable for a while after they give up so ask for your family's support and understanding. If they know you've quit smoking they might be more willing to forgive a grouchy mood.
- Tell people you've stopped. Ask them to help by not smoking in front of you.

- Choose a significant date to stop – such as New Year's Day, National No Smoking Day or your birthday.
- Sit in no-smoking areas in restaurants.
- Resist the urge to smoke by chewing vegetables, sugar-free chewing gum or other healthy snacks.
- Spend at least some of the money you save on yourself, such as on a holiday.

Quitline★ as well as Action on Smoking and Health (ASH)★ offer advice, information and support.

If these measures fail, you can try one of a number of smoking cessation aids. These don't replace the self-help strategies outlined above. However, they markedly increase your chances of giving up, and fewer than five per cent of users need to stop because of side effects. Indeed, the various approaches seem to offer the same benefit. Hughes notes that they roughly double your chances of quitting – although you still need to be motivated.

Replacing the nicotine in cigarettes can help people quit. Nicotine replacement comes in several forms – gums, inhalers, nasal sprays and patches – so you can probably find one that suits you. These are available either on prescription or from your pharmacist. A doctor can also prescribe a drug called bupropion, originally developed as an antidepressant, to help you quit. Some nicotine replacements are available only on prescription as part of a programme to help you stop. Treatment may be for a short period only, and depends on your progress.

While nicotine replacements can help, the likelihood of stopping smoking using such aids declines sharply over time. This under-scores the importance of preventing relapses, known as the 'maintenance phase' in the stages of change model (see pages 56–63). In spite of the hurdles, through a combination of willpower and smoking cessation aids, you can have a good chance at quitting. There are many success stories of people who give up and never look back.

Further reading

Johnstone, N. 2002. *A Head Full of Blue*. Bloomsbury

Chapter 6

Stress and physical diseases

In this chapter, we will look at some of the physical diseases that stress contributes to, either directly or by making symptoms worse. The examples used allow us to explore the evidence suggesting that stress is closely linked with illness, and show you how to cut down your risk of experiencing physical symptoms. If you suffer from a particular physical complaint, we give some hints on how to manage the condition.

The medical advice and lifestyle tips in this chapter should be read in conjunction with the coping strategies in the rest of the book. There isn't space to discuss the medical options in depth – each of these topics could fill a book in its own right. So if you have concerns about an illness, ensure that you talk to your doctor about the issues raised in this chapter.

The truth about stress and illness

The relationship between stress and physical disease is surrounded by myths and misconceptions. Many people think, for example, that stress directly causes heart disease, cancer or any number of life-threatening conditions. However, with a few important exceptions, such as some infections and irritable bowel syndrome (IBS), stress causes physical illness only rarely. Nevertheless, stress can undoubtedly worsen the symptoms of several diseases. For instance, stress can trigger exacerbations of the skin complaint psoriasis, and a patient's psychological state can influence how quickly he or she recovers following a heart attack. Weisberg and colleagues found that people suffering from post-traumatic stress disorder (see pages 195–96) were more likely to suffer several diseases including anaemia, arthritis, asthma, back pain, diabetes, eczema, kidney disease, lung conditions and ulcers.

As we saw on pages 16–17, stress can cause a variety of unpleasant and sometimes distressing symptoms. If you are worried that a particular symptom might be caused by a potentially serious disease rather than stress, you should consult your GP. If you already suffer from a physical disease and want to reduce your stress levels, talk things through with your GP or consultant. He or she might recommend assertive coping strategies (see Chapter 3), or refer you to a counsellor, psychologist or psychotherapist. Patient groups can offer valuable advice and support. Ask your nurse, doctor or local library for details of relevant groups or contact NHS Direct.* We have also made a few suggestions at the end of each section.

Check that your complementary therapy is safe

It is especially important to discuss any alternative or complementary therapies you are contemplating with your GP or consultant. In most cases, your doctor won't raise any concerns and the complementary therapy might help you manage your stress. However, some physical therapies could exacerbate your condition – if, for example, you suffer from arthritis – while some herbal remedies may interact with conventional medicines. Not all doctors are aware of the risks and benefits offered by complementary medicine. However, it is better to ask your GP's advice than run the risk of taking a dangerous treatment. At the very least he or she might be able to explain whether there is any scientific or medical justification for the approach.

While complementary and alternative therapies can help you regain a sense of control and help you relax (see Chapter 10), there are charlatans and cranks who prey on the vulnerable. If your doctor suggests that a particular complementary approach might be inappropriate, ask him or her to explain the reasons, and proceed cautiously if you decide to ignore medical advice. See Chapter 10 and The Which? Guide to Complementary Therapies for more information about complementary and alternative remedies.

Two-way traffic: stress and the immune system

Our body plays host to a large reservoir of micro-organisms, which live in symbiosis with us and prevent us from contracting an infection. However, we are surrounded by bacteria, viruses, fungi and parasites. When one of these organisms invades our body, cells in our immune system try to eradicate any harmful infections.

Stress can undermine the immune system through a complex pathway linking the mind and the body. Some chemicals released by the cells as part of our immune defences also activate nerves that stimulate the brain. The brain feeds back on the immune system through nerves supplying the bone marrow, thymus gland, spleen, lymph nodes and other organs. This influences the production of white blood cells – the main line of defence against infection. In other words, the immune system influences the brain and *vice versa*. This highlights that stress can at least contribute to physical disease.

Acute and chronic stress can produce differing effects on immune function.

- **Acute stress** Acute stress is the fear you feel when confronted with a physical threat or shock. The changes that take place during acute stress may reflect the action of stress hormones, which enhance our immune function to protect against wounding or infection when we fight or take flight. For instance, adrenaline and some related chemicals (the catecholamines) can produce short-term changes in immune function, including influencing white blood cells. Dhabhar noted that during acute stress, leukocytes (a type of white blood cell) accumulate in the skin. This demonstrates that stress can influence some aspects of the immune system. However, chronic stress (see below) suppresses this leukocyte mobilisation. 'During acute stress, the brain may send a warning signal to the immune system, just as it does to other fight/flight systems in the body,' Dhabhar comments.
- **Chronic stress** (or long-lasting stress) is what you might face if you're seriously ill or feel trapped in a job or situation that you find difficult but can't leave – such as caring for a patient with Alzheimer's disease. Again chronic stress can have marked biological effects. For example, chronic stress seems to slow

wound healing by between 24 and 40 per cent. Possibly, as Kiecolt-Glaser and colleagues noted, stress may alter the activity of certain important biological chemicals – called mediators – that control the immune response and are important in the early stages of healing. This slow recovery might be a manifestation of the 'exhaustion' phase in the stress response (see page 21).

Stress and your likelihood of suffering an infection

As stress influences the immune system, it can predispose us to suffering an infection. Cohen, for example, found a direct link between cortisol levels in the blood and the risk of developing a cold, 'flu or other upper respiratory tract infection. (Cortisol is one of a number of hormones and chemicals released as part of the fight-or-flight response – see pages 19–21.)

Patients with high cortisol levels reported experiencing a large number of stressful life events, and seemed to be especially vulnerable to suffering upper respiratory tract infections. High cortisol levels do not directly cause an infection. However, cortisol may act as a marker for a range of changes in the immune system that increase our susceptibility to infection. Those patients who experienced fewer stressful life events, or who reacted less when they faced a stressor, contracted fewer infections. (The large number of people who suffer a cold or 'flu each year makes these infections ideal to study the effects of stress. You would need a much larger study to assess the effect of stress if you used a more serious but less common disease.)

In another study, Schaubroeck and colleagues found that people with demanding jobs were more likely to suffer upper respiratory tract infections than those who face less pressure at work. A high level of job control partly protected people with demanding jobs from the risk of an infection. But this difference emerged only in those who *felt* themselves to be in control. This, again, underscores one of the central themes in this book: being in control protects against stress. Those patients whom the researchers felt had a high level of control – but who did not recognise this themselves – were at increased risk of developing the infection.

Kiecolt-Glaser and colleagues concluded that stress (or immuno-logical changes caused by stress) *can* influence your risk of developing certain diseases. However, other factors are important.

Stress might increase your chances of contracting an infection, but you need to be exposed to the bacterium or virus first, for example. In addition, your age is significant. The immune system becomes weaker with advancing age, so older people have less reserve in their immune system. As a result, stress could depress the system enough to mean they develop an infection. Younger people might experience the same stress, but have a stronger immune system and sufficient reserve to counter the infection.

Against this background, interventions that reduce stress might offer partial protection from some diseases. This book provides some strategies that will help bolster your defences.

Stress and vaccines

Vaccines work by priming the immune system to mount a response against a virus, bacteria and so on. For example, your doctor might inject you with a vaccine to protect you against 'flu. Because it impairs the immune system, stress may affect how well vaccines work. Van Loveren and colleagues comment that several factors – including age, nutrition and psychological stress – impair the effectiveness of some vaccines. (However, exactly how these factors react with vaccines is not fully understood.)

Other studies show that your psychological state influences the success of vaccination. In some patients, feelings of well-being and belonging seem to increase the likelihood that some vaccines will protect them from disease. Morag and colleagues, for instance, found that girls who experienced prolonged periods of negative emotions – essentially depression – and had low self-esteem mounted an impaired response to the rubella vaccine.

As we saw in Chapter 4, the caregivers of people with severe diseases often experience marked stress. And according to two studies – one published by Kiecolt-Glaser and colleagues and another by Vedhara and co-workers – people looking after a spouse with dementia are less likely to mount a protective response following the 'flu vaccine than non-caregivers. So carers might be more susceptible to catching 'flu than their less stressed peers – even if they have received the vaccine.

However, having a close network of friends and family may help the body respond successfully to some vaccines. Glaser found that students with better levels of social support – which helps to counter stress – showed a stronger response to hepatitis B vaccines than those with less support.

Cancer

The immune system does more than protect us from infections. It also seems to destroy some of the abnormal cells that could develop into cancers. Each day, some 35 billion cells divide in a healthy adult – each producing a new cell. Invariably, some of these new cells are defective. Certain immune cells – natural killer cells, for example – act as a quality control system, selectively eradicating potentially cancerous cells. So based on the findings already discussed in this chapter, you might expect that chronic stress, which undermines the immune system, would predispose people to cancer.

Nevertheless, the jury is still out. Cancers usually take several years to develop from a cancerous cell to a diagnosable tumour. People smoke and sunbathe for many years before developing lung or skin cancer, for example. Some studies suggest that a stressful event can predate the diagnosis of cancer by several years, even decades. This makes assessing the effect of stress on cancer especially difficult. One theory suggests that as stress can undermine the immune system, it might increase the risk of developing those cancers triggered by viruses (including Burkitt's lymphoma and cervical cancer).

To confuse matters further, cancer isn't really a single disease. Cancer is a general term for a multitude of conditions, with various causes. Indeed, while all cancers arise from the uncontrolled proliferation of abnormal cells, most researchers believe that a tumour only develops following several cumulative events. So stress might have different effects depending on the cancer.

Breast cancer

Doctors now know that certain women are at high risk of developing breast cancer, including:

- women whose mother or sister had breast cancer
- childless women
- those women who had their first baby during their 30s
- those who had a late menopause.

Ironically, the stress associated with being at high risk might mean that a woman is less likely to examine her breasts regularly or go for mammography (an example of denial – see page 38). For instance, Schwartz and colleagues studied a group of women who had a first-degree relative with breast cancer. They found that the more distressed women were less likely to undergo mammography than their less stressed counterparts. However, women who had undergone counselling were more likely to attend the screening that could save their lives.

If you are a woman at high risk of breast cancer, counselling can dramatically reduce your level of distress and keep your fears in perspective.

You should see your doctor without delay if you find a lump or any abnormality in your breasts. After the initial investigation or screening you may be called back for more tests. This can be a worrying time, but it is important to follow medical advice and stay as calm as possible. The stress management therapies in Chapter 10 – such as relaxation, massage or alternative treatments – may help.

Sandin and colleagues found that, not surprisingly, women called for a second-stage breast cancer screen suffered more emotional distress than those attending for the first mammogram. The women who needed further assessment were more worried and scared, and held inappropriate beliefs about breast cancer. However, these feelings did not persist once the women received the all-clear. So it's worth dealing with the short-term stress while waiting for the results of the medical investigation – use some of the suggestions in this book to alleviate your worries. A negative result can put your mind at rest. A positive result means that you will get the treatment you need to extend or save your life.

The impact of stress on breast cancer

Scientists have not found any conclusive evidence that stress increases your chances of getting breast cancer. Some studies suggest that experiencing traumatic events might increase a woman's likelihood of developing the disease much later on. For example, Jacobs and Bovasso found that women whose mothers died from any cause during their childhood were 2.6 times more likely to develop breast cancer than other women. Furthermore, severe episodes of chronic depression increased the risk of breast cancer fourteen-fold in these women. These stressors preceded the cancer's onset by at least 20 years. Some other studies suggest a 20-year lag between the cause of breast cancer and the diagnosis. Nevertheless, the research couldn't show that stress as such caused the increased risk for the women: some other factor might be responsible, such as exposure to a carcinogen not yet identified. And other studies paint a different picture, failing to find any important associations between breast cancer and stressful life events. Clearly, further work is needed to define fully the relationship between stress and cancer.

Being diagnosed with any form of cancer can be devastating (see opposite). The impact of stress after the discovery of cancer is, perhaps, best studied in breast cancer. Koopman and colleagues found that 'traumatic stress symptoms' (essentially, very severe stress) were relatively common following a diagnosis of breast cancer. Certain patients seemed especially vulnerable to developing traumatic stress:

- younger women
- those who needed further treatment following their operation for breast cancer
- women who tended to be emotional
- those in whom the cancer markedly affected their lives.

Indeed, in an earlier study, Koopman and colleagues found that, on average, women considered their breast cancer diagnosis to be one of the four most stressful life events they ever experienced. Many women were not sure how to cope, felt hopeless and dwelt on the diagnosis.

On a more positive note, Landmark and Wahl found that women newly diagnosed with breast cancer channelled all their energy 'into a tenacious fight for life' – which can be construed as a beneficial response to stress. In other words, experiencing stress may encourage women to take all the steps they can to beat the disease, such as adhering to treatment, joining support groups and learning about the disease.

Certainly, stress management can help many women. Antoni and collaborators, for instance, used cognitive behavioural techniques (see pages 232–34) in 100 women undergoing breast cancer treatment to help them deal with stress. The programme, which lasted 10 weeks, reduced the number of women who suffered moderate depression compared to another group that had not undergone stress management training. Furthermore, more women in the stress management group reported that breast cancer had made a positive contribution to their lives (for example, suffering from a serious disease can help you get events in perspective.) In general, the women who learnt stress management techniques felt more optimistic than those who had not. The benefits were especially marked in women who had held the most negative views and were the least optimistic at the beginning of the programme.

Women can consult Breast Cancer Care★ for support and advice.

Dealing with a diagnosis of cancer

Whether stress directly causes cancer is uncertain. However, being diagnosed as having cancer is one of the most stressful events you are ever likely to face. And you don't even have to develop cancer to suffer from its stressful effects. Being at high risk of developing the disease – for example, having a family history of breast cancer – can be enough to cause some people considerable distress.

A diagnosis of cancer, the realisation that a malignancy is likely to prove fatal, a feared treatment or being present at the death of a cancer patient can all cause severe stress symptoms. Some people even develop symptoms of post-traumatic stress disorder (PTSD) – see pages 195–96. Patients with severe stress endure extreme fear, helplessness and horror. They may endure nightmares, flashbacks and interfering thoughts. They may have sleeping problems or be overly defensive, watchful or irritable. Guilt or a sense of overwhelming loss are also common reactions.

Although a diagnosis of cancer seems to be a death sentence to many people, the reality is that doctors can now cure many cancers, especially if they are detected during the early phases. It is important to stay positive and find out as much as you can about treatment options. Stress management strategies such as the ones in this book can help you deal with a diagnosis of cancer and other traumatic events.

Learning the skills to cope

Studies reinforce the suggestion made above that stress management helps people live with cancer. For example, Fawzy and co-workers educated patients suffering from malignant melanoma (a type of skin cancer) about the condition, as well as improving their problem-solving skills and stress management techniques. After a six-week course, patients reported less psychological distress and the authors found several favourable immunological changes in these people compared to those who did not take part in the programme. Over six years, deaths were higher among those who had not received the training than in those who had taken part in the programme.

Some of the benefits associated with stress management might not be due solely to any direct effect on the cancer. People who feel less depressed, isolated and frightened are more likely to eat better, sleep soundly and exercise than those who feel traumatically stressed. They are also more likely to follow their doctors' instructions – which can involve taking unpleasant treatments. Such differences might contribute to reduced morbidity and a better quality of life in cancer patients who take part in stress management programmes.

As a result, psychosocial therapies that aim to alleviate the depression, anxiety and stress surrounding cancer are now a standard part of cancer management in many hospitals. For instance, some centres offer massage or other forms of complementary therapies for stress relief. Patients may undergo group therapy to explore their feelings and emotions about cancer. They may be offered marital therapy if they feel their marriage is under strain. Some patients require individual therapy to deal with specific problems, such as excessive crying and refusing to eat.

People sometimes find it easier to talk to someone who is not directly involved with their care. You may find that seeing a counsellor helps. Patients' groups such as CancerBACUP,★ Cancerlink★ and Tenovus★ offer general advice and support for cancer patients and their families. There are also specialist groups for individual cancers, including Breast Cancer Care,★ the Lymphoma Association★ and the Leukaemia Care Society.★

Heart disease

Cancer might be the most feared disease, but heart conditions remain the UK's leading cause of death. Despite advances in surgery and medicines, despite greater understanding of the causes of heart disease, despite greater awareness of the risk factors among doctors and patients, it still kills a third of men and a quarter of women. A further two million suffer symptoms of heart disease, such as angina.

What causes heart disease?

The commonest form of heart disease arises when fatty deposits – known as atherosclerotic plaques – build up on the walls of the blood vessels supplying the heart. This narrows the blood vessels and starves the heart muscles of oxygen. The crippling pain of angina signals that the heart is not getting enough oxygen. The pain forces angina patients to slow down and, thereby, helps balance oxygen supply and demand.

In some cases, plaques rupture and expel their contents into the blood. This causes the blood to clot. The clot further reduces or totally blocks the blood supply to the heart and the patient suffers a heart attack (also called a myocardial infarction). Many people at high risk of suffering a heart attack – for example, those who have experienced a myocardial infarction in the past – take a daily dose of aspirin, which makes the blood less likely to clot. But don't take aspirin in this way without talking to your doctor first. There is a small risk that regular aspirin may trigger bleeding in the stomach or duodenum (part of your intestine) or, less commonly, a haemorrhagic stroke (see pages 142–44).

The links with stress
The evidence for a link between stress and heart disease is mixed. Several factors seem to influence the risk.

- Smith and Ruiz reviewed the evidence that psychosocial factors can influence the risk of developing heart disease. They found that hostility – one aspect of a type A personality (see pages 29–32) – seems to be linked to an increased risk. For tips on managing your anger and hostility, see page 225. Furthermore, depression and anxiety can hinder recovery following a heart attack (see opposite). Social isolation, conflict with other people and job stress might also confer an increased risk of developing heart disease.

- Alfredsson and colleagues looked at the link between job strain and biological markers that might indicate an increased risk of heart disease – such as high blood pressure and abnormal levels of cholesterol – in 10,382 people. As discussed on pages 94–95, job strain arises when people are in demanding occupations with little ability to take decisions. In this study, job strain was linked to neither high cholesterol levels nor increased levels of fibrinogen, which triggers blood clots. (As mentioned above, blood clots inside the coronary vessels can trigger a heart attack.) There seemed to be a link between job strain and hypertension in women, but not men. Both women and younger people with high levels of job strain also showed low levels of a type of fat called HDL (high-density lipoprotein cholesterol). This carries cholesterol to the liver for destruction, so low levels increase the risk of heart disease. These results hint that job strain might be linked to an increased risk of heart disease in some people. But it's hard to draw hard-and-fast rules for everyone from these findings.

- Blumenthal and colleagues studied men with established heart disease. In these patients, activity or stress seemed to reduce the blood flow to the heart – a phenomenon called ischaemia. Some men participated in a weekly class on stress management that lasted one-and-a-half hours for four months. Compared to men who didn't take part, the number of heart attacks and other disease symptoms in patients were lower after both two and five years. However, these findings might apply only to men with stress-induced ischaemia – and it is difficult to show this without extensive testing.

- Intensely traumatic events might increase the risk of developing heart disease, even many years later. Li and colleagues found that parents whose child died unexpectedly were much more likely to fall prey to heart disease. Parents who lost a child were 36 per cent more likely to die from a heart attack than others who were not bereaved, for instance. Bereaved parents were also 28 per cent more likely to suffer a first heart attack. The increased risk seemed to last for up to 17 years following the child's death.

- Several studies suggest that people who become depressed following a heart attack or heart transplant have a poorer outcome than those that do not develop depression – in other words, they are more likely to die or suffer a serious complication (such as another attack). For example, Zipfel and colleagues followed 103 patients for more than four years following a heart transplant. Those patients who were markedly depressed before the operation were more likely to die following the transplant, even allowing for other factors. This is one area where there does seem to be broad agreement, and many cardiologists (doctors specialising in the treatment of heart disease) now advocate screening for and managing depression in people with heart disease.

Keep stress in proportion

It's important to realise that the heart disease risk directly associated with stress for most of us is not that great. On the other hand, many heart disease risk factors are intertwined – stress may make you smoke or eat poorly, for example – and the risk from some of these factors greatly outweighs that from stress alone. For example, smoking more than 20 cigarettes a day doubles the risk of heart disease compared to non-smokers. Indeed, stopping smoking is the single most effective thing you can do to lower your risk of heart disease. Smokers' risk of suffering heart disease declines almost to that among non-smokers within five to ten years of stopping, for example. We offer some more advice about smoking cessation on pages 120–24.

How to reduce your risk of heart disease

Even if stress is not of major factor in heart disease for most people, there is no room for complacency. Heart disease still kills more people than any other condition. The lifestyle advice offered below should help you limit your risk of developing heart disease. Over the years, studies have linked more than 250 factors – including infections, diet and depression – with an increased risk of developing heart disease. You cannot alter some risk factors – including being male, having a family history of heart disease or getting older, for instance. But you can reduce the risk associated with a number of other factors such as smoking, inactivity, high blood pressure, diabetes and high cholesterol. So exercise regularly (see pages 247–49), and eat a healthy diet. For example:

- Try to fill up on bread, cereals, potatoes, fruit and vegetables. They tend to be relatively low in calories, while still being filling.
- Fat has roughly twice the amount of calories as the same weight of foods rich in starch or protein. So switch to low-fat foods and eat more carbohydrates, such as baked potatoes, pasta and wholegrain bread.
- Ban table sugar completely. It's simply empty calories and is devoid of any nutrients.
- Replace puddings, biscuits, cakes, chocolate and so on with low-fat, low-sugar yoghurt or fresh fruit.
- Use butter, margarine, low-fat spreads and mayonnaise sparingly.
- Avoid sweetened juices and other drinks.
- Ensure that your alcohol consumption is within the current recommended limits (see page 110).

If following these measures doesn't adequately control your cholesterol levels, you may need to take drugs. Your doctor and some pharmacists can test your cholesterol level.

Arrhythmias and palpitations

A pounding heart is one of the commonest symptoms of stress. So the chances are that you have already experienced palpitations when you have felt stressed, anxious or scared. In certain circumstances – before giving an important presentation at work, for example – you may feel that your heart is beating furiously. This heightened awareness of your heartbeat is known as palpitations – although your heart may be beating fast, the rhythm is normal. Palpitations are usually harmless, although they can be unpleasant and even frightening.

Medicines prescribed by your doctor, alcohol, nicotine and caffeine can all cause palpitations in some patients. If any of these factors are affecting you, review your medication with your doctor, drink less alcohol and stop smoking (see Chapter 5). Palpitations can also be a symptom of a number of diseases, including thyroid disease and heart conditions. If palpitations persist or become severe, or you experience breathlessness or chest pains during an attack, you should consult your GP. Once you have ruled out any medical causes, using stress management techniques or relaxation can reduce the frequency of palpitations. If relaxation fails, look at your lifestyle.

Arrhythmias are disordered heartbeats: the heart rhythm becomes erratic and disorganised. As a result, the heart may not fill properly. Everyone seems occasionally to experience short-lived arrhythmias from time to time, although some arrhythmias cause no symptoms and may be found by accident. Protracted periods of arrhythmia can be dangerous, even life-threatening. If you are concerned you need to seek advice from your doctor.

Hypertension

Hypertension – or high blood pressure – is one of the more common chronic diseases. According to the British Heart Foundation, 41 per cent of men in England and 33 per cent of women either have, or are being treated for, hypertension. The condition becomes more common with increasing age.

However, hypertension is detected in relatively few patients. It rarely causes symptoms, and is often picked up during routine health scans or when patients consult a doctor about another problem. The British Heart Foundation estimates that less than 80 per cent of men and 70 per cent of women with hypertension are treated for the condition. Primatesta and colleagues reported that in 1998, 37 per cent of adults were hypertensive, but only 32 per cent of these were being treated and just 9 per cent attained the target blood pressures (see overleaf). So you should ensure that a doctor or a nurse checks your blood pressure at least once every five years if you are over 35. All too often hypertension is a silent killer.

How doctors measure blood pressure

Doctors take two blood pressure measurements, known as the systolic and diastolic. Each heartbeat sends a wave of blood into the arteries. The blood pressure produced at the peak of this wave is determined by the amount of the blood expelled and the flexibility of your veins and arteries. Blood vessels tend to be most elastic in younger people, stretching to accommodate the surge in blood. As a result, the blood pressure remains stable and relatively low. In general, blood pressure tends to be higher in older people with more rigid vessels.

The blood pressure when the heart contracts is known as the 'systolic'. The pressure while it is relaxed is called the 'diastolic'. Each is expressed as the pressure in millimetres of mercury (mmHg). A young person might have a systolic blood pressure of 120mmHg and a diastolic of 80mmHg – expressed as 120/80. However, there is no clear cut-off point where blood pressure becomes unacceptably high, and whether a patient has 'hypertension' partly depends on their age. A systolic blood pressure of 145mmHg in a teenage girl is considered abnormal, but it would be acceptable in her grand-mother. As a rule of thumb, doctors consider a systolic blood pressure above 140mmHg and a diastolic below 90mmHg as abnormal. They use these as targets for treatment.

In at least 90 per cent of cases, doctors cannot identify a physical disease underlying high blood pressure. Doctors call this essential hypertension. In the remaining cases, other conditions such as kidney disease lead to hypertension. However, doctors recognise that a number of factors conspire to increase your risk of developing essential hypertension. If your parents had hypertension, your blood pressure is also more likely to be high. Being overweight or drinking excessive amounts of alcohol can also tend to drive blood pressure up. Stress may also increase blood pressure, at least over the short term.

During the fight-or-flight response (see pages 19–21), your heart rate increases and blood pressure rises – at least in the short term. Even the stress of having your blood pressure measured by a doctor or nurse can cause it to rise – a problem doctors call 'white coat' hypertension.

Around a quarter of people with high blood pressure may have 'white coat' hypertension: outside the surgery, their blood pressure is normal. In some cases 'white coat' hypertension can lead to patients being treated unnecessarily. However, most GPs are now aware of this syndrome. The effect wanes as patients become used to having their blood pressure measured. So you may have your blood pressure measured by the GP or practice nurse on two or three occasions before the doctor decides you have hypertension.

As mentioned above, short-term (acute) stress can drive up your blood pressure. Whether long-term stress causes chronic hypertension, rather than just a short-lived rise in blood pressure, is less clear. Some studies suggest a link between chronic stress and hypertension. Others deny any association. However, if you have hypertension you need treatment with a combination of lifestyle changes and, if necessary, drugs (see overleaf).

Hypertension dramatically increases your risk of suffering a stroke or heart attack, which can leave you disabled or prove fatal. A 40-year-old with hypertension is 30 times more likely to suffer a stroke than someone with normal blood pressure, for example. Furthermore, middle-aged men with a diastolic blood pressure above 90mmHg are at least 1.5 times more likely than someone with normal blood pressure to die from heart disease. Above 100mmHg the risk increases to 2.5 times.

Ways to reduce high blood pressure

You can change your lifestyle to reduce high blood pressure. These changes will also help any drugs you take for high blood pressure to work more effectively. Occasionally, if lifestyle changes are very effective, you might be able to stop taking your tablets. However, you should only stop treatment under medical supervision.

- **Lose weight** Carrying excess weight means that your heart needs to work harder to pump blood around your body. So losing weight reduces blood pressure. The healthy eating suggestions on page 138 should also help you lose weight. However, you might also need to go on a calorie-controlled diet, which, combined with regular exercise, can help you lose weight.
- **Take regular exercise** (see pages 247–49). However, people with hypertension should talk to their doctor first. Walking, cycling, swimming or other dynamic exercises can help lower

blood pressure. It's relatively easy to fit such changes into even a busy life. Don't take the bus or car on short trips, for instance. If you need to take a bus or train, whenever possible get off the stop before and walk the rest of the way. Park further from the shops, work or station. Use the stairs rather than an escalator or lift. Go to the park, leisure centre or swimming pool regularly.

- **Reduce your salt intake** Avoiding salt can prove difficult, but you can stop using it at the dinner table and cut back on high-salt foods such as crisps, peanuts, canned foods and bacon.
- **Limit your alcohol intake** Government guidelines suggest that men drinking three to four units a day and women who drink up to two to three units daily do not face a significant health risk. Remember, these are maximum limits. They are not an encouragement to drink this much, and you should not drink any more than the recommended amounts. A unit is one glass of wine, one measure of spirits or half a pint of ordinary-strength lager. (Look on the side of the can. Some lagers and beers are deceptively strong – perhaps five or even nine per cent.)
- **Relaxation**, which means 'active' relaxation (see pages 228–30), not just sitting in front of the TV, produces a short-lived reduction in blood pressure. However, relaxation's most important benefits are in the long term: an enhanced feeling of control and a more positive outlook. Both blunt the fight-or-flight reflex. This feeling of control can help you implement some of these lifestyle changes using the techniques outlined in Chapter 3.

If these lifestyle modifications fail to adequately control blood pressure, you may need to take one of the so-called anti-hypertensives, which lower blood pressure. Unfortunately, these can cause a range of side effects including (depending on the drug) cold hands and feet, fatigue, impotence, rashes and cough. If you experience anything abnormal after taking the medication, talk to your doctor. Doctors can choose from a large number of anti-hypertensives available and changing the drug may alleviate the side effect.

Strokes

Strokes are the third most common cause of death after cancer and heart disease. Strokes are also the commonest cause of disability in the UK. Fortunately, we can take several steps to reduce our risk of suffering a stroke.

There are two types of stroke: ischaemic and haemorrhagic. Ischaemic strokes, which account for 85 per cent of strokes, are 'brain attacks'. Ischaemic strokes arise from a process similar to that underlying heart attacks: fatty plaques build up in the blood vessels supplying the brain. If these plaques rupture, the blood clot can starve areas of the brain of oxygen, which destroys brain cells. The less common haemorrhagic strokes arise when blood vessels burst. Blood leaks into the brain and clots, destroying brain cells. In both cases, the brain damage is irreparable. Indeed, strokes result in death or severe disability in two out of three cases.

As with heart attacks, you can take several steps to reduce your risk of suffering a stroke:

- Uncontrolled hypertension is a leading cause of strokes. So you need to reduce any raised blood pressure with drugs and lifestyle changes (see pages 141–42).
- Quit smoking (see pages 123–24). Cigarette smoking increases the risk of stroke threefold.
- Ischaemic strokes result from the same process that causes heart attacks. So following the advice to prevent heart attacks (see pages 137–38) also helps prevent strokes.
- Keep your alcohol consumption within the recommended safe limits (see page 110). In particular, binge drinking increases the risk of a stroke, so spread your drinking out during the week.

Caring for a loved one who survives a stroke can impose an immense burden on the carer. Indeed, Thommessen and colleagues found that the stress experienced by spouses caring for people with strokes was similar to that seen with dementia and Parkinson's disease. Many of the problems facing the carers – such as disorganised household routines, difficulties with holidays and a restricted social life – emerged irrespective of the disease. However, patients' mental abilities were also important. The carers of people with better mental function tended to be less stressed than those with worse mental functioning. We have suggested some ways to help carers cope with the stress of looking after an ill relative or partner on pages 106–108. The Stroke Association* offers further information, advice and support.

Stress and the stomach

We have all suffered from the effects of stress on the stomach. Butterflies in your tummy, diarrhoea, feeling you have a lump in your throat, vomiting, nausea and irritable bowel syndrome (IBS) can all be gastrointestinal manifestations of stress.

Ulcers

A peptic ulcer (an erosion in the stomach or duodenum) was once assumed to come with the company car, gold credit card and key to the executive toilet. Doctors even described an 'ulcer personality'. People predisposed to developing ulcers were supposedly thin, hungry-looking, highly competitive and conscientious. Despite their seemingly self-sufficient personalities, ulcer sufferers, the doctors argued, were 'hungry' for attention, recognition and support. Some psychologists viewed ulcers as a sign of emotional immaturity. In recent years, this view has come under attack. Overall, there is no convincing evidence that people with certain personalities are more likely to develop ulcers.

At least one in ten people develop a stomach ulcer some time during their lives. An ulcer is an erosion in the wall of the stomach or duodenum – the foot-long section of gut immediately below the stomach. Acid in the stomach irritates this erosion, causing a number of symptoms. In a few cases, the erosion reaches the network of blood vessels in the stomach or duodenal wall, which may lead to life-threatening gastrointestinal bleeding. There is also a risk of perforation of the ulcer, when the ulcer penetrates the wall of the stomach or duodenum and damages other organs or the abdominal space.

The evidence linking stress and peptic ulcers is at best mixed. In 1833, doctors discovered that stress increased the blood flow in the stomach and stimulated acid secretion. Around 50 years later, financial ruin was associated with an increased risk of developing an ulcer (although this doesn't prove that stress caused the ulcers). Over the years, several studies suggested that stress predisposed people to develop ulcers. However, other studies have failed to link stress and ulcers. Some of these failed to account for the effects of smoking. Some people smoke to alleviate stress, and smoking predisposes people to stomach ulcers.

The link between stress and ulcers was dealt a fatal blow with the discovery of the bacterium *Helicobacter pylori*. Doctors recognised for decades that stomach ulcers tended to run in families. They also noted that stomach ulcers were more common among people living in air-raid shelters or prisoner of war camps during the Second World War. But doctors attributed this to the intense stress rather than an infection. Few researchers seriously considered that a bacterium could be responsible for ulcers or dyspepsia (indigestion). Stomach acid, which evolved in part to sterilise food and drink, makes the stomach one of the most inhospitable parts of the body.

Then in 1983, the Australian microbiologist Robin Warren and the physician Barry Marshall made a discovery that revolutionised gastroenterology. They isolated *H pylori* from the stomach of patients suffering from dyspepsia and ulcers. The bacterium survives by burrowing beneath the thick mucus and producing a cloud of ammonia that protects the stomach wall from attack by acid. However, this burrowing bacterium allows the acid to erode the stomach.

Doctors now know that *H pylori* causes at least eight out of ten stomach ulcers and possibly all duodenal ulcers. Alcohol abuse and non-steroidal anti-inflammatory drugs – widely used to treat arthritis and other inflammatory diseases – cause the remainder.

Dyspepsia (indigestion)

While the jury was out studying the evidence linking stress and ulcers, doctors began questioning another long-held link: the association between stress and dyspepsia (indigestion or heartburn caused by excessive acid production). Dyspepsia is also very common. Holtmann comments that in Western countries, between 10 and 30 per cent of the population suffers from gastro-oesophageal reflux disorder, the medical name for many cases of dyspepsia.

The symptoms of dyspepsia (see below) follow over-indulgence with fatty food and alcohol. However, in up to a fifth of dyspepsia cases, doctors cannot identify a cause for the symptoms – despite intensive investigation. So, many doctors came to believe that dyspepsia in people who do not have stomach ulcers was caused by mental factors rather than by anything in their guts. More recent studies have suggested that *H pylori* might cause some cases of non-ulcer dyspepsia.

Non-ulcer dyspepsia symptoms include:

- upper abdominal pain or discomfort
- heartburn
- tasting acid in the mouth
- vomiting
- nausea.

Treatments for stomach disorders

Traditional antacids alleviate symptoms by reducing the acidity of the stomach. More recently, the government approved a group of drugs known as H2-antagonists – such as cimetidine, famotidine, nizatidine and ranitidine – for sale by pharmacists. Formerly prescription-only medicines, these drugs reduce acid production in the stomach, which relieves the symptoms of dyspepsia. In general, the H2-antagonists are safe and effective treatments for dyspepsia. However, you should consult your GP if your symptoms persist for more than a month.

GPs can prescribe a wide range of treatments for ulcers and dyspepsia, including higher doses of H2-antagonists and a group of drugs known as the proton pump inhibitors, which includes omeprazole and lansoprazole. These rapidly relieve symptoms and may heal some ulcers, as well as alleviating dyspepsia that does not respond to over-the-counter medications. A short course of antibiotics combined with a proton pump inhibitor or ranitidine bismuth citrate will probably eradicate the infection and prevent recurrence. If these don't alleviate the symptoms, or they recur, you should ask your GP to make further investigations.

Irritable bowel syndrome

After dyspepsia, irritable bowel syndrome (IBS) is perhaps the commonest gastrointestinal disorder. As many as 14 per cent of adults suffer from IBS. However, after reviewing the evidence, Lydiard concluded that less than half of people with IBS seek treatment from their doctor. We'll return to this later.

Despite being so common, IBS – also called spastic colon – is poorly understood. Over the years, studies have linked IBS to refined low-fibre diets, disordered gastrointestinal motility (bowel movements) and a hypersensitivity to having a distended bowel. But stress and other psychological factors undoubtedly play a part.

However, IBS isn't really a disease, which may be one reason why doctors find it so difficult to identify a cause. Rather, IBS is a collection of symptoms arising from a number of causes. For example, Tougas notes that IBS is an 'arbitrary' diagnosis that lacks any 'specific biologic markers'. 'IBS is … no more a disease than dyspnoea (breathlessness) or fatigue,' he claims. And, Tougas notes, the pain characteristics of IBS can both cause and be caused by the other symptoms such as diarrhoea and constipation. To confuse matters further, mental factors such as stress, and physical factors – such as intestinal infection – can produce similar symptoms to IBS (see box below).

IBS symptoms

- abdominal pain, sometimes eased by defecation
- changes in bowel habit
- dyspepsia
- frequent loose stools
- feelings of incomplete defecation
- weight loss
- mucus with stools
- nausea and vomiting
- eating often exacerbates pain
- rumbling, gurgling stomach
- urgent stools.

IBS symptoms: beyond the gut

- fatigue
- headaches
- insomnia
- muscle pains.

Abdominal pain and altered bowel patterns are the hallmarks of IBS. However, the disease can be associated with a wide variety of other symptoms, both in the gastrointestinal tract and more widely in the body. Many of these symptoms are vague and very similar to the effects of stress. This further underscores the overlap between stress and IBS.

In general, IBS sufferers endure painful contractions of their stomach, feel bloated and experience changed bowel habits – they may expel 'pellet-like' or 'ribbon-like' stools. IBS patients with diarrhoea often report morning frequency, an urgent need to defecate after meals and a sense of incomplete evacuation. IBS's gastrointestinal symptoms are fairly non-specific and most people have probably suffered at least some of them at one time or another. So doctors consider the change to be an IBS 'symptom' only if patients experience it for at least three months and if it interferes with normal life.

Of course, many people misinterpret bowel actions as being abnormal when there is nothing wrong. Being unable to defecate every morning before breakfast isn't a sign that you're unhealthy. Indeed, in healthy people stool frequency ranges from three times daily to three times a week. Many sufferers improve once they recognise this. Only persistent changes in your normal bowel habits are abnormal.

Stool consistency is also important. For example, changing from one to two movements a day does not count as diarrhoea unless the consistency becomes more watery. Likewise, constipation implies both reduced frequency and stools that are difficult to pass. Some people with IBS experience both symptoms at different times.

So when should you worry? In general, if the changes in your bowel habits are more marked than those described above, it might be worth talking to your GP. Stools with the consistency of 'rabbit droppings' or 'toothpaste' may be abnormal. Mucus passage with the stool is almost certainly abnormal. Rectal bleeding definitely is. If you are over 40 years old, you should always report any new change in bowel habit to your GP.

Stress and IBS

As mentioned above, stress and other psychological states are strongly associated with IBS. Several studies now underscore the intimate relationship between stress and IBS. For example, Pinto and colleagues enrolled 30 IBS patients and the same number of healthy people to act as controls. They assessed the number of stressful life events each group experienced, as well as their coping mechanisms.

- IBS patients were more stressed than controls.
- Around half of the IBS patients showed clinically significant anxiety or depression or both.
- The coping strategies used by IBS patients who also showed depression tended to be negative compared to IBS patients without anxiety or depression.

Monnikes and colleagues noted that psychological stress could precipitate an exacerbation of symptoms. Indeed, there is now clear evidence that acute stress can change the speed at which food passes through your gastrointestinal tract. This might contribute to dyspepsia and IBS that is linked to stress. Moreover, stress seems to make you more sensitive to changes in the bowel, such as a feeling of fullness. This contributes to the increased likelihood that your symptoms will worsen during stressful times.

Furthermore, the person's mental state may influence whether or not they present for treatment. You will recall that less than half of people suffering from IBS seek treatment from their doctor. The evidence suggests that suffering from psychiatric symptoms in addition may determine whether people suffering from IBS present for treatment or not. Lydiard estimated that between 50 and 90 per cent of people with IBS suffer from psychiatric disorders, including panic disorder, generalised anxiety, post-traumatic stress disorder, and major depression. People with IBS who do not suffer psychiatric disease tend not to see their doctor.

Ways to relieve IBS

Some people find that some simple dietary changes may help alleviate some of the symptoms of IBS:

- **Eat more fibre** Eating at least 30g of fibre – around six slices of wholemeal bread – a day helps relieve constipation. Prunes, leeks, onions and garlic may also alleviate constipation.

- **Switch to a plain diet** such as simple fish and meat and a few vegetables. This benefits up to 70 per cent of IBS sufferers. Sticking to the diet can prove more of a problem.
- **Cut out milk and wheat** In a few people, milk and wheat trigger IBS symptoms. So if your symptoms start after milky breakfasts try a wheat or milk substitute.
- **Exercise regularly** Lustyk and colleagues found that exercise improved IBS symptoms in women. Among women with IBS, those who took exercise were less likely to report a feeling of incomplete evacuation following bowel movements, and they were less fatigued than those who weren't so active. The authors of the study interpret these findings as suggesting that physical activity might reduce your risk of developing IBS as well as alleviating some of the symptoms.

Doctors can choose from a limited but growing number of drugs for IBS. And many people report that complementary and alternative therapies alleviate their symptoms and help them live with the disease. However, remember that mental states can cause or exacerbate IBS. So, not surprisingly, a positive outlook can also make you feel better. As a result, IBS patients show a very marked placebo response (see box opposite).

The studies show that active drugs do help to alleviate the symptoms of IBS in some patients. In other words, their benefits are not solely due to the placebo effect. However, IBS can produce a wide range of symptoms. So you need to find a combination of treatments that works for your particular pattern.

Indeed, Villanueva and co-workers noted that the choice between dietary changes, anti-diarrhoeal agents and muscle relaxants (also called antispasmodics) will depend on the predominant symptom the sufferer displays. So, for example, high-fibre diets may help to alleviate constipation. Anti-diarrhoeal drugs, obviously, counter diarrhoea, while muscle relaxants can reduce pain. Nevertheless, they add that no single treatment is likely to help every IBS patient. The range of symptoms, which can change over time, means that many patients need to employ several strategies. A number of other drugs in development at the time of writing might further offer IBS sufferers some relief. However, these need to be tested in rigorous studies.

Placebos show IBS may partly be in the mind

Many clinical trials compare a test drug against an inactive placebo. The placebo looks and tastes the same as the drug, but doesn't contain any active drug. However, many people respond to the placebo, highlighting the potent effect mind can have over matter. This is true of most diseases. But the placebo effect is particularly marked among people suffering from IBS. As a result, many patients with IBS respond to a pill containing no active drug. Moreover, they also respond to any alternative therapy, no matter how bizarre. That's not to say some alternative and complementary treatments don't have a direct effect. Hypnotism, for example, can help restore normal bowel function. But the sizeable placebo effect may mean that it's your mental state – rather than the therapy itself – that's producing the benefit.

For example, Poynard and colleagues reviewed several studies assessing the effectiveness of muscle relaxants in IBS. Thirty-eight per cent of patients reported an overall improvement while taking a placebo compared to 56 per cent who were on relaxants. And 41 per cent of the patients reported that their pain improved on placebo compared to 53 per cent in those taking the relaxants. In other words, four out of every ten patients with IBS responded to an inactive placebo. Furthermore, even with the active drug another four out of ten patients showed no benefit.

IBS is an unpleasant and common disease. It's one of the few physical diseases in which stress seems to be a significant contributory factor. Fortunately, it is also one that can be effectively treated. The Digestive Disorders Foundation* and the IBS Network* can offer advice and support to IBS sufferers.

Migraine and tension headaches

Around one in ten people suffers from migraine attacks that last from a few hours to two or three days. Often the attacks are unpredictable. Some patients suffer only one migraine attack each year.

Psychogenic vomiting

Almost everyone has felt sick with fear sometime during their lives. However, in a few people, emotional problems cause recurrent and persistent regurgitation of food – also called rumination or psychogenic vomiting. Rumination is common in infants and people with mental disabilities, but can also be a manifestation of distress over, say, bereavement, separation or abuse. In some patients, vomiting becomes a form of communication – a way to express their anxiety and anger or to escape from stressful situations.

During rumination patients repeatedly regurgitate small amounts of food from their stomach. They then chew, swallow or expel (vomit) the regurgitated food. Khan and colleagues examined 12 otherwise healthy adolescents who suffered from rumination. All could effortlessly regurgitate food after eating, suffered weight loss and complained that they experienced abdominal pain. Most of these patients responded to psychological treatment, however, suggesting that their condition was stress-related. In 10 of the 12 children, therapy with antidepressants and anxiolytics (drugs that alleviate anxiety), cognitive behavioural therapy with biofeedback or relaxation, and pain management resolved or improved symptoms. If you suspect that you or your child suffers from psychogenic vomiting, talk to your healthcare professional who should be able to recommend appropriate treatment.

Others have two or three attacks a week. However, on average, sufferers experience about one attack a month.

Migraine sufferers endure an intense, throbbing headache, usually over one side of the head. However, migraine is more than a headache. For example, most migraine sufferers say that they feel washed out after an attack and in some cases it can take a day or two before they feel totally back to normal. Most migraine sufferers also endure nausea, sometimes vomiting, and find light and sound intensely uncomfortable. These patients suffer from so-called 'common migraines'. Most others experience 'classical migraine' –

the headache and other symptoms are preceded by a visual 'aura', which includes flashing lights and other visual hallucinations. The aura can last for an hour before the headache starts.

The symptoms of tension headache differ from those of migraine. Patients suffering from tension headaches report feeling as if they have a tight band around their heads, experience pressure behind their eyes and say that it seems their throbbing head is about to burst. Their scalp and neck muscles may feel tender. However, muscle tension probably does not directly cause tension headaches.

What triggers migraine?

Numerous factors can trigger migraine including stress, alcohol and changed sleeping habits (see box on page 155). In particular, many migraine sufferers seem to be over-sensitive to tyramine, an amino acid (one of the building blocks of protein) which is found in particularly high levels in cheese, red wine, beer, chocolate, beef and several other common foods and drinks. You can determine the factors that trigger your migraines by keeping a diary noting the frequency of your attacks and what you were doing and eating in the hours before the headache emerged (see case history overleaf).

According to one widely held theory, the combination of the trigger factors ultimately causes blood vessels supplying the brain to swell. This swelling produces the throbbing headache characteristic of migraine. In classic migraine, blood vessels in the part of the brain controlling vision temporarily constrict; this produces the visual aura. However, after the initial constriction, a dilation leads to the headache.

In some people, a single factor triggers a migraine. However, in most migraine sufferers, two or three triggers act together to precipitate the headache. Once the number of trigger factors passes a critical threshold, the patient develops a migraine. Moreover, the threshold for a migraine can change over time. For example, some women find that migraines become more common as they approach the menopause or at certain times of the month – around menstruation, for example.

Shared triggers in migraine and tension headaches

Stress is a common trigger for tension headaches. However, several other factors seem to trigger tension headaches, including heat, noise and concentrated visual effort, such as staring at a computer

---

Case history: Rebecca

Rebecca suffered from migraines – but only at weekends. After keeping a migraine diary, she traced her headaches to the Bordeaux wine she drank in the local wine bar after work on a Friday night, her later bedtimes on Friday and Saturday, the long weekend lie-ins and the change in stress levels after finishing work for the week. Like some migraine sufferers, Rebecca gets a migraine when the pressure lifts rather than during the stressful time.

---

screen. In some cases, tension headaches can be a physical manifestation of depression. Indeed, there seems to be a considerable overlap between the triggers for the two types of headache. Spierings and colleagues found that stress and tension, not eating on time, fatigue and lack of sleep were the commonest factors that precipitated both migraines and tension headaches. However, only people with migraine reported that certain types of weather, some smells, smoke and light were triggers for their headaches.

When to visit your doctor

Often there is no need to consult your GP for migraine or tension headache. Indeed, around three-quarters of migraine sufferers treat their headaches themselves with over-the-counter treatments. However, you should consult your doctor if you suffer severe headaches for the first time, if headaches start after a blow to the head or persist, or when your symptoms are different to normal.

You should also check with your GP that you really do suffer from migraine or tension headache. Often, the fear that the headache heralds a serious illness can cause stress. Treatment for patients suffering from tension headaches usually involves reassuring them that their symptoms do not mean they are suffering from a sinister disease, advice on avoiding trigger factors, and painkillers. Many patients find that relaxation, massage, meditation and other stress management techniques reduce the severity and frequency of headaches.

Migraine triggers

- alcohol
- certain smells
- certain types of weather
- changes in sleeping pattern
- coffee
- driving
- drugs
- exercise
- fatigue
- certain foods, e.g. chocolate, citrus fruits and cheese
- hunger
- low blood sugar levels, e.g. missing a meal
- menstruation
- stress
- travel.

How to help yourself

You can take a number of steps to alleviate the misery of migraines and tension headaches.

- Look at your lifestyle. Eat regularly, drink plenty of fluids and follow regular sleep patterns. Try not to lie in too long over the weekend, for example, if that precipitates your headaches
- Exercise is a good way to relax. However, during exercise your blood sugar levels can drop dramatically, which can trigger a migraine. Ensuring that you eat foods rich in complex carbohydrates (such as fruits, vegetables, breads, cereals and pastas) can help prevent this.
- Follow some of the stress reduction approaches, such as relaxation (see pages 228–30).
- Keep a diary: note the date, day, time, symptoms, intensity and duration of the attack. You should also note anything you feel contributed to the attack, such as stress, diet or alcohol consumption. After identifying your trigger factors, split them into those you can control (such as missing a meal or drinking

red wine) and those you cannot (such as your period). Cut out the controllable trigger factors one by one.

- If you suffer from migraine or tension headache and over-the-counter treatments don't offer adequate relief (see below), consult your GP. There are a number of drugs and other approaches that might help. Furthermore, the Migraine Action Association★ and the Migraine Trust★ offer advice and support.

- To relieve the pain of a migraine attack, lie down in a dark, quiet room and take simple painkillers, such as soluble aspirin or paracetamol (but note that children under 16 years old should take aspirin only under medical supervision). Many people find that anti-sickness medicines settle their stomach. Experiment with the migraine remedies available from your pharmacist, which differ in their formulation. To gain the most benefit, these over-the-counter remedies should be taken as early as possible during the attack. Other migraine drugs, such as sumatriptan, rizatriptan and zolmitriptan, are available on prescription. These are thought to constrict the swollen blood vessels and alleviate the attack. However, you can't use them if you have taken other migraine therapies and they can cause a number of side effects, ranging from a tingling feeling to chest tightness and difficulty breathing. Doctors tend to prescribe these drugs – which are expensive – only if your migraines are particularly debilitating or you experience more than two attacks a month.

Complementary treatments may help

Some patients with migraine and tension headache also benefit from complementary and behavioural therapies. For example, behavioural interventions – such as relaxation, biofeedback and stress management – reduce the severity and frequency of migraines and tension headaches by between 30 and 50 per cent. Indeed, the effectiveness of these approaches may rival results obtained with some widely used headache drugs, according to Penzien and co-workers. And Lake notes that cognitive behavioural therapies (in which relaxation is one element) can be roughly as effective as a widely used drug called propranolol, sometimes used to prevent frequent migraine attacks.

Back pain

Back pain is common – which is not surprising if you consider that poor posture and a sedentary lifestyle can further weaken one of the weakest parts of the skeleton. You can suffer pain anywhere along your spine. However, the lower back is the most common site of discomfort. If one of the discs of cartilage between the vertebrae bulges – a so-called 'slipped' disc – it can press on the sciatic nerve. This means pain can radiate from the lower back to the buttocks, legs and feet – a problem known as sciatica.

Around one in five people consult their doctor because of low back pain at some time during their lives. Around a fifth of these claim their back pain was caused at work, and low back pain does impose a major economic burden, accounting for almost 100 million lost working days a year. However, even this may underestimate the scale of the problem. Surveys suggest that 60 per cent of people experience back pain during any fortnight.

Low back pain is a disease that tends to affect middle-aged manual workers. This partly reflects the nature of the job – it is easier to damage your back if you are spreading asphalt than if you are constructing a spreadsheet. However, a sedentary job is also a risk factor, along with pregnancy and shift work. Even improving the back's strength, fitness and flexibility does not seem to protect you from low back pain. Often, the severity of symptoms does not seem to reflect the true extent of spinal damage. For example, X-rays reveal that some people without symptoms have prominent 'slipped' disks. This led doctors to search for causes of low back pain elsewhere than in the spine's physical architecture.

For a while, stress was strongly suspected of at least contributing to low back pain. Some doctors believed that anxious people had a lower pain threshold, so they were more likely to report suffering low back pain. Moreover, stress often causes muscle tension, and physical trauma can act on a back already weakened by muscle tension if, say, you lift a heavy object. However, doctors now regard anxiety and depression as the consequences – rather than the causes – of low back pain. These conditions may however influence the patient's ability to cope with low back pain. For example, depression can undermine a patient's motivation to get better. Anxiety can also exacerbate pain. So while anxiety, depression and stress probably do not cause low back pain, they can slow your recovery and exacerbate your suffering.

Traditionally, patients suffering from low back pain received analgesics (painkillers) and were told to lie on their back for between two and three weeks. However, lying in bed for as little as a week reduces muscle mass and strength. This approach further weakens the back even though sufferers experience pain relief. Recommendations of bed rest are now largely replaced by physiotherapy, osteopathy, chiropractic and other manipulative techniques. Avoiding bed rest and staying active is most important. If you remain active, you might not need any manipulation. If the techniques mentioned above fail, you might need further medical treatment, including an operation (although it is rare to need surgery).

Contact your GP or BackCare★ for further information and advice.

Impotence

Impotence – which doctors describe as erectile dysfunction – tends not to be talked about. However, it's likely that you or someone you know suffers from impotence at least occasionally, and with the advent of Viagra (the brand name of a drug called sildenafil) the condition has become more widely discussed.

Indeed, around one in ten men cannot either obtain or sustain an erection firm enough for penetrative intercourse at some time during their lives. Not surprisingly, erectile dysfunction can cause considerable stress for men and their partners. Moreover, your risk of impotence increases markedly with advancing age. Around 5 per cent of men in their 40s suffer erectile dysfunction. This increases to 10 and 20 per cent of men in their 60s and 70s. Between 30 and 50 per cent of men over the age of 80 years experience erectile dysfunction.

The relationship between stress, psychological problems and physical factors in impotence is complex. And doctors' attitudes have shifted markedly over the last few years. In the 1970s, most doctors believed the vast majority of erectile dysfunction cases were essentially psychological. Obviously, psychological factors can exacerbate the problem. For example, depression and some antidepressants can undermine sexual performance. (There are ways around this. Talk to your doctor for guidance.) However, in the late 1980s and 1990s, overwhelming evidence that most cases of impotence are physiological forced a change of view. The majority of doctors now consider that non-psychological factors are the main cause of impotence.

For example, smoking, high blood cholesterol levels and some drugs can cause or contribute to erectile dysfunction. Raised cholesterol levels can lead to blockages forming in the blood vessels supplying the penis. The process is the same as that which leads to the blockages in the heart's circulation that trigger angina (see page 135). So, treating the other diseases and quitting smoking could help to improve the situation. In rare cases, surgeons might be able to unblock the artery. In general, if you treat the physiological problem underlying erectile dysfunction, the psychological aspects often improve.

However, even if the impotence arises from a physical cause, men with erectile dysfunction can become trapped in a cycle of poor performance. If you expect to have problems obtaining or sustaining an erection, you are more likely to fail to attain an erection. A sympathetic partner and counselling can help alleviate so-called performance anxiety. Indeed, if you gain erections when you masturbate, but not with your partner, the problem could be psychological rather than physiological.

Doctors' attitudes towards sexuality in older people have also changed in recent years. Doctors once often behaved as if sexual activity stopped after middle age. Of course, it doesn't. The frequency and form of intercourse and sexual activity might change as you get older, but many couples have fulfilling sex lives well after middle age. The increasing recognition of sexuality among older people meant that doctors were no longer able to dismiss older men who wanted help with impotence.

Despite these fundamental shifts in medical attitudes, many men do not seek treatment for impotence, either from embarrassment or because they have an impression that doctors cannot help. Fortunately, the launch of Viagra has led increasing numbers of men to seek help for erectile dysfunction. Even if Viagra is not appropriate for you – and there are numerous men for whom it isn't – doctors can offer a range of other effective approaches. The choice depends on the preferences of you and your partner, as well as any medical limitations.

Oral treatments

Several drugs can effectively treat impotence in some men. However, all the drugs used to treat erectile dysfunction have the same effect, although they act in different ways: they increase the amount of blood that enters two sacs (the corpus cavernosa) that run the along the shaft of the penis. The drugs allow the two corpus cavernosa to become engorged with blood, which initiates and maintains the erection.

Viagra is by far the best-known treatment for impotence. You take Viagra, which contains a drug known as sildenafil, as a tablet approximately one hour before sexual activity. This may reduce the spontaneity of intercourse. Nevertheless, Viagra helps many men attain a satisfactory erection. Indeed, in a recent UK study Sairam and collaborators found that Viagra was successful in 91 per cent of men – although some doctors believe that the success rate may not be so high in 'real life' cases.

In general, few men taking Viagra develop side effects. Some men experience dyspepsia (indigestion), headaches, flushing or visual disturbances, for example. More seriously, Viagra needs to be used carefully if you have heart disease. Indeed, researchers originally developed sildenafil to alleviate angina, but men on the angina trials told researchers that the drug improved their erections.

Following Viagra's success, a new generation of oral impotence treatments has been developed. One of these, apomorphine (Uprima), acts through a different mechanism to Viagra and so might be effective when Viagra fails to produce adequate erections. You place the apomorphine tablet under your tongue, where it

---

Avoid Internet Viagra

It may be dangerous to buy Viagra on the Internet. A doctor needs to check that the drug will not affect your heart before you take it. So never use Viagra unless you have been fully assessed by a doctor. Men with heart disease should use Viagra only under close medical supervision, and those taking nitrates for angina should avoid it altogether.

melts. Apomorphine acts more rapidly than Viagra. Typically, men attain satisfactory erections within 20 minutes. Altwein and Keuler tested apomorphine in a group of men who attained an erection firm enough for intercourse on only 24.3 per cent of occasions without treatment. Apomorphine increased the proportion of times the erection was satisfactory to 49.4 per cent. The side effects can include nausea, headache and dizziness. However, in general, it is well tolerated and only a few men find that the side effects are a significant problem.

Other drugs for impotence

There are two other ways that drugs for impotence can be administered. Firstly, you can inject certain drugs – such as papaverine (which is used by some doctors but is not formally approved) or alprostadil – into the base of the penis. The drugs are injected using a very fine needle, which means that the injections are not as traumatic or painful as they sound. Indeed, some men allow their partner to inject the drug. The injections can produce erections that satisfy both patients and their sexual partners. If the erection is not adequate, doctors might be able to increase the dose.

Men with diabetes are especially likely to develop impotence. Tsai and colleagues found that 76.5 per cent of diabetic patients said that the injections produced erections that allowed satisfactory sexual activity. However, not surprisingly, the injections can cause penile pain and irritation as well as prolonged erections. In the study by Tsai and colleagues, 61 per cent of patients experienced tolerable penile pain, which declined with continued treatment over time. Furthermore, 6.5 per cent suffered prolonged erections. If any erection lasts for more than four hours, you should seek help as soon as possible since this is considered a medical emergency. Very few of the diabetic patients treated with injections – perhaps around one per cent – suffered side effects in the rest of their body, such as low blood pressure or dizziness.

Alprostadil (MUSE) takes a different approach and offers an effective alternative to oral drugs and injections for many men. With this method, you insert a small pellet into the urethra (the tube that carries sperm and urine along the penis) before sex. Obviously, this is more inconvenient than a pill – although MUSE is effective.

Khan and colleagues found that MUSE successfully treated 35 per cent of patients. However, only 43 per cent of patients continued to use MUSE after six months; usually because it became less effective or because they suffered side effects. MUSE can cause pain in the penis and testicles, irritation of the urethra, headache and several other side effects. You will also need to wear a condom if your partner is pregnant.

Mechanical treatments

If oral drugs fail or cannot be used – for instance, if you suffer from another medical condition – you can try several mechanical devices to help you attain and maintain an erection. Vacuum devices, first used in 1917, are among the most popular of these mechanical treatments. The man or his partner places a plastic tube over his penis and, using a hand pump, creates a vacuum. This vacuum forces blood into the penis, making it erect. The man places a ring at the base of the penis to prevent the blood escaping once he releases the vacuum.

Vacuum devices produce satisfactory erections in up to 80 per cent of men. The erections last for up to half an hour before the penis swells to the point that the ring becomes uncomfortable. However, using the device can be inconvenient. The ring can also be uncomfortable and hinder ejaculation, and some men find that the device reduces penile sensation.

Some men prefer surgically implanted penile prostheses – this might take the form of a flexible rod that is permanently rigid and allows intercourse. In another approach, the surgeon inserts small inflatable bladders that the user fills with air or fluid. New devices give a normal appearance when flaccid.

Such devices are implanted during an operation, which can lead to complications. Between 3 and 5 per cent of men suffer infections following penile implantation, for example. Fluid can leak from the device, which might mean a further operation. Despite this, implants are an effective and appropriate approach for a few men.

Some of these treatments for impotence might mean that you lose sexual spontaneity. However, with understanding from your partner and a little imagination, you can overcome the embarrassment. You could even include the mechanics of, for example, inflating the bladder or using the vacuum device in your foreplay.

If erectile dysfunction is causing stress and friction in your relationship, you should speak to your doctor. He or she should be able to find at least one approach that suits you and your partner.

Premenstrual syndrome

Many women experience irritability, fatigue and other mild symptoms in the week or so leading up to their period. These symptoms (see box below), which can cause stress to the woman and her partner, tend to develop as progesterone levels increase between days 14 and 28 of the menstrual cycle, and are relieved by menstruation. Some researchers believe that some women are 'hypersensitive' to normal hormonal changes, although this theory has not been proven.

Common PMS symptoms

- breast tenderness
- bloating
- craving for food, especially carbohydrates
- depression
- feeling out of control
- headaches
- irritability
- tension
- tearfulness
- tiredness and lethargy.

Psychological factors seem to be important. Once a woman believes that she will suffer PMS each month she becomes more aware of the symptoms around that time, whether they are linked to menstruation or not. The anticipation of PMS can also cause stress. As PMS symptoms can overlap with general stress symptoms as well as those of several other disorders, you need to identify whether or not the timing coincides with your menstrual cycle. You could try keeping a dairy of the symptoms for at least two cycles to discover if there is really a link with menstruation.

Advice and support are the first step in treating PMS. Many women feel frightened and confused by their symptoms. Understanding the cause of the problem often takes the edge off the symptoms. It is essential to get to the cause of the stress. Many women blame PMS instead of admitting to problems at work or at home – an example of projection (see page 39). But attributing behaviour to your hormones can mean not facing up to the reality of your situation and taking responsibility for your actions.

For women with 'true' PMS (whose symptoms coincide with the menstrual cycle and don't seem to be caused by other factors), cognitive behavioural therapy (see pages 232–33) can help. Many women also report benefiting from complementary treatments. For example, some women find that evening primrose oil – which contains gammalinolenic acid (also known as gamolenic acid) – reduces breast pain, depression and irritability. Morrow found that evening primrose oil relieved symptoms in between 38 and 58 per cent of women. However, the response can take between 8 and 12 weeks to fully emerge in some women. Other sources of gammalinolenic acid, such as medicinal borage and starflowers, may also alleviate breast pain, although doctors are split about the effect of gammalinolenic acid on other PMS symptoms. In October 2002, the government withdrew the product licences for gammalinolenic acid. So doctors can no longer prescribe the drug for breast pain, although it remains available in health food shops.

Some women may feel better simply because they are doing something to help their symptoms, otherwise known as the placebo effect (see page 150). If these self-help remedies fail, talk to your GP or contact the National Association for Pre-menstrual Syndrome.★ Doctors may prescribe a number of treatments for PMS, such as (in a few cases) diuretics for water retention. Some antidepressants are also effective; these must be taken throughout the menstrual cycle. Some doctors give progestogen (proges-terone) by various routes. At high doses, progestogen can cause insomnia and drowsiness, and results with the drug are mixed: some women benefit, although others feel worse. As a result, progestogen is rarely used for PMS.

The menopause

The two or three years around the menopause – the time when a woman's periods cease – can be intensely stressful. Hormonal changes during this time, which is also called the climacteric, cause a variety of symptoms (see box overleaf). For example, most women suffer hot flushes and many experience sweating. More disturbingly, declining bone density as a result of declining oestrogen levels increases the risk of developing osteoporosis.

You can relieve your symptoms using several self-help methods (see 'Helping Yourself', overleaf). Alternatively, using hormone replacement therapy (HRT) to increase oestrogen to pre-menopausal levels can relieve hot flushes and sweats, and help to prevent osteoporosis. At the time of writing, recent research has cast doubt on HRT's benefits on heart disease. Indeed, HRT may increase the risk of heart disease. You should discuss the pros and cons of HRT with your doctor before deciding whether it is suitable for you.

Women who have undergone a hysterectomy (an operation that removes all or part of the womb) can take oestrogen HRT alone. Women with intact wombs must also take progestogen (proges-terone) for 10 to 13 days each month to protect the womb lining (the endometrium). Oestrogen increases the thickness of the endometrium – which may predispose you to endometrial cancer. So doctors add progestogen to induce withdrawal bleeds (periods), which sheds the endometrium and eliminates the increased risk of endometrial cancer.

You should determine whether HRT is right for you in consul-tation with your doctor, preferably as you approach the menopause. It may have side effects – taking HRT may increase your risk of breast cancer, for example. If you decide on HRT, there are a number of treatment options. You can choose from several HRT formulations, including tablets, vaginal creams and pessaries and skin patches. Your doctor can help you decide on the right one for you.

WellBeing★ and the Women's Health Concern★ offer advice and support tailored to women's problems, and the Amarant Trust★ focuses on HRT.

Menopausal symptoms

- anxiety
- cystitis
- genital dryness
- hot flushes
- insomnia
- irritability
- palpitations
- painful intercourse
- poor concentration
- sweats
- vaginal dryness and bleeding
- weakness.

In addition, some women report a variety of other symptoms at or around the menopause. It isn't always easy to attribute these directly to the menopause – a number of other factors can cause them. These symptoms include:

- aching joints
- dizziness
- faintness
- headaches
- itchy skin
- loss of confidence
- loss of interest in sex
- mood changes
- memory loss
- weakness.

Helping yourself

HRT can alleviate many menopausal symptoms. However, you can take a number of other measures to limit the impact of 'the change'. For example, if you cannot sleep follow the suggestions on good sleep hygiene (see pages 210–12). A healthy lifestyle including eating a healthy diet, taking regular exercise, not smoking and limiting excess alcohol consumption reduces the impact of the menopause. Increase your self-esteem by getting a job or studying for some qualifications with the Open University,★ or enrol as one of the growing number of mature students. Your library will have details of most further education colleges and universities. *Which? Way to Manage Your Time – and Your Life* also offers some suggestions.

Some women experience hormonally driven changes in mood, which may be exacerbated by stressful life events such as bereavement or divorce. The relaxation techniques outlined in Chapter 10 can protect against the stress surrounding the menopause. You should consult your GP if you develop any symptoms of depression (see Chapter 7), as happens to some women during their menopause – depression might not directly result from the hormonal changes, but the life changes and events that can happen at the time of the menopause can trigger the condition. Perhaps most importantly, try to maintain a positive outlook on life. You will probably spend almost as much time as a post-menopausal woman as you did in your childbearing years. The menopause doesn't close the book on your life – it starts a new chapter.

Asthma

Suffering from any potentially serious disease can cause stress for the patient and their family. Asthma is a good example of this. According to the National Asthma Campaign,★ more than five million people suffer from asthma. One in every thirteen adults and one in every eight children currently takes medicines for asthma.

What is asthma?

Asthma is caused by a chronic inflammation of the airways. A variety of factors – for example, exercise and irritants such as smoke – can either trigger or worsen this inflammation. Allergens (substances that most people find innocuous, but which trigger allergies in susceptible people) including pollen, the faeces of the house dust mite, or cat and dog dander (particles of animal hair and skin) can also trigger the inflammation. As a result, the lining of the airway becomes inflamed and swollen, which reduces the airway's diameter and limits the amount of air getting to the lung. As a result, patients have problems breathing and often develop a bad cough. In severe cases, patients may suffocate during severe asthma attacks. While some asthma sufferers go through symptom-free periods most people experience periodic exacerbations throughout their lives.

Asthma sufferers usually need to take drugs to control the underlying inflammation and to relieve the symptoms of an acute attack. Fortunately, modern medicines can alleviate and prevent most attacks in the majority of people with asthma. Bronchodilators (or 'relievers') re-open the airways. However, bronchodilators do not reduce inflammation, so relying on them alone is dangerous and may even prove fatal. Unless you suffer from very mild asthma – for example, if you only wheeze during exercise – you probably need to take regular anti-inflammatories (or 'preventers') including inhaled steroids (such as budesonide, fluticasone and beclomethasone – also called beclometasone), the 'leukotriene receptor antagonists' (montelukast and zafirlukast), sodium chromoglycate (cromoglicate) or nedocromil. These reduce the risk of a future attack.

These medicines should allow most people with asthma to lead relatively normal lives. Used correctly, they could prevent many serious or life-threatening attacks. However, some patients who experience a serious asthma attack show high levels of denial. For instance, Campbell found that 57 per cent of a group of patients who suffered a near-fatal attack showed strong symptoms of this trait, concluding that 'high levels of denial in asthmatic subjects may be life threatening'. Among patients who do enter denial, a small number may stop taking the drugs that control their asthma, Buston and Wood remark. High levels of stress also seem to undermine some patients' perception of their symptoms, as Steiner and colleagues reported. So a number of asthmatics may take only the bronchodilator, which does not control the underlying inflammation, despite alleviating the symptoms. If you are frightened about asthma or have problems acknowledging your condition, it is particularly important to take medical advice and follow treatment guidelines.

Links with stress
Although asthma is usually caused by an allergy, stress can trigger an attack or make your symptoms worse. For instance, Schmaling and

collaborators examined a group of 32 people with asthma who kept a diary of both their lung function and the possible triggers of their asthma attacks for around 140 days. Half showed a strong relationship between a decline in lung function and psychosocial factors, such as mood and stress levels.

Asthma can also cause stress directly, and augment the effect of other stressors. For example, Gillaspy and colleagues found that asthma exacerbated the problems facing teenagers and young adults who were already at risk of developing poor adjustment (essentially, behavioural difficulties) due to poverty, poor educational attainment or vocational problems. Adolescents with asthma showed higher levels of anxiety, depression and overall psychological distress than those without asthma but who faced the same socio-economic problems.

Effects of trauma on asthma

According to US government figures, based on a telephone survey of Manhattan residents, 27 per cent of asthma sufferers reported experiencing more severe symptoms during the fifth to ninth weeks after the terrorist attacks of September 11 2001 on the World Trade Centre. The US government attributed the increase to 'psychological distress associated with the attacks and/or difficulty breathing because of smoke and debris'.

Staying in control

Despite several advances in management over recent years, serious asthma attacks are common. Asthma can be life-threatening, and should always be taken seriously – never underestimate your symptoms. According to the National Asthma Campaign, hospitals still deal with some 74,000 serious attacks each year. Not surprisingly, serious asthma attacks can leave patients and their families experiencing anger, anxiety and considerable stress.

It is possible to educate yourself about the condition and stay on top of symptoms. A discussion with your GP or practice nurse may help reassure you. Following the advice of your health practitioner, properly using the appropriate drugs from the growing number of effective treatments now available, taking sensible precautions and watching for signs of deteriorating symptoms ensure that most people with asthma can live a normal, active life.

Contact the National Asthma Campaign* for further information and advice.

Eczema

Eczema is an unpleasant and, in severe cases, disfiguring disease where the suffering is, literally, on display. Sufferers endure dry, itchy, inflamed skin that can blister, weep, thicken and crack. As a result, moderate or severe eczema can cause considerable stress to patients and their families. Indeed, Kemp commented that the family stress associated with moderate or severe eczema in children seemed to be greater than that caused by caring for a child with insulin-dependent diabetes (of course, as with any disease the amount of stress experienced will depend on the severity of the condition and the individual's perception). Many people regard skin diseases with distaste, which can induce further stress in the person with eczema.

Many eczema patients are children, who can make their condition worse by scratching. (They often can't help this, so shouldn't be scolded for it.) Most children suffering from eczema first develop symptoms between the ages of six months and two years, so they are too young to understand their disease and its treatment. They may be unable to sleep, and make constant demands on their parents – which can leave the entire family tired and irritable. While severe eczema can be an intensely stressful experience for parents, they can draw some comfort from the long-term outlook. Around half of children with eczema improve by school age, and around 90 per cent of cases resolve during adolescence. However, some eczema patients suffer outbreaks for the rest of their life.

What is eczema?

Eczema can be broadly divided into contact or allergic eczema. Contact eczema is essentially triggered by an environmental irritant, such as a chemical. It may be worth changing your bubble bath or washing powder, as this causes the eczema to disappear in a few cases. Allergic eczema (also called atopic dermatitis), by contrast, results from a hypersensitive immune system that overreacts to the allergen.

The suffering caused by eczema can be more than skin deep, however. Children with eczema seem to be more likely to show behavioural problems than those without the condition, as noted by Duad and colleagues – which may reflects their stress. But these problems tend to be minor, such as excessive dependency and clinginess, fearfulness, and sleep problems. There is an effect on the parents, too. Thirty per cent of mothers of children with eczema reported feeling particularly stressed about parenting, and thought they were less efficient in disciplining the child with eczema. However, the women were more empathic towards sons or daughters with eczema.

Treating eczema

At the time of writing, eczema cannot be cured. You can try to avoid trigger factors, but this can prove difficult – it's hard to avoid pollen, for example. Instead, treatment can soothe inflamed skin. You could try the following:

- Emollients are specially formulated creams, ointments and bath oils that soothe and smooth crusty skin scales and moisturise skin. You can apply emollients directly to the areas affected by eczema after a bath. Also try applying emollients before swimming in a pool – chlorine can worsen eczema. You may have to try several emollients before finding one you or your child prefers. Fortunately, there is a huge range available. So talk to your doctor or pharmacist.
- Try to bathe daily; pat rather than rub yourself dry.
- Heat exacerbates the itching, so keep the skin cool.
- Try different types of soap, such as liquid, unperfumed or hypoallergenic varieties.
- Antihistamine tablets may relieve itching. Some antihistamines make you drowsy and so may help you sleep.
- Steroid creams and ointment are highly effective. However, the risk of side effects means that they are usually applied only to limited areas for a short time.

- Keep nails cut short. This means any inadvertent scratching is less likely to damage the skin (damaged skin is more likely to become infected). Children may prefer wearing mittens.
- Many people are allergic to the house dust mite, which lives in warm, damp places and feeds on shed skin cells – beds are their ideal habitat. Dusting, vacuuming, covering mattresses and pillows with plastic sheets (available from chemists), and keeping the sufferer's room cool and well-ventilated can help. Putting soft toys in the freezer for six hours every week can reduce the number of house dust mites using teddy as a home.
- Fur and flakes of skin shed by household pets are another common eczema trigger, so make sure you or your child wash after stroking the animal, and keep pets off bedding.
- Sleep on cotton bedclothes.

Minimising stress can also help alleviate the discomfort associated with eczema. Try some of the techniques outlined in Chapter 10 – relaxation reduces scratching and alleviates anxiety, for example. Indeed, Ehlers and colleagues assessed the effect of relaxation and a cognitive behavioural treatment programme on people with eczema. Encouragingly, both techniques helped patients to relax, control their scratching and manage stress. They both also improved patients' skin condition and allowed the dose of topical steroids to be reduced.

If eczema does not respond to the treatments outlined above, your GP may refer you to a dermatologist, who can instigate more aggressive therapies. The National Eczema Society* offers further advice and support.

Bed wetting

Most children gain control of their bladders as toddlers. So three-quarters of children are dry overnight by the age of three-and-a-half years. By the age of five, 80 to 90 per cent are dry. However, some children start wetting the bed again after this age. Indeed, bed wetting (or nocturnal enuresis) can be a sign of stress among children. In a few cases, enuresis arises from urinary tract infections, bladder disorders or diabetes. This means that a doctor should investigate all cases of persistent bed wetting. In many cases, the enuresis arises from immature bladder muscles and sphincters. However, some children who wet their beds do so in response to emotional or psychological stress.

For instance, Eidlitz-Markus and co-workers found that children involved in motor vehicle accidents could develop nocturnal enuresis. Some children develop enuresis as a result of an injury, especially to the head. However, in others bed wetting seems to be a manifestation of psychological distress. More commonly, Jarvelin and colleagues found that parental divorce or separation were common causes of enuresis. And the more life stress the children faced, the greater the risk of bed wetting (although stress didn't seem to be linked to daytime enuresis). The birth of a new baby may result in older siblings bed wetting – an example of regression (see pages 40–41).

Nocturnal enuresis tends to inflict considerable distress on children – which they may be unable to express – and undermines their self-confidence and self-esteem, as well as sometimes causing behavioural problems. Not surprisingly, enuresis also causes considerable stress for sufferers' families. For instance, Chang and colleagues found that children with enuresis were more likely than children who didn't wet the bed to show poor attention and school performance. It was also probable that the children with nocturnal enuresis would be more aggressive and show worse social skills. Parents of such children were also more highly stressed than those of children who didn't wet the bed. As Potter and co-authors remark, bed wetting can lead to feelings of guilt, frustration and anxiety, reflecting the lack of control felt among parents and children.

In many children, nocturnal enuresis is a short-lived problem – most grow out of it. A number of approaches can help children regain control of their bladders. Alarms that sound when the child wets the bed may help to retrain the bladder. You could also try charts with stars awarded for staying dry and other incentives. In more difficult cases, doctors can prescribe drugs, although many children relapse once the drug stops. Nevertheless, drugs can also help keep children dry in potentially embarrassing situations – going on holiday or to camp, for example.

Drugs and counselling are the best combination

Dittmann and Wolter found that the drug desmopressin combined with bladder retraining reduced the number of wet nights among children with enuresis. However, bed wetting usually returned to pre-treatment rates when the drugs stopped. Moreover, around a quarter of patients did not respond to treatment. The drugs tended to be less effective in those children that showed the highest levels of psychological distress. The authors argue that combining desmopressin with counselling, psychotherapy or both might improve the outcome for children who wet the bed.

The Enuresis Resource and Information Centre* offers an information pack and helpline.

Chapter 7

Treating depression and clinical anxiety

This chapter focuses on depression and clinical anxiety (and related conditions), which are two of the commonest stress-related disorders. Depression and anxiety are distinct illnesses that are far more serious than an 'attack of the blues' or a 'touch of nerves' respectively. Their symptoms can dramatically undermine sufferers' quality of life and their ability to cope with everyday living.

Although many people suffer symptoms of both diseases, they are different conditions. The term 'anxiety' is sometimes used synonymously with stress. However, as Chapter 1 explains, stress refers to our level of biological arousal – the fight-or-flight mechanism – and is entirely normal and healthy. It is not the same as the psychiatric condition 'anxiety'. Nevertheless, it is a risk factor for both depression and anxiety, in the same way that it is a risk factor for heart disease, irritable bowel syndrome (IBS) and other physical diseases (see Chapter 6).

There is now no doubt that stress can both trigger and exacerbate clinical anxiety and depression. Indeed, researchers increasingly recognise that stress can induce changes in the brain that seem to predispose people to depression and anxiety. Several studies show that stressful life events and having a lack of social support (or few people to rely on) can affect the risk of suffering both conditions. Wildes and co-workers found that negative life events and a lack of social support may make depression worse. In particular, poor social support – which can undermine your stress defences – seems to have a strong effect on how well people cope with potentially stressful life events. Men and women differ in their susceptibility to these disorders. Roughly twice as many women suffer from depression as men, although bipolar disorder (see page 182) seems to affect both men and women equally.

Everyone experiences fluctuations in mood or a touch of the blues from time to time. And we all get anxious on occasion. However, it is important not to dismiss depression and anxiety as 'trivial' or tell someone to 'pull themselves together'. Depression and anxiety are potentially serious medical conditions that need effective treatment. They may reduce life expectancy (both are linked to an increased risk of suicide, for example) and increase the risk of physical illness. However, many people often do not seek help for various reasons. Some people suffering from depression may not even realise they are ill. Others hope the symptoms will go away, or fear the stigma that still, wrongly, surrounds psychological (mental) illness. Often sufferers believe that they are weak, lazy or feeble and must not give in. They struggle on enduring a poor quality of life. And many people regard depression as an appropriate reaction to a life event such as unemployment or bereavement. To a certain extent this is true. However, a person might need professional help if his or her symptoms are severe or continue for long periods.

It is very important to seek advice sooner rather than later if you feel that you suffer from depression or serious anxiety, or if someone close to you is affected. A delay can reduce the chance of treatment alleviating symptoms, leading to 'resistant depression' when thoughts and responses associated with depression, as well as the underlying physiological mechanisms in the brain, contribute to the condition's persistence.

Unless you have suffered from depression it is hard to appreciate the psychological, spiritual and emotional devastation that the condition can cause. Depression is a strong risk factor for suicide, which makes it particularly important to treat the condition. Fortunately, modern treatments can do much to alleviate patients' suffering.

Are you depressed or anxious?

So how do you know if you suffer from depression or anxiety? Doctors use a number of techniques and scales. Psychiatric conditions are notoriously difficult to self-diagnose, but you can use the test on pages 178–79 as a guide to help you decide whether you need professional help (see also the boxes describing the symptoms of depression, below, and those of anxiety on page 191). Psychiatrists sometimes use this questionnaire, called the Hospital Anxiety and Depression Scale, to distinguish between the two conditions. For each question, circle the answer that most applies to you. The scores for each response are on pages 257–58.

The test is only a guide, since depression and anxiety can overlap. Many patients with serious depression also suffer significant levels of anxiety, which may mask underlying depression. However, if you score more than eight overall or on either scale, or if you feel markedly depressed or anxious, whatever your score, you should seek your doctor's advice. Indeed, the closer you score to eight, the stronger your depressive or anxious trait. So you may still want to consult your doctor, especially if you have had the symptoms for more than a month.

Depression

Depression is far more than the 'blues' or feeling a bit low. Depression is a crushing feeling of being unable to cope with life that produces a number of symptoms (see box below). It may occur following a stressful event, especially in people with a genetic tendency to develop the condition.

Symptoms of depression

- loss of interest and enjoyment in life
- inability to enjoy things that are normally a source of pleasure
- feeling useless, inadequate, bad and helpless
- a sense of worthlessness
- loss of self-esteem
- feeling inappropriate or excessive guilt or remorse about past actions
- lack of drive and motivation
- avoiding meeting people

- agitation or restlessness
- irritability
- change in appetite or weight
- feeling worse at certain times of the day
- insomnia or excessive sleepiness
- waking earlier than normal
- feeling that life is not worth living; suicidal thoughts
- fatigue
- loss of sexual interest
- few displays of affection
- loss of self-confidence.

DEPRESSION

1. **I still enjoy the things I used to enjoy:**
    Definitely as much
    Not quite so much
    Only a little
    Hardly at all
2. **I can laugh and see the funny side of things:**
    As much as I always could
    Not quite so much
    Definitely not so much
    Not at all
3. **I feel cheerful:**
    Not at all
    Not often
    Sometimes
    Most of the time
4. **I feel as if I am slowed down:**
    Nearly all the time
    Very often
    Sometimes
    Not at all
5. **I have lost interest in my appearance:**
    Definitely
    I don't take as much care
    I may not take quite as much care
    I take just as much care as ever
6. **I look forward with enjoyment to things:**
    As much as ever I did
    Rather less than I used to
    Definitely less than I used to
    Hardly at all
7. **I can enjoy a good book or radio or TV programme:**
    Often
    Sometimes
    Not often
    Very seldom

Scores for each response are on pages 257–58

ANXIETY

1. **I feel tense or wound up:**
   Most of the time
   A lot of the time
   From time to time, occasionally
   Not at all
2. **I get a sort of frightened feeling as if something awful is about to happen:**
   Very definitely and quite badly
   Yes, but not too badly
   A little, but it doesn't worry me
   Not at all
3. **Worrying thoughts go through my mind:**
   A great deal of the time
   A lot of the time
   From time to time, not too often
   Only occasionally
4. **I can sit at ease and feel relaxed:**
   Definitely
   Usually
   Not often
   Not at all
5. **I get a sort of frightened feeling like 'butterflies' in the stomach:**
   Not at all
   Occasionally
   Quite often
   Very often
6. **I feel restless as, if I have to be on the move:**
   Very much
   Quite a lot
   Not very much
   Not at all
7. **I get sudden feelings of panic:**
   Very often indeed
   Quite often
   Not very often
   Not at all

Depression is common. Middleton and colleagues found that during 1998 GPs wrote 23.4 million prescriptions for antidepressants. As noted above, women are at least twice as likely to be prescribed antidepressants as men. This may be the result of social conditioning. Men may be less likely to admit their feelings to themselves, let alone a doctor. They may bottle up their emotions, or express their distress as bouts of aggression or drinking. Racial differences also appear to be significant. According to Nazroo, six per cent of people of Caribbean descent suffer depression in any given week compared to almost four per cent of white people. However, disentangling social and genetic factors is difficult.

The baby blues

Having a child is often one of the most remarkable, but one of the most stressful, times in our life. Most people cope with the changes remarkably well – despite the baby blues.

New mothers normally suffer a bout of the post-natal baby blues between the third and the tenth day after birth. This is different to post-natal depression (see below) and occurs in between 50 and 80 per cent of women. The mother may be tearful, irritable and distressed. She may cry uncontrollably or be argumentative. These emotions probably reflect the sudden change in hormones following childbirth. There is usually no need to call in a doctor unless the symptoms are severe.

While a tearful few days (the baby blues) are a normal part of childbirth, post-natal depression certainly is not. This condition, which begins later than the baby blues, often goes unrecognised and has all the hallmarks of major depression (typical symptoms are described on page 177). The baby's constant demands, changes in the woman's relationship with her partner and a loss of independence can all contribute to post-natal depression. The risk is especially marked if the woman already suffers from a psychological illness. It is especially important not to dismiss post-natal depression as 'just' the baby blues. If a depressed mood continues for more than three days it is worth seeking help from the GP or midwife.

It's not only the mother who suffers stress-related symptoms following a birth. Skari and collaborators found that 37 per cent of mothers and 13 per cent of fathers develop 'clinically important psychological distress' a few days after childbirth. Nine per cent of mothers and two per cent of fathers experienced severe intrusive stress symptoms. However, the level of psychological distress and depression declined to that in the general population over the next few weeks and months.

Many of the self-help and problem-solving strategies outlined in the book should help you adjust to the new birth (see Chapters 3 and 10). Counselling or talking to the midwife or health visitor can also help, especially if you are worried about your health or that of the child. In some cases, anti-depressants and other medications might help. You may also find the suggestions below useful.

- Ignore the housework or get your partner to do it – you are more important than an immaculate home.
- Arrange for a babysitter so you can devote some time to yourself.
- Share night-time tasks with your partner. Get treatment if you need it. If you don't get help, you're not only hurting yourself, you're hurting your baby. You can take some antidepressants even if you are breastfeeding without any risk to your baby.
- Breastfeeding reduces the levels of stress hormones released when you are confronted with a number of stressors and hassles.
- Many women feel isolated after giving up their job to look after a baby. A phone call from your partner at lunchtime may help, and you could join local mother and baby groups.
- Don't return to work too quickly. Give yourself time to recover.
- Stressful life events including bereavement and marital difficulties can exacerbate post-natal depression. You may want to get specific help for these problems.
- Contact the National Childbirth Trust* for further advice.

Manic depression (bipolar disorder)

Some people experience periods when they are intensely depressed and periods when they seem elated and over-excited. During the latter phase, patients may formulate grandiose plans that they are simply unable to carry out. Their judgement fails – so they may become involved in dubious business deals or even crimes. They tend to talk fast, drink heavily, get into fights or become promiscuous. Many then crash into depression.

When the mood swings begin interfering with work or social life or when they endanger the patient's life, doctors describe the condition as manic or bipolar disorder. These mood swings have all the features of a psychosis – the individual loses touch with reality and becomes unreachable. Bipolar disorder is a painful condition for sufferers and their families.

Lithium is widely used to reduce the severity and frequency of the mood swings, but may cause a number of side effects including nausea, vomiting, diarrhoea and tremor. Patients undergo regular blood monitoring to ensure blood levels of the drug stay within safe limits. Research is under way into a number of new agents that might help people with manic depression. Some of the drugs used to treat schizophrenia, for example, are showing considerable promise in people with bipolar disease. The Manic Depression Fellowship* offers a network of self-help groups for sufferers and their families.

Seasonal affective disorder

The advent of spring can help lift the mood of many of us. However, people suffering from seasonal affective disorder (SAD) are especially likely to welcome the spring. SAD sufferers experience mild-to-moderate depression during the autumn and winter. They may sleep more, crave carbohydrates, lack energy, feel fatigued and suffer headaches during these months. However, symptoms tend to resolve in the spring and summer. Sufferers also improve when they sit under a special strong light (domestic light fittings are not powerful enough). The Seasonal Affective Disorder Association* helps patients with this type of depression.

Treating depression

Depressed patients show abnormal brain chemistry, which antidepressants, the mainstay of treatment, aim to normalise. These changes in chemistry are believed to underlie the symptoms exhibited by a depressed person. The exact way this translates into, for example, loss of self-confidence, isn't clear. Nevertheless, restoring the balance in the brain's chemistry seems to ameliorate symptoms in many cases.

In mild depression, drugs, psychotherapy and counselling seem to be equally effective. You can discuss the pros and cons of each with your doctor. Antidepressants tend to be more effective for most cases of moderate and severe depression, although psychotherapy and counselling can augment the effect of the drugs. Very severe depression may require a stay in hospital – if patients are likely to harm themselves, for example – in addition to a course of medication.

Doctors can choose from a growing number of antidepressants with a variety of actions and side effects. So if one drug doesn't alleviate symptoms it might be worth trying an alternative. The large number of drugs available allows doctors to tailor treatment to the patient's pattern of symptoms.

How antidepressants work

Understanding how antidepressants work means making a brief diversion into pharmacology, the science that studies the biological effects of drugs. Nerves carry messages to and from the brain. These messages are transmitted along nerves as electrical impulses. When an electrical impulse reaches the end of a nerve it triggers the release of chemical messengers, known as neurotransmitters. These diffuse across a small gap to another nerve where they bind to specialised proteins – called receptors – on the nerve's surface. This binding is specific, rather like a key fitting into a lock. The binding switches on a complicated chemical cascade in the nerve cell and the message continues its journey around the nervous system.

Some neurotransmitters increase the nerve's activity. Other neurotransmitters inhibit the nerve's activity. The balance between these rival neurotransmitters determines whether the electrical impulse is passed along to the next nerve. Many drugs work by binding to the receptors, thereby changing the balance of nervous activity. Some drugs, known as antagonists, bind to the receptor without stimulating it. This blocks the natural neurotransmitter from binding to the receptor. In contrast, agonists bind to and stimulate the receptor. In other words, agonists mimic the action of the natural transmitter.

One major group of neurotransmitters, known as the monoamines, contains adrenaline, noradrenaline, dopamine and serotonin. Low brain levels of monoamines may underlie depression as well as playing a role in a variety of other disorders, including obsessive-compulsive disease, panic disorder, alcoholism and obesity. Low levels of serotonin and noradrenaline seem to be especially important in depression.

Antidepressants probably act by normalising monoamine levels. The actions of monoamines are curtailed in part by being taken back up into the nerve ending from which they were released (a process called re-uptake). This lowers levels around the receptor so the nerve's activity declines. In people with depression, the levels around the receptor fall too far. One group of antidepressants – the tricyclic antidepressants – act by blocking the re-uptake of serotonin and noradrenaline. Another group, the selective serotonin re-uptake inhibitors (SSRIs), block only the re-uptake of serotonin, as their name suggests. Yet another group of drugs – the noradrenaline re-uptake inhibitors (NARIs) – reduce noradrenaline uptake. An enzyme called monoamine oxidase also curtails the monoamines' actions. Monoamine oxidase inhibitors (MAOIs) increase levels of the neurotransmitter by inhibiting this enzyme. All these mechanisms ultimately increase levels of monoamines in the patient's brain.

However, restoring the brain's chemical balance takes time, so patients have to take antidepressants for up to four weeks before their depressed mood begins to lift markedly. In some cases, symptoms such as anxiety, insomnia and tension may improve more rapidly. There is little to choose between the antidepressants for efficacy – although patients may respond to some and not others. The differences emerge when you look at their side effects.

- **Tricyclic antidepressants** – for example, dothiepin, amitriptyline, imipramine and desipramine – can cause blurred vision, disorientation, drowsiness, lethargy and sedation, as well as reducing hand-eye co-ordination. They may interact with alcohol. These side effects can make it dangerous to drive.

- **MAOIs** inhibit an enzyme called MAO, which comes as two types, designated 'A' and 'B'. MAO-B normally breaks down an amino acid (one of protein's building blocks) called tyramine. High tyramine levels can trigger a potentially dangerous rise in blood pressure. So patients taking some MAOIs have traditionally been advised to avoid certain foods that are rich in tyramine, such as cheese, red wine and Marmite. More recently developed MAOIs are more selective for MAO-A, the enzyme that underlies the antidepressant action. This leaves MAO-B to metabolise tyramine, so patients don't have to avoid these foods.

- **Selective Serotonin Re-uptake Inhibitors (SSRIs)** – of which Prozac (fluoxetine) is the most familiar – do not inhibit MAO-A or -B, so patients do not have to restrict their diets. As SSRIs are more selective, they cause fewer and less serious side effects than the tricyclics. For example, SSRIs are non-sedating, don't cause a dry mouth and blurred vision, do not promote weight gain and do not interact with alcohol to the same extent as tricyclics. However, the SSRIs can cause side effects such as impotence in men and an inability to experience an orgasm in women, as well as nausea, diarrhoea and headaches.

Once you are over the acute symptoms of depression, you will probably need long-term treatment to prevent relapse. Typically, patients continue to take antidepressants for around six months after recovering from a bout of depression. However, you can take a few simple steps that may help reduce the risk of a relapse (see 'Self-help measures to beat depression', overleaf).

Other therapies

In the rare cases where drugs fail, doctors still have a few options. One option is to combine an antidepressant with lithium, a drug more commonly used to manage manic depression. Another option is to use electro-convulsive therapy (ECT). ECT can literally shock depression into submission – but it also seems to run counter to common sense, as we protect ourselves from electric shocks during the rest of our lives.

The image of ECT has been undermined by movies such as *One Flew Over The Cuckoo's Nest*. However, ECT is an effective and generally safe treatment. ECT is generally reserved for patients with severe, intractable depression who are unresponsive to other therapies. Patients are given a light anaesthetic and a drug that relaxes muscles, which makes them feel that they have gone to sleep. An electrical current is then passed through their brain for a split second. For reasons scientists don't understand, this often alleviates even severe, psychotic depression – one suggestion is that ECT increases monoamine levels. Patients commonly report memory loss for events just before the ECT and may have patchy memory loss during the following two or three weeks. Many patients also feel nauseous, confused and restless or experience headaches after a session.

Self-help measures to beat depression

The strategies below can help you cope if you are becoming depressed, or are recovering from depression. Some of these suggestions might be enough to resolve mild depression. Don't underestimate your symptoms however, and seek a doctor's advice if you score more than eight on the Hospital Anxiety and Depression scale (see pages 178–79), or are concerned about your wellbeing, whatever your score.

- Try to develop social supports. Friends and a sympathetic family make handling difficult situations easier and so you're less likely to develop depression. Indeed, Zhang and colleagues found that married persons were less likely to report loneliness and depression compared with divorced, widowed and never-married people. Not surprisingly, the study also confirmed that higher levels of education, better physical health and more economic resources reduced the likelihood of loneliness and depression.
- Talk to someone. Work through your pain. Cry (ideally with someone rather than on your own). Simply telling someone how terrible you feel can help. You could consider counselling or psychotherapy (see Chapter 10), which may help you understand the source of your stress and depression and offer a new perspective on your problems. Both require a degree of

commitment that is difficult when depression leaves your motivation and energy at a low ebb. However, antidepressants can give you a window of opportunity to tackle the underlying problems.

- Depression can result from relationship difficulties or bereavement. Relate★ provides counselling to couples and individuals, while Cruse★ and The Compassionate Friends★ support the bereaved and parents who have lost a child respectively. Remember the Samaritans★ are always at the end of a phone.

- Learn about depression: the Royal College of Psychiatrists★ publishes information leaflets on depression. Groups such as the Depression Alliance★ and MIND★ also offer advice and support. Education can be effective in its own right. For instance, Honey and colleagues found that educating new mothers about post-natal depression and helping them develop coping strategies markedly reduced the intensity of depressive symptoms.

- Don't just sit there brooding. While motivating yourself can be difficult, try to walk around the shops or through the country, do some housework or gardening. This will keep you fit and help you sleep. Exercise also distracts you from your worries and helps lift your mood. Sitting worrying makes you feel worse.

- Sleep disturbances are common in people with depression. Following the tips on good sleep hygiene may help (pages 210–12).

- You can't drown depression in alcohol. Rather, depression feeds on alcohol. Even moderate drinking can be dangerous for people with depression: alcohol interacts with certain antidepressants, increasing your likelihood of developing side effects. If you suffer from depression, don't drink.

- Do your best to stay optimistic, although this can be very difficult. Remember that thousands of people have recovered from depression. Indeed, you can emerge better able to cope with life than before. You may gain a new perspective, and depression can act as a spur to change your life. For some people, depression improves the rest of their lives.

- Gail Feldman's book *Taking Advantage of Adversity* exemplifies how to use the energy wrapped up in life crises and move to improved self-expression.

Suicide

Suicide – or a suicide attempt – is, arguably, the ultimate condemnation of society's care of people with depression and psychological illness. Despite the millions of pounds spent on treatment, despite the best efforts of doctors and the care of the family, even minor psychological illnesses seem to be linked to an increased risk of suicide. Men are particularly at risk, according to Gunnell and colleagues who followed a group of men and women for 20 years.

According to the Department of Health about 5,000 people take their own lives in England each year. Women are more likely to attempt suicide than men. However, men are more likely to succeed. Indeed, around 1,300 of the suicides are among men under 35 years old, and suicide is the commonest cause of death in this age group.

Suicidal thoughts seem to be remarkably common. They may even cross the minds of normally well-balanced adults after an intensely stressful event such as the death of a parent or spouse. However, suicidal thoughts are most strongly linked to people suffering from psychiatric disease. Depression, anxiety, personal tragedy and alcohol abuse all increase the risk of suicide. Substance abuse and a tendency to impulsive behaviour are among the most powerful factors predicting the risk of suicide in depressed people – Pezawas and collaborators found that impulsive behaviour played a major role in some 81 per cent of suicide attempts.

Parasuicide – deliberate self-harm without intending to die – is often a cry for help. However, it's a cry that often goes unheeded. Even some health professionals feel that parasuicide detracts from 'real' medical problems. And while suicide is no longer criminal, it conflicts with many moral and religious codes. Some people still regard suicide as an unforgivable sin. These attitudes hinder attempts to help some of society's most vulnerable and distressed members.

Clearly, people living with or caring for depressed patients need to watch for the signs of suicide and, where necessary, encourage sufferers to get help before it's too late. (Some further advice targeted at adolescents is on page 87.) Ironically, recovering from depression temporarily increases suicide risk. When depressed patients are at their lowest ebb, many lack the energy and motivation to kill themselves. However, antidepressants can increase a person's energy before they lift the person's mood. As a result, patients are more likely to kill themselves as their energy levels begin to rise. A number of other risk factors may signal someone is contemplating suicide (see box below).

Suicide risks and signals

- people who have deliberately hurt themselves in the past
- people who verbally threaten suicide
- the unemployed
- people working in certain occupations, such as doctors, farmers, vets
- people living alone, divorced or separated
- people suffering from physical illness
- drug addicts and alcoholics
- depression
- insomnia
- weight change – usually a loss
- general loss of interest
- lethargy
- hypochondria.

Anxiety disorders

Case history: Jane

One summer day, the tube stopped between stations. It was the rush hour and Jane was crushed on all sides. She was hot, claustrophobic and intensely anxious. Jane began to feel sweaty and breathless, her condition made all the worse by the stifling lack of air in the tube. She had been delayed getting her children off to school and was running 15 minutes late. Her heart began pounding and Jane began to worry that she might be having a heart attack. She felt terrified of breaking down in front of everyone and began to feel disorientated and faint. Her vision began to swim. Suddenly the train started moving again. Jane left the tube at the next station and walked the rest of the way to the office where she regained her composure.

Jane's feelings of anxiety are familiar to everyone – especially during times of great stress. Many of us experience the occasional panic attack. However, at the other end of the scale anxiety disorders include the enslaving rituals of obsessive-compulsive disorders and the frightening effects of post-traumatic stress disorder. In rare cases, anxiety can be serious and contribute to suicidal feelings. Khan and colleagues estimated that every year one in 500 people with anxiety will kill themselves and seven in every 500 will attempt suicide.

Stress may either cause or contribute to this spectrum of anxiety-related disorders. And living with anxiety can, in turn, cause considerable stress. Indeed, events that would hardly bother a healthy person can have an enormous impact on the anxious. The National Phobics Society★ and Triumph over Phobia★ provide advice and support to people suffering from anxiety disorders and their families.

Anxiety symptoms

Anxious people experience a range of symptoms (see box opposite). Many result from an over-stimulation of the autonomic nervous system, which controls the fight-or-flight reflex (see pages 19–21). Others are so-called 'somatic' (bodily or physical) symptoms – patients convert their anxiety into symptoms including headaches, bowel disturbances and muscle tension. Many generalised anxiety disorder patients suffer from mainly somatic symptoms, usually in their gut or chest.

A number of conditions may mimic the symptoms of anxiety. For example, high levels of caffeine – between 10 and 15 cups of coffee daily – can produce symptoms similar to those of anxiety. One patient complained of severe anxiety that did not respond to tranquillisers. Doctors were stumped until they discovered he drank 50 cups of coffee a day. But some people may develop anxiety following just five cups of coffee, depending on their sensitivity. Excessive alcohol, certain thyroid diseases and low blood sugar can also mimic anxiety. Moreover, some people experience panic attacks when they stop taking certain drugs, including barbiturates, benzodiazepines and amphetamines. Your doctor can help determine if any of these other factors contribute to your anxiety.

Anxiety symptoms

- feeling on edge and keyed up, easily startled, irritable
- restlessness
- difficulty concentrating
- fatigue and insomnia
- dry mouth
- nausea
- trouble swallowing
- feeling there is a lump in the throat
- shaking, twitching or trembling uncontrollably
- breathlessness or feeling smothered
- pins and needles in the fingers and toes
- dizziness, feeling unsteady, faintness
- chest pains or palpitations
- hot flushes or blushing
- chills, sweating, cold, clammy hands
- muscle tension, aches and pains
- an urge to urinate or defecate
- feeling they are dying or having a heart attack
- feeling they are about to go crazy or lose control
- a sense of unreality – which strengthens the feeling of going mad
- avoidance behaviour: anxious people go out of their way to avoid situations or people that trigger the symptoms.

Types of anxiety

As mentioned above, there are several types of anxiety and related disorders.

Generalised anxiety and panic attacks

Generalised anxiety is characterised by an unshakeable feeling that something terrible is going to happen. Sufferers can't put their finger on the cause of their anxiety and stress. Nevertheless, people with generalised anxiety show certain characteristics. They worry habitually, feel apprehensive, are constantly vigilant, always seem on edge, have difficulty concentrating, and are easily startled. Not surprisingly, this heightened vigilance can cause considerable stress.

Panic attacks are periods when the patient experiences debilitating and overwhelming 'fear'. The feelings are usually much more intense than in generalised anxiety, but are shorter-lived and subside within a few minutes. During a panic attack, sufferers may feel dizzy, faint or think they are dying; others may feel breathless and convinced they are having a heart attack.

Panic attacks start suddenly and reach a peak within 10 to 20 minutes. Longer attacks tend to be a feature of generalised anxiety. Once the panic has passed, patients feel weak and exhausted. Panic attacks are distressing rather than dangerous. Some patients suffer attacks for only a few weeks or months. In others, the attacks recur.

Panic attacks often develop in response to a certain situation, such as agoraphobia or social phobia, for example. However, panic attacks may strike without warning. Nevertheless, sufferers may begin to associate certain events with suffering a panic attack and will go out of their way to avoid these triggers. For example, some people find travelling in underground trains intensely stressful and develop panic attacks. As a result, they either take slower overground transport or avoid working in areas where they need to travel by underground. Nevertheless, the situation does not invariably cause a panic attack, in contrast to a phobia. Cognitive behavioural therapy, psychotherapy and drugs can all alleviate the suffering caused by panic disorders.

Phobias

Phobias are fears out of all proportion to their cause and attached specifically, but irrationally, to identifiable objects or situations. Snakes, blood, bees, heights or flying scare many of us but we usually overcome these fears as we grow older. People with phobias experience a fear so intense, so debilitating, that it affects the way they lead their lives. Agoraphobics may be unable to leave the house. A tiny house spider may terrify arachnophobia sufferers. Ironically, sufferers often recognise that their fears are unrealistic or excessive, but they are unable to do anything about it.

Patients with simple phobias experience intense panic when confronted with a specific object or event – such as animals, closed spaces (claustrophobia) or heights (acrophobia). People suffering from arachnophobia may feel panicky, sweaty and breathless when they see a spider. Their anxiety increases the closer they get to the spider and is more intense the larger the spider. Simple phobia sufferers also experience anxiety when they anticipate facing their fear. A person with acrophobia (fear of heights) may suffer anticipatory anxiety when entering a tall building – even though his or her feet are firmly planted on the ground floor. Simple phobias rarely dramatically impair patients' lives, although claustrophobia may be more debilitating and stressful if, for example, patients can't enter a tube train.

Agoraphobia, which tends to develop in a patient's 20s or 30s, is a fear of being in places where escape might be difficult or embarrassing or where help might be unavailable if the person experiences a panic attack. As a result, people with agoraphobia commonly fear being alone outside the house, in a crowd or travelling by public transport. People with agoraphobia find these situations intensely stressful and they experience a panic attack. This can leave sufferers terrified of going outside the house in case they experience another attack. Other sufferers fear that the symptoms will incapacitate them – even if they have never experienced a panic attack.

Everyone gets nervous before an important meeting, performing on stage or giving a presentation. It is abnormal *not* to feel tense, and the fight-or-flight reflex ensures that we give our best performance (see pages 19–21). Most of us learn to handle the stress surrounding these difficult social situations. However, social phobia sufferers go out of their way to avoid social gatherings. These people may be so nervous beforehand that they drink before meeting their friends down the pub or at a party. Many people – even the sufferers themselves – dismiss their symptoms as shyness.

However, social phobia is more than being intensely shy. People with social phobia develop many typical stress-related symptoms when they need to face their fears (see box overleaf). Many are concerned about an anxiety-provoking event – sometimes for weeks before. They may lie awake at night worrying to the extent that lack of sleep undermines their performance and exacerbates stress and anxiety. This constant tension means that many people with social phobia are unable to relax – sometimes for years on end – and traps sufferers in a cycle of fearing fear. So perhaps it's not surprising that people with social phobia feel stressed, anxious and depressed. Many people with social phobia turn to drink and drugs to mask their anxiety and to provide them with the 'Dutch courage' to socialise. Fortunately, social phobia can be treated with behavioural therapies, or with drugs.

Typical fears in social phobia

General

- being introduced to strangers
- meeting people in authority
- eating or drinking in public
- participating in small groups
- entering a party group
- being teased.

Performance

- speaking in public
- writing in front of others
- acting or playing a musical instrument in public
- giving a report to a group
- expressing disagreement.

Obsessive-compulsive disorder

Around one per cent of the population suffers from obsessive-compulsive disorder. Many more suffer from mild obsessions or compulsions – repeatedly checking that the gas is turned off or that the front door is locked before going to bed, for example. Others have an obsessive-compulsive personality – perfectionist, stubborn, indecisive, devoted to work and emotionally flat – that may be an advantage in certain jobs requiring, for example, an intense attention to detail. While many medical textbooks lump obsessive-compulsive disorder with the anxiety states, many psychiatrists regard them as different diseases.

- **Obsessions** are persistent ideas, thoughts, impulses or images that a person recognises as senseless and tries to resist. A vicar may repeatedly experience perverted thoughts. A businesswoman may fear becoming infected through shaking her clients' hands. Not surprisingly, these thoughts cause considerable stress and anxiety.

- **Compulsions** are repetitive actions performed to alleviate the stress generated by an obsession. Examples are repeated hand-washing, counting, checking and touching. The sufferer derives no pleasure from these unrealistic and time-consuming actions. Even if you are scrupulous about avoiding infection, there is no need to wash your hands 50 times a day.

At first, when patients feel compelled to behave in a certain way they try to resist as they recognise their behaviour is unreasonable. However, resisting the compulsions causes intense and increasing stress and psychic internal tension. Yielding to the compulsion releases tension. After repeated failures to counter the compulsion the sufferer may give in and no longer resist the compulsion. However, they will try to avoid situations likely to trigger the obsession. A housewife obsessed about dirt may avoid public toilets, or the businesswoman obsessed about contamination may avoid shaking hands. So in effect, the disorder may slide into a phobia.

Obsessive-compulsive disorder usually begins in adolescence or early adulthood and symptoms tend to wax and wane throughout the patient's life. It is equally common in women and men. However, it may also emerge during pregnancy. Some women find pregnancy stressful and this may maintain, trigger or exacerbate obsessive-compulsive disorder.

As with other anxiety diseases, a combination of drugs and behavioural therapies is used to treat obsessive-compulsive disorder.

Post-traumatic stress disorder

The idea that intense stress can leave sufferers traumatised for long periods, if not for life, first emerged during the horrors of the First World War. Soldiers returned suffering from a number of 'hysterical' symptoms that doctors attributed to the pressure of exploding shells – so-called 'shell shock'. However, during the Second World War doctors recognised that shell shock had its roots in the mind rather than the body. They renamed the syndrome 'combat neurosis' or 'combat fatigue'. Doctors now describe the tragic psychological legacy of intense stress as post-traumatic stress disorder (PTSD).

Post-traumatic stress disorder follows an intensely stressful, often life-threatening, 'trigger' event that falls outside the range of normal human experience, such as being involved in a war, man-made or natural disaster, being raped or seeing a serious accident. In contrast to other anxiety disorders, the fear experienced by post-traumatic stress sufferers is not out of proportion to its cause. Anyone would find a major disaster, a serious earthquake or a war stressful. But in PTSD the fear and anxiety persists for months and even years after the original event. It is now recognised as occurring after more common stressful events, such as an emergency caesarean.

Following the stressful incident some survivors develop intense fear, terror and helplessness. They either repeatedly run through the event in their minds or avoid anything that reminds them of the tragedy. Others become apathetic and 'numb' to life generally, agitated or dependent on other people. Most can't sleep properly.

Most patients have to undergo psychotherapy or exposure therapy to face the fear underlying post-traumatic stress disorder. In many cases, this treatment is supported with drugs. At the time of writing, SSRIs (see page 184) are the treatment of choice for PTSD. However, a number of other drugs are currently being investigated for PTSD.

Take control of your anxiety

Many people endure the torment of intense anxiety for years, but it's never too late to take control. You may need professional help from your GP, a counsellor or a psychiatrist. The doctor or therapist will probably choose some of the various elements discussed below to develop a treatment programme that meets your needs.

- Initially, doctors aim to provide support, reassurance and counselling. They may also prescribe a short course – perhaps a week or fortnight – of benzodiazepines if you suffer from very severe anxiety or panic attacks. Alleviating symptoms helps put you in the 'right frame of mind' to embark on a course of non-drug treatment. So behavioural therapies may work hand-in-hand with drugs, rather than being an alternative. Drugs alleviate symptoms in the short term, while psychological therapies control anxiety in the longer term and so reduce the risk of relapse.

- Counselling often alleviates anxiety after only a few sessions. Counsellors encourage 'problem solving' – similar to that outlined in Chapter 3 – to tackle the source of stress. Self-help materials, such as those provided by the Royal College of Psychiatrists★ and Triumph over Phobia★ support counsellors' attempts to break the cycle of stress that fuels anxiety. So patients are taught, for example, relaxation and stress management or meditation (see Chapter 10). Some of the behavioural techniques used to overcome phobias can be intensely stressful. Relaxation and stress management techniques help patients remain calm during treatment.

- Cognitive behavioural therapy replaces a destructive thought pattern with a more realistic and positive approach. By reinterpreting anxiety-provoking thoughts and events, cognitive therapists change patients' behaviour. Patients undergoing cognitive behavioural therapy for social phobia may watch a video of themselves. This gives patients an insight into how they appear – rather than how they think they appear. For example, people with social phobia often believe that they sweat heavily. When they watch the video it is clear that they don't. However, patients need to see this for themselves, rather than relying on someone else telling them. Cognitive behavioural therapy can be effective. For example, Piacentini and colleagues found that 79 per cent of children with obsessive-compulsive disorder responded to cognitive behavioural therapy. On average, symptom severity declined by 45 per cent.

- During exposure therapy patients learn to control their anxiety while they confront their fears. For example, people suffering from arachnophobia try to relax as a spider crawls over their hand. During each session the exposure gradually becomes more intense and frightening. In the first session, agoraphobics may walk down the road. During the next session they walk to the local supermarket, then take a bus ride, and so on. Similar techniques are used to gradually desensitise patients with post-traumatic stress disorder to the trigger event.

- In 'flooding' the patient learns relaxation techniques and then is suddenly exposed to an intense form of the anxiety-provoking event. The patient tries to relax and waits for the anxiety to abate. So someone scared of crowds goes shopping in a crowded shopping centre.

- Aversion therapy: clients are punished if they perform a certain act. Combined with positive approaches, this can break unpleasant habits. Disulfiram, used to treat alcoholism (see pages 119–20), is a classic example of aversion therapy – it causes disagreeable physical symptoms in people who drink.
- Social skills training can help people with social phobia feel relaxed and confident in company by learning simple social skills, such as how to start a conversation. Social skills training usually means role-playing in front of a video camera.
- Psychotherapy reaches into a patient's psyche to examine and dispel repressed feelings. This may undermine the beliefs that sustain the phobia. See Chapter 10 for more information.

Depression and clinical anxiety are common and can be devastating for sufferers. There's no simple pill that frees everyone from the conditions. However, a combination of non-pharmacological measures and drugs mean that most people with depression and anxiety are able to live normal lives.

Further reading

Feldman, G. 2002. *Taking Advantage of Adversity.* Time Warner
Styron, W. 1991. *Darkness Visible.* Jonathan Cape

Chapter 8

Other psychological disorders linked to stress

We have already seen how depression and anxiety are linked with stress. In this chapter, we'll look briefly at a few conditions that further exemplify this inter-relationship between stress and psychological disease – schizophrenia, eating disorders, dizziness, vertigo and tinnitus. According to Esch and colleagues, stress 'plays a major role' in many psychological disorders, and these particular conditions are no exception. Sufferers can become trapped in a cycle whereby stress exacerbates their condition, which causes further stress. We show here how stress management techniques can help.

Schizophrenia

Schizophrenia affects about one per cent of the population. However, despite being relatively common the condition is surrounded by myths and misconceptions. To many people, 'schizophrenics' are homeless vagrants with Jekyll and Hyde personalities, ready to explode into violence at the slightest provocation. But rather than having 'split' personalities, people with schizophrenia live with a split between their internal thoughts and external reality. For example, people with schizophrenia may believe their actions are controlled by a radio-transmitter implanted in their brains by aliens. The reality is that most people with the condition live lives of quiet desperation, and they are far more likely to hurt themselves than others. The film *A Beautiful Mind* explored the effect of the illness on the life of the Nobel prize-winning mathematician John Nash.

Thirty per cent of patients suffer a single episode of schizophrenia and then recover. However, in around 70 per cent of patients the first episode – usually in late adolescence or early adulthood – marks the beginning of a number of relapses and remissions throughout the patient's life. The relapses undermine the person's ability to make social relationships and enjoy the usual benefits of adulthood: an intimate relationship, social networks and employment. As a result, most patients take medication known as antipsychotics for much of their life. It is important that schizophrenia is diagnosed as soon as possible. The longer the delay in treating symptoms, the poorer the outcome tends to be, and sufferers are less likely to respond well to medication.

The older medicines for schizophrenia – the neuroleptics – can cause a number of debilitating side effects ranging from fatigue to movement disorders reminiscent of Parkinson's disease. Newer agents – the so-called atypical antipsychotics – are less likely to cause these Parkinsonian side effects. However, they still cause a number of other adverse reactions, including weight gain, sexual side effects, dizziness and cardiovascular changes.

Over the years, researchers have linked numerous factors – including stress – with an increased risk of schizophrenia, at least in some patients. In particular, the stress associated with an excessively critical, hostile family or with life events such as the breakdown of a relationship or losing a job may also provoke a relapse.

However, stress management can improve the prospects for people with schizophrenia. For example, Norman and collaborators found that training patients in stress management techniques helped them cope with acute stress, and might reduce the likelihood of a relapse requiring hospitalisation. While stress management isn't a replacement for drugs, it might offer supplementary support for some patients with this disease. However, people with schizophrenia should practise such techniques only under medical supervision. As a starting point, you can use the strategies outlined in this book.

Contact SANE,★ Rethink★ (formerly the National Schizophrenia Fellowship), the Royal College of Psychiatrists★ and MIND★ for further information.

Eating disorders

Newspaper articles focus on tragic or high-profile cases of people with eating disorders, and many parents and teenagers are very aware of the dangers. However, it is important to keep food fads in perspective. Dieting is common among adolescents and most teenagers who diet do not become anorexic. Indeed, government statistics suggest that around six per cent of girls are on a diet at any time. Between the ages of 15 and 18 years, this proportion increases to 16 per cent. A smaller number of teenagers, adults and even children suffer from serious eating disorders.

Anorexia sufferers show persistent, deliberate weight loss and may refuse to eat, often to the point of emaciation. However, in their view they never attain their ideal weight. No matter how thin they become, they still see themselves as overweight. Yet, by definition, a person with anorexia believes themself to be overweight despite weighing at least 85 per cent less than what is expected for their age and height. This massive weight loss means that people with anorexia can suffer numerous health problems including heart disease, menstrual problems, long-term infertility, anaemia and osteoporosis (brittle bone disease). Around 1,000 people in the UK die from anorexia each year.

The Eating Disorders Association* found in 1994 that one in 500 girls in state schools suffers from anorexia. (One boy suffers from anorexia for every 10 girls.) This increases to:

- one in 100 girls at independent schools
- one in 55 at university
- one in 10 at dance and drama schools.

The association believes these numbers could have doubled between 1994 and 2000. The frequency of anorexia in these institutions could reflect the impact of pressure to succeed, an emphasis on over-achieving, and media pressure to conform to a possibly unattainable stereotype. The British Medical Association, for example, found that many models and actresses viewed as role models had about 10 to 15 per cent body fat (a healthy woman usually has between 22 and 26 per cent body fat). When Katzmarzyk and Davis assessed *Playboy* centrefolds between 1978 and 1998 – regarded by the general public as the ideal female shape – they found that 70 per cent of women were underweight by today's standards.

Certain personality traits seem to predispose people to anorexia. For example, girls with anorexia tend to be high achievers, perfectionists, meticulous and obsessive. They are also likely to have rigid mental views, be socially inept, avoid risk, and conform to authority. In some cases, anorexia may reflect an unwillingness to face up to sexual maturity – sufferers lose body fat giving them a childlike silhouette, and their periods may stop. In other cases, anorexia may be a means of protest through sexual regression, with some instances possibly reflecting the higher rates of child sexual abuse among anorexics.

People with bulimia, like anorexics, have an extreme dread of fatness although most are around normal weight. Bulimics eat vast quantities of food, then get rid of it by vomiting, using laxatives or over-exercising. In extreme cases, bulimics eat around 6,000 kilo-calories a day (more than treble the necessary amount) and binge and vomit up to 30 times a day. This can lead to numerous compli-cations including erosion of tooth enamel, menstrual problems, anaemia and ulcers.

Some psychiatrists believe that bulimia expresses depression, anxiety, sexual problems and stress in our food-obsessed culture. Bingeing and vomiting may help bulimics cope with anxiety and depression. Bingeing is associated with guilt and anxiety; purging brings relief.

Eating disorders and stress

The way in which anorexics and bulimics react to stress differs, partly as a result of the personality traits outlined above. In two studies, Troop and collaborators found that women with anorexia tend to avoid thinking about a crisis. In contrast, people with bulimia tend to ruminate on a difficulty and blame themselves for the problem. (Quite how these differences relate to the eating disorder isn't clear.) Overall, women with anorexia or bulimia were less likely to cope effectively with their problems than those without eating disorders. 'Women with eating disorders were less likely to be masterful in response to crises than women without eating disorders,' the authors write.

We have seen throughout the book that feeling in control is a powerful weapon in the fight against stress. Adopting some of the strategies in Chapters 3 and 10 may help you face up to difficult situations if you have an eating disorder. However, you are likely to need professional help.

Eating disorder warning signs

Several tell-tale signs might suggest that a person you know is suffering from an eating disorder:

- they tend to be preoccupied with food, weight or calories. In some cases, they may not be able to hold a conversation without mentioning food
- they may weigh themselves frequently and be excessively concerned about their appearance and attractiveness
- they also show eating disorder patterns such as eating in secret, frequent binges, strict dieting and so on
- they may disappear after a meal to vomit or use laxatives or diuretics
- they may complain of feeling nauseated or bloated after eating a normal amount of food.

If you or someone you know has these symptoms, it is important to see a doctor urgently. In particular, you should act if someone displays rapid and continuous weight loss combined with a lack of recognition that they are getting thinner.

Treatment

The management of anorexia or bulimia requires specialist help. Combining medication, cognitive behavioural therapy (see page 232) and an eating plan can help manage the underlying problem. In the case of many adolescents under 19 years of age, family therapy is the most successful form of intervention. Some psychiatrists believe that anorexia should at times be treated with antipsychotic medication – body dysmorphia (false belief about one's weight and size) is a form of delusion or psychosis. Around half of people with bulimia taking an antidepressant cut down on bingeing, although most still eat abnormally. In some cases, high doses of the selective serotonin re-uptake indicators (SSRIs), used in depression, can help – they may influence appetite in high doses.

Psychotherapy helps sufferers face the cause of their poor body image and lose their pathological fear of being fat. Problem-solving

Are you overweight?

The best way to find out whether you are overweight is to estimate your body mass index (BMI) or have your body fat measurement taken (this is probably best performed by a doctor or a gym). To estimate your BMI you need to multiply your height in metres by itself. Then divide your weight in kilos by this figure.

Body mass index (kg/m²)	Range
Less than 13	Anorexic
Less than 18.5	Underweight
18.5 to 24.9	Desirable (healthy) range
25 to 29.9	Overweight
30 to 34.9	Moderate obesity
35 to 39.9	Severe obesity
40 or over	Very severe (morbid) obesity

If your BMI is between 20 and 25 you are not overweight. If despite this, you feel that you are overweight, especially if you are in the middle to low end of the range, you might be vulnerable to eating disorders. It is probably worth seeking professional help from your doctor or charities such as the Eating Disorders Association.* The closer you are to the upper end of the normal range, the more you need to watch your calorie consumption and energy use to avoid becoming overweight. If your BMI is over 25, you're already overweight. A BMI of above 30 suggests that you're obese. So you're at significantly increased risk of suffering from numerous health problems. If your BMI is over 35, you should consult your doctor as soon as possible. You might need professional help to bring your weight back under control.

The principle of weight loss is simple. Eat healthily, reduce the amount of calories you consume and increase your exercise and you will lose weight. A slow and steady approach is more likely to succeed than trying to crash diet. It's important to maintain the lifestyle changes. Around 98 per cent of people who diet regain all the weight they lost, plus another 10 pounds (4.5 kg) within five years.

and cognitive behavioural therapy can help reinforce the positive aspects in their lives (for more information see Chapters 3 and 10). However, recovery takes time – perhaps between one and five years for a person with anorexia to reach, and stay, at a reasonable weight. Contact the Eating Disorders Association★ for further information.

Dizziness, vertigo and tinnitus

Dizziness, vertigo and tinnitus are common stress-related symptoms. At times of stress, some people feel their head is swimming or that the room is spinning. Others hear the unpleasant, persistent and intrusive ringing or hissing in their ears known as tinnitus.

The link between stress, dizziness and vertigo – the feeling that the room is spinning, which can herald a blackout – was first studied scientifically in the 1940s. Since then, researchers have found that stress can provoke three reactions that increase your likelihood of feeling dizzy or even fainting:

- **a short-lived fall in blood pressure** in situations that provoke fear or anxiety but from which escape is impossible or impracticable. For example, some people faint before a blood sample is taken
- **hyperventilation** – rapid, shallow breathing – increases levels of carbon dioxide in your blood. This reduces the amount of oxygen getting to your brain and so you feel light-headed
- **a 'hysterical faint'** – this conjures up the rather clichéd image of a highly-strung young woman who passes out at the slightest – usually sexual – provocation.

Tinnitus is another common reaction to stress. 'Tinnitus often entails severe psychological distress … Tinnitus may be considered as a chronic stressor,' Weber and colleagues remark. However, you should see your doctor to find out whether there is a physical cause, as tinnitus is also linked to some viral infections and Menière's disease, for example.

Tinnitus shows the typical pattern of a stress-related disease. Stress may contribute, at least partly, to causing some cases of tinnitus. And tinnitus undoubtedly exacerbates stress, causing considerable emotional distress and fatigue. The incessant noise means that tinnitus sufferers often find relaxation impossible and experience difficulty falling asleep. In the still of the night, even mild tinnitus can seem deafening. As a result, tinnitus undermines sufferers' concentration and leaves them tired and irritable – a combination that conspires to cause considerable stress. So it's perhaps not surprising that sufferers frequently feel depressed, anxious and irritable. This can heighten the acuteness of their perception, so they hear their tinnitus all the more acutely. For example, Folmer and co-workers found that people with depression seemed to experience louder tinnitus than those without. Treating the depression may reduce the tinnitus severity experienced by many of these patients – for more on depression see Chapter 7.

Against this background, it would seem logical that stress management techniques could help people with stress-related tinnitus. And Weber and colleagues found that a ten-week relaxation programme decreased patients' perception of feeling stressed, anxious, depressed and angry, and reduced the disturbance caused by tinnitus. On the other hand, Dineen and colleagues compared learning about the condition, relaxation training and a therapeutic noise strategy (which employs white noise to get people used to tinnitus). None of the strategies seemed to be more effective than the others in helping patients to cope or become used to tinnitus. However, 37 per cent of subjects given long-term low-level white noise stimulation reported benefit. It might be that different patients respond to different strategies.

Contact the British Tinnitus Association* or the Royal National Institute for Deaf People* for further information.

When to see your doctor

Dizziness, vertigo and tinnitus are often stress-related, but they can also signal diseases including brain tumours, inner ear problems or multiple sclerosis. Moreover, a number of drugs – including antihypertensives (blood pressure-lowering medicines), antihistamines and antidiabetic drugs – can cause dizziness, vertigo or both. So if symptoms persist consult your doctor. You should also see your GP if you suffer blackouts or a seizure.

Chapter 9

Beating insomnia and fatigue

Insomnia and fatigue are both common in people suffering from stress. The link between stress and sleep disturbances was strikingly underlined by Galea and collaborators, who found that 24.5 per cent of people living in Manhattan suffered from insomnia following the September 11 terrorist attacks of 2001. Indeed, in a detailed assessment of insomnia sufferers, Hall and co-workers found that even when subjects managed to fall asleep, the number of stress-related intrusive thoughts, the overall stress burden and depression all increased the risk of insomnia and undermined sleep quality. However, in many cases there is no need to take a sleeping pill. Simple self-help strategies can help you get a good night's sleep.

Everyone suffers from insomnia at one time or another. Jet lag, nerves, bereavement and general stress can lead to a few sleepless nights, for example. Indeed, Leger notes that a quarter of adults say that they suffer from insomnia (although only around one in four complains about their disordered sleep to a doctor). Insomnia leaves sufferers worn out, irritable and stressed. It can also prove dangerous. A sleepless night reduces alertness, concentration and your ability to cope with stress. And for some occupations – pilots, taxi and lorry drivers and doctors, for example – poor concentration or falling asleep during the day may threaten the lives of themselves and others.

What is sleep?

Considering that we spend a third of our lives asleep we know remarkably little about it. Some specialists believe that sleep helps us recuperate. Other researchers see sleep as 'mental downtime' which allows us to process the day's input of sensations, information and experiences. Still others suggest that sleep evolved to keep us out of danger at night. (Of course, these theories aren't mutually exclusive.) But there is no doubt that sleep is more complex than unconsciousness punctuated by dreams.

Recordings of the brain's electrical activity reveal that sleep consists of five main stages. One stage, rapid eye movement (REM) sleep, is associated with dreaming and may contribute to learning, memory and mood. REM sleep usually accounts for around a quarter of normal sleep. Another stage, called slow wave sleep, occurs during two of the four non-REM stages we go through each night and may assist rest and recuperation. In normal adults, there are five non-REM/REM cycles, organised into a pattern known as the sleep architecture.

How much sleep is normal?

Most of us sleep for around seven or eight hours a night, but the amount of sleep we need varies widely. Some people get away with five or six hours, while others need ten. The amount of sleep we need changes with age. Babies sleep for up to 16 hours a day; teenagers need about 10 hours; young adults need eight hours; and the middle-aged and elderly less than seven hours. As we get older, the biological clock controlling the sleep-wake cycle begins to wind down. As a result, many elderly patients nap during the day, so they sleep less at night and complain of insomnia. Sleep quality is more important than quantity: you are getting enough if you don't feel sleepy, tired, lethargic and apathetic during the day.

What is insomnia?

Strictly speaking, insomnia is a total inability to sleep. However, most people who say that they suffer from insomnia do get some sleep. Time drags during the night and insomniacs often overestimate the amount of time they spend awake. Insomnia is highly subjective and attitudes about how much sleep is normal colour patients' expectations. Insomnia also takes various forms:

- **initial insomnia**: patients experience difficulties falling asleep. This is especially common with stress or anxiety

- **sleep maintenance insomnia**: patients wake frequently during the night
- **terminal insomnia**: patients wake early in the morning and cannot fall asleep again – this is a hallmark of depression
- **conditioned insomnia**: patients sleep terribly at home, but well on business trips or in front of the TV – in other words, they associate their bed and bedroom with not sleeping. Entering the bedroom makes them more alert, which makes it harder to sleep.

Stress, anxiety, depression, chronic pain and a variety of other diseases can either cause or contribute to any of the four types of insomnia.

How to get a good night's sleep

The first step is to treat any underlying condition that could contribute to insomnia. For example, the chronic pain of arthritis can leave patients unable to sleep. Similarly, Elsenbruch and colleagues found that suffering from irritable bowel syndrome (IBS) – a physical disease closely associated with stress (see pages 146–51) – undermined sleep quality and increased daytime fatigue. Patients reported both insomnia and that sleep wasn't restful. However, managing the underlying condition helps the sufferer get a good night's rest (the treatments for IBS are explained in Chapter 6).

Similarly, approaching the menopause proves a stressful time for many women. And Owens and Matthews found that 42 per cent of women reported sleep disturbances around the menopause (which might arise from hot flushes, for example). Being anxious, depressed, stressed, tense and self-conscious in public increased the likelihood that the woman would experience sleep disturbances. Jones and Czajkowski suggest the management of sleep disturbances in menopausal women should incorporate stress management, coping strategies, improving relationships, and good sleep hygiene. Some women might find that hormone replacement therapy (HRT), which alleviates many common symptoms around the menopause (see page 165), can help them sleep better.

Sleep apnoea

Sleep apnoea can leave sufferers – and their partners – tired, stressed and irritable. People with the condition snore loudly and stop breathing for a several seconds. Obese and overweight people are especially prone to develop sleep apnoea, partly because fat in the neck may squeeze the windpipe. Most people with sleep apnoea have no recollection of waking many times in the night. However, they complain of feeling excessively tired during the day. Sleep apnoea can contribute to serious medical conditions such as hypertension and heart disease. It may also lead to road traffic accidents because of tiredness at the wheel. Weight loss, as well as avoiding alcohol and sleeping pills can help manage sleep apnoea. If you suffer from sleep apnoea – if you have a partner, he or she will be able to tell you – consult a doctor. A technique called continuous positive airway pressure (CPAP) can keep the airways open at night and resolve the tiredness. The British Snoring and Sleep Apnoea Association* provides information about the condition.

Good sleep hygiene

You can take a number of steps to help you sleep better without resorting to sleeping pills. Following these good sleep hygiene tips should help tackle your insomnia.

- Create wind-down or relaxation time at the end of the day, so you don't go straight to bed while your mind is still active.
- Go to bed at the same time each night and set your alarm for the same time each morning – including weekends. This helps re-establish a regular sleep pattern.
- Try not to take your troubles to bed with you. Stress keeps you awake. Brooding on your problems makes them seem worse, exacerbates stress, keeps you awake and – as you're tired in the morning – means you are less able to deal with your difficulties.
- Don't worry about anything you've forgotten to do. Get up. Note what you have to do. This should help you forget it until

the morning. You could keep a notepad by your bed if this proves a persistent problem.

- If you're going to have a heavy discussion, try not to have it just before you go to bed. Emotional upsets can lead to a disturbed night.
- Avoid naps during the day.
- Avoid stimulants such as nicotine and caffeine for several hours before bed. The amount of time will depend on your sensitivity to these substances – you might have to avoid from mid-afternoon, for example. Remember that tea, coffee, cocoa, cola, energy drinks and some over-the-counter medications contain caffeine (check the label).
- Try hot milk: milky drinks help some people sleep. However, too much fluid in the evening can mean regular nocturnal trips to the bathroom.
- Avoid heavy drinking during the evening or alcohol at bedtime. Many insomniacs believe that an alcoholic nightcap helps them sleep. In fact, alcohol has the opposite effect. A nightcap may help you fall asleep and enable you to sleep more deeply during the first third of the night, but as blood alcohol levels fall sleep becomes lighter and more fragmented, and drinkers tend to wake repeatedly during the latter half of the night. Furthermore, alcohol increases the volume and amount of snoring, which can leave your partner unable to sleep.
- Try eating a light meal in the early evening rather than a curry an hour before bedtime. Heavily spiced meals often disrupt sleep. Some people find, however, that a light snack before bed staves off any hunger pangs that keep them awake.
- Regular exercise during the day helps you sleep, but exercising just before you go to bed can make insomnia worse.
- A hot bath helps, and relaxation techniques (see pages 228–30) can relax tense muscles.
- Use the bed for sleep and sex only. Don't work or watch TV in bed. This helps you associate the bed with sleep.
- Make the bed as comfortable as possible. Sleep on a comfortable mattress, with enough bedclothes.
- Make sure the bedroom isn't too hot, too cold or too bright. Blackout curtain lining can help.
- Try to limit sudden noise. You can sleep against a considerable amount of background noise – provided the volume is constant.

Indeed, some people find that white noise – the random sounds produced by a fan, for example – aids sleep.

- If you still can't sleep, don't lie there worrying about your insomnia: there's nothing worse for keeping you awake. Get up and read or watch TV until you feel tired. Then go back to bed.

Good sleep hygiene often helps overcome insomnia without the need for sleeping pills. However, even after sticking to the rules a 'hard core' of insomniacs remain unable to get a good night's rest. If you find that the good sleep hygiene techniques don't work and there is a specific cause for insomnia, such as bereavement, consider taking a short course of sleeping tablets. These can help re-establish a normal sleep pattern while the sleep hygiene techniques begin to work. But it's important not to rely on sleeping pills as a long-term solution to your insomnia. We'll return to the role of sleeping tablets in treating insomnia later.

Beating jet lag

Worldwide plane travel for business and pleasure is now commonplace. However, travel can be associated with a number of health problems. For example, Rogers and Reilly commented that between 36 and 54 per cent of international business travellers experience health problems such as traveller's diarrhoea and insomnia, while 6 to 18 per cent suffer accidents and injuries while abroad. Poor sleep quality resulting from jet lag can contribute to accidents. Fortunately, a few simple steps can help you beat jet lag.

- Avoid stimulants during the flight, including coffee, tea and cola.
- Avoid caffeine after arriving at your destination.
- Avoid alcohol during the flight – alcohol promotes dehydration. As mentioned above, alcohol can also disrupt sleep.
- Take some exercise, especially outdoors. Light helps to reset your internal biological clock.
- Try to keep going once you arrive; sleep as little as possible until the night after landing or until the local bedtime.
- A sleeping tablet, such as zopiclone and zolpidem, can help establish a local sleep pattern. These can only be obtained from a doctor on prescription.

A brief history of sleeping pills

We have been searching for ways to get a good night's sleep for millennia. Our ancestors tried blood letting, elaborate ceremonies to local gods, and concoctions made from snakes and geese as insomnia remedies. The Ancient Egyptians drank wine and probably used opium in sleeping potions. Insomniacs continued to use opium well into the nineteenth century. Victorian England overcame insomnia with bromide, paraldehyde, laudanum and chloral hydrate. Only chloral hydrate is still used today, and then only very rarely. The early years of this century saw the launch of the first barbiturates, but at a price. Barbiturates are highly addictive, interact with alcohol and other drugs, and are lethal in overdose.

In the 1960s the benzodiazepines were launched. The first benzodiazepines, including chlordiazepoxide (Librium) and diazepam (Valium), were tranquillisers. The first benzodiazepine specifically for insomnia was nitrazepam (Mogadon) launched in 1965. Benzodiazepines are much safer than barbiturates and, at the time, doctors believed incorrectly that they were non-addictive. They quickly became the nation's favourite sleeping pills.

Despite their popularity, sleeping pills have a limited impact – they cause a 15-minute reduction in the time it takes people to fall asleep and enable them to spend perhaps 30 or 40 minutes longer asleep. Furthermore, over the years doctors have recognised that benzodiazepines had important disadvantages. For example, they can cause rebound insomnia. In other words, when long-term benzodiazepine users stop taking the tablets, the insomnia returns: sometimes worse than ever.

Benzodiazepines are highly addictive. Their effect on sleep begins to decline in as little as three weeks. Some patients take higher doses to get the same effect, but most remain on the same – possibly ineffective – dose. This cycle of reduced effect leading to increasing dose can lead to addiction. Furthermore, many benzodiazepines are long-acting. As a result, a user's blood concentration in the morning can be high enough to produce a 'hangover' and affect daytime performance, such as driving ability. Less commonly, benzodiazepines can cause amnesia, especially of short-term memory.

So is there ever a role for sleeping tablets? Newer sleeping pills, such as zaleplon, zopiclone and zolpidem, are prescribed for only 10 to 14 days at a time. They are not approved for long-term use and zopiclone and zolpidem can lead to dependence in some patients. Nevertheless, by relieving the burden of insomnia, these short courses give you time to deal with your underlying stress and give the sleep hygiene techniques a chance to work. However, it is worth stressing again that you can't rely on sleeping pills as a long-term solution to insomnia.

Using herbs to treat insomnia

Western herbalists still use a number of plants, including hops, skullcap and valerian, to treat insomnia. Some of the herbal remedies undoubtedly work. But the same criticisms apply to many herbal remedies as to sleeping pills: they don't tackle the cause of the insomnia and can cause side effects. If you want to try a herbal remedy you might do better to consult a qualified medical herbalist rather than buying a formulation from a health shop.

Beating fatigue

If you don't get a good night's sleep, you'll probably find that you feel fatigued. However, you can give yourself a boost. Coffee, for example, which contains caffeine, is the most widely used way to provide stimulation. According to legend, an Ethiopian holy man discovered coffee when he noticed that goats eating the bush's berries frisked all night. Yemeni farmers cultivated coffee in the ninth century and it was introduced to the West about 700 years later. But coffee was not welcomed with open arms. Seventeenth-century Parisians were warned that coffee shortened life. Germans in the eighteenth century could be caned for drinking coffee and King Frederick II of Prussia tried to get his subjects to switch from coffee to beer for the good of their health.

You can also drink teas, colas and energy drinks that contain caffeine. Some energy drinks can contain quite high levels of caffeine, though there is no evidence that they offer any benefit over that produced by coffee. So look at the label.

> **Go easy on guarana**
>
> Brazilian Indians drink guarana in the same way we consume coffee or tea. However, guarana contains around twice as much caffeine by weight than either coffee beans or dried tea leaves. Coffee beans and tea contain 1 to 2 and 1 to 4 per cent caffeine respectively. Guarana contains between 3 to 5 per cent. So some drinks and other products containing guarana can pack a considerable caffeine punch – read the can or packet carefully.

Caffeine is valued for its effects on the mind. Doses of caffeine between 85 and 200mg reduce drowsiness and fatigue, and improve alertness and productivity. A cup of brewed coffee contains around 100 to 200mg, a cup of instant coffee 60 to 80mg and a cup of tea 40 to 100mg. Energy drinks may contain far more. The more tea and coffee you drink, the greater the improvement. However, too much caffeine – over about 600mg per day – can cause headaches, irritability, tremor, palpitations and nervousness. Regular drinkers become tolerant to caffeine's effects – so you may need to brew stronger coffee to get the same effect – and caffeine's effects are short-lived. Nevertheless, caffeine remains the most popular way to boost flagging energy levels and is safe in small doses.

Food to fight fatigue

Skipping breakfast, gobbling a chocolate bar at coffee time or grabbing a sandwich on the run between meetings and flushing it down with cola isn't the best way to beat fatigue. The sugar in chocolate and soft drinks is called sucrose. Sucrose is rapidly absorbed and broken down into glucose, which your cells use to fuel their activities. The body absorbs and metabolises the complex carbohydrates in pasta, potatoes and whole grains more slowly. So the supply of glucose from these foods is more constant. In other words, sugary drinks or chocolate provide an instant boost – but it is quickly burned off. After reaching a 'peak', blood sugar levels plummet. Some researchers believe these fluctuating blood sugar levels can promote fatigue. They can make you feel hungry quicker. If you want to give yourself a longer-lasting energy boost, take a tip from athletes who eat vegetables, whole grains and fruits before a race. This can help you overcome daytime tiredness.

Insomnia is common and can dramatically undermine quality of life. In some cases, the daytime fatigue can be dangerous, contributing to accidents, for example. However, the few simple steps outlined in this section should help you get a good night's sleep.

Part 3

Stress-busting techniques to put you in control

Chapter 10

The anti-stress toolkit

The preceding chapters have examined the causes of stress and explored the link between excessive stress and physical and psychological illnesses. They have also suggested ways you can identify the problems that cause you stress and develop a plan to tackle them using assertive coping. This chapter looks at 25 ways you can bolster your stress defences, which might form an element of your personal coping plan.

You can regard this chapter as a toolkit. Read through it until you find those approaches that you feel could help you either counter the causes of your stress or bolster your defences generally so you can deal more effectively with the ups and downs of modern life. Then implement the changes in your life – you might find that the stages of change model in Chapter 3 helps.

In some ways, waiting until you develop symptoms of excessive stress means you have left it too late. Many of the techniques listed in the directory can act as first-aid for stress, but the majority are most effective when used to prevent excessive stress.

(1) Time management

Poor time management is a major causes of stress. So time management techniques can reduce stress, boost productivity and help you get more out of life at work and at home.

Despite what some books and courses suggest, there are no rules in either time or life management. What works for one person may fail hopelessly for another. And some of the most widely quoted time and life management 'rules' seem ideal in theory, but simply do not work in our day-to-day lives. This means that you need to think about every piece of advice and see whether it applies to you, and then take what is useful. Nevertheless, certain principles should help you improve your time management skills. These are discussed in more detail in *Which? Way to Manage Your Time – and your Life*, from Which? Books.★

Perform a time audit

A business truism states that 20 per cent of the effort produces 80 per cent of the results. For example, about 80 per cent of a company's sales probably come from approximately 20 per cent of their customers. One could argue about the exact percentages. However, you could aim to rewrite this equation so that you spend around 80 per cent of your time on your priorities.

It is up to you to decide what these priorities are and what proportion of your time you need to spend on each activity. However, before you can decide this, you need to know where the time goes, whether you are in an office or at home.

Performing a time audit is the most effective way to examine your commitments, although it can be laborious and takes some self-discipline. However, it is worth making the effort because it tells you, for example, how you *really* spend your time, as opposed to how you *think* you spend your time. The two can be very different. There are two ways to audit your time:

- Note how long you spend performing *each* task, without changing to something else. This means *everything*. For a few days, you need to note how long you spend making coffee, chatting about the football and even going to the loo. You need to include interruptions, checking your mail and making calls. In some cases, you may find that you spend only a few minutes on a task before becoming distracted. You will probably only be motivated to do this for a couple of days. However, it is a powerful way to underline just how uncontrolled your daily life is and how minor interruptions can have a profound impact on your time and your stress levels. Remember that a sense of being 'out of control' is a key factor driving stress.

- Divide a piece of paper into 15- to 30-minute sections. At the end of each hour, write one description of how you spent each chunk of time. The problem with this method is that it fails to detect minor time thieves, such as interruptions that may take only two or three minutes, but which soon add up over the course of the day. It is often difficult to get going again once you have been disturbed, so such interruptions can be disruptive out of all proportion to their duration.

It is also worth performing a time audit if your main role is at home. How much time do you spend at the supermarket? How many times do you visit it each week? How much time do you spend at school coffee mornings? How much time do you spend on your hobbies? Note it all down. You should then be able to see why you cannot get a few minutes to yourself.

Enhance your productivity

Once you have performed your time audit, you can work towards enhancing your productivity. List the core tasks uncovered by your time audit and add up the time they currently take. This should allow you to see whether most of your time goes on the tasks that are both important and urgent (see box on page 223). Now set yourself a target time for each task. Try not to be over-ambitious – you do not want to sacrifice quality in the pursuit of speed. However, most of us can shave between five and ten per cent off each task, especially by limiting the impact of the smaller time thieves (interruptions and so on).

Over the next couple of weeks, record how you are doing. Some tasks will prove impossible to perform more quickly. Others you will find you can do in much less time. For example, you may be able to save several hours by going to the supermarket once a week instead of daily. The only way you will know is to track your time.

Use your diary

You probably already have a diary. Indeed, you may have several. However, it is better to use one diary for both your business and personal commitments. This avoids confusion and clashes, as well as helping you balance your work, family and personal life. You can also use your diary to plan long-term projects and use the year-to-view to mark on holidays, conferences and so on. You should set or agree your long-term deadlines in line with this view. As soon as you know which meetings you are expected to attend, mark your holidays.

Keep a 'to do' list

A 'to do' list is fundamental to effective and efficient time management. Obviously, this lists your tasks along with any deadlines. Most time management books suggest that you should have a master list as well as a daily list, which you update each night. Advocates of this approach argue that the daily update helps clear your mind of any problems and stops you worrying overnight. So you might find it reduces your stress levels and helps you sleep. Your 'to do' lists could also categorise certain tasks: writing, calls, emails and personal priorities. It is worth considering this if you need to perform a number of similar tasks – you tend to be more effective if you perform these in batches.

You should also break each large task down into smaller, more manageable pieces. This applies just as much to a major report analysing a market as it does to moving house. Try to define the task in a sentence. Then work out the broad stages that will allow you to reach the aim. For a report, for example, these stages might include: research, discussions, writing, revising and presentation. Then break each of these stages down into tasks. So, for the research stage, the tasks might include: visits to other companies; going to libraries; Internet searches; and so on. Then order these tasks in a logical progression and add these to your 'to do' list. In this way, a large project suddenly becomes much less daunting – and, therefore, less stressful.

Once you have your master list, you need to establish your priorities. In some cases, this may mean simply picking the highest-priority job from the list and working your way down. You also need to prioritise your daily list. It is worth, if you can, interspersing dull tasks with interesting ones as well as alternating physical and mental tasks.

There are several ways in which you can prioritise your 'to do' list. The simplest is to mark each task from '1' (highest urgency) to '10', or whatever is the least urgent. A more sophisticated approach considers whether each task is urgent, important, both or neither (see box opposite). Many people tend to tackle urgent jobs first, irrespective of their importance. As a result, they need to devote less quality time to their important tasks. So the quality of their work inevitably suffers. Assigning a value to each of these helps us to stop performing urgent or routine tasks simply out of habit.

Is it urgent? Important? Or both?

Mark each task on your daily and master lists as follows:

- **A important and urgent** You should do these tasks now.
- **B important and less urgent** These are tasks that you need to do in the next couple of days, but at a time you are at your most efficient and effective.
- **C less important but urgent** These are tasks that you need to do in the next couple of days, but do not require you to be at your best.
- **D less important and less urgent** You can do these tasks at your convenience. Consider delegation.
- **E unimportant and not urgent** If it needs to be done some time, delegate. However, it might be better to bin it.

When you prioritise your work the first few times, you will probably find that almost everything on your 'to do' list is a high priority. However, with practice you will find that you are better able to assess a task's priority accurately. On the other hand, if, after careful consideration, you still face a number of important and urgent jobs, you have two choices. You could go for the shortest first; many people find that finishing a job gives them a psychological boost and the momentum carries over into other jobs on their list. Or you could tackle the most difficult and boring first – at least this way the dullest job is dispensed with. The choice is really up to you – go for whichever approach causes you the least stress.

You need to keep your prioritisation up-to-date. In many cases, this may mean that you need to spend time each day rewriting the list, transferring the undone tasks to the next list, reassigning priorities and deciding how important and urgent new tasks are. The time you spend organising your workload pays itself back in improved effectiveness. However, if this takes up a considerable amount of time each day, consider investing in a personal information manager or palmtop computer. But, if you continually fail to reach your objectives, ask yourself:

- Am I trying to do much in too short a time?
- Could I have been better prepared?
- Did I assign the priorities correctly?
- Was there an unexpected interruption that threw my plans?
- Did I lack self-discipline?
- Were the tasks boring or too demanding?
- Did I procrastinate?
- Am I having problems with a particular person?

If a pattern emerges, see if you can identify what is stopping you from meeting your priorities, and whether there is anything you can do to improve the situation.

Be flexible

In our constantly changing world you need to remain flexible. If an unexpected problem upsets your carefully devised schedule, deal with the immediate problem and then re-evaluate your schedule. At home, try being more flexible in some of your expectations of your relationships with your spouse and children. Your kids probably know how you will react to a certain situation. Indeed, they may use this knowledge to provoke an argument or land the first strike. So relaxing your expectations defuses many potentially stressful problems before they arise. But, remember: being flexible is not the same as being a walkover. Transactional analysis (pages 64–66) might help you avoid problems at home and at work.

Learning to 'just say no'

Agreeing to an unreasonable demand from a boss, partner or child is probably one of the leading time-wasters and a major cause of stress. How many hours and weeks do you waste simply because you do not say no when you have the chance? No doubt you say 'yes' to please someone. But who are you trying to please? How effective will you be if you are doing something that you do not really want to do? And how much does this contribute to your stress?

You have to learn to say no to any demand that you feel is unreasonable, either because you do not have sufficient time or because the demand does not fit with your personal ethical view. You may even gain respect for knowing when to say no. After all, it is far worse to agree to a request and then back out. Therefore, before agreeing, ensure that you know what you are letting yourself in for. Some tasks can be more time-consuming than they appear. (As a rule of thumb, add between 10 and 25 per cent to any time estimate to help cover the unexpected.) You could also put a time limit on your commitment – say that you will be able to help only for a couple of hours a week, for example – and stick to it.

If your boss makes an unreasonable demand, remind him or her of your other high-priority tasks, and ask which need to be sacrificed. Do not feel guilty about this – deciding between competing high-priority tasks is a key management skill. If you are the manager, try to decide which aspects of the work you need to perform and which you can delegate or reassign among your staff.

It is also worth helping out your boss. Explain, for example, that you cannot work on a particular project immediately but will be able to the following week. This can be difficult to broach, especially given the pressure placed on people at work, but it will become easier with practice. Again, the techniques of transactional analysis (pages 64–66) can help.

Which? Way to Manage your Time – and Your Life explores further the techniques you can use to control your time – and your life in general.

(2) Dealing with anger

When you're stressed, anger can soon follow. However, it is generally an inappropriate reaction. There is some evidence that anger can contribute to certain diseases (see pages 155–6). And getting excessively cross can make you feel more stressed out. So try these approaches to deal with anger.

- Think of the consequences: is it worth losing your temper at a child's tantrum or because you've been cut up at a road junction?
- Use visualisation. Imagine situations where you become angry. Imagine the situation in enough detail and you will probably feel anger and annoyance welling up inside you. So try to remain calm. Staying calm when you imagine a stress-provoking situation makes it easier to stay calm when you face the reality. Sportspeople often use a similar technique to help them cope in stressful situations (see pages 245–46).

- Some people find that regular exercise reduces a tendency to become angry.
- Take several deep breaths when you feel your temper rising. Counting to ten really can help.
- Meditation (see below) might help you develop a calmer approach to life.
- Try to identify and change type A forms of behaviour (see page 29), such as time urgency, hostility and anger. If you want to know whether you suffer from time urgency, try taking your watch off at work one morning or afternoon when you don't have a meeting. Then see how tense you feel. Time management techniques can help modify this sort of behaviour.
- Take up creative leisure pursuits that provide a healthy diversion from the daily routine. Do something that cannot be rushed, such as yoga, pottery or gardening.

(3) Meditation

Meditation is undoubtedly an effective way to help you relax and build your defences against the daily onslaught of potentially stressful events. We've seen how stress can worsen numerous physical and psychological conditions. Many people find that meditation can help to alleviate the symptoms of a number of stress-related diseases including hypertension (high blood pressure), insomnia, addictions and asthma. (However, don't stop taking – or reduce the dose of – any medication without consulting your doctor first.). Meditation can also offer an effective counterbalance to stress in our lives generally.

Classically, meditation involves sitting quietly on a mat, legs crossed and focusing on your breathing or a saying (mantra) for a total of 20 to 60 minutes a day. Transcendental meditation (TM) requires two daily sessions of between 15 and 20 minutes. This may seem a considerable time commitment in a busy life. However, meditators usually find that taking the time to meditate helps them to achieve more with less effort. After a while, meditation can become part of the coping strategies that you can call on when stressed.

To learn to meditate correctly, you really need to seek instruction from a teacher. However, you can try meditation for yourself before investing time and money on a course. Many people teach themselves using tapes, for example. Ideally, meditation is done in a quiet space. Sit comfortably: this does not need to be the full, cross-legged lotus position – a chair is fine. Alternatively, sit on a cushion on the floor with your back against the wall. Avoid lying down as it is easy to fall asleep. You need to ensure that you are able to sit still for around 20 minutes without being distracted by cramps and other aches and pains.

Now breathe deeply. Meditation teachers emphasise that most people tend to breathe into their chest instead of their abdomen. The teachers argue that by concentrating on breathing into the abdomen, we can learn to breathe slowly and deeply in stressful situations. Imposing this internal control seems to help meditators master external stresses. As a result, stress and difficult situations are less likely to seem overwhelming.

Now focus your attention – which, as anyone who has tried meditation knows, is much easier said than done. TM practitioners use a mantra – a personal phrase or saying given to them by their teacher. However, for this experiment, choose your own mantra. It does not have to be an exotic phrase. You could try 'om' but any simple, non-emotive word or sound will do, even if it is nonsense. The aim is to focus your attention on a single point. Repeat the phrase over and over in your mind. If your mind starts to wander bring it back to focusing on the mantra. The aim is to focus your mind on the repeated word. This brings your attention down to a single point and it is this, meditators believe, that is the key to the benefits of meditation.

Alternatively, you could also try focusing on your breath as it moves in and out of your nose and mouth. You could also focus on a candle flame or crystal. These all concentrate your mind and exclude distractions. 'Mindfulness' meditation involves four stages: counting up to ten after each breath; counting up to ten before each breath; focusing on the movement of breath in and out of your lungs; and focusing on the movement of breath in and out of your nostrils. Each stage lasts for five minutes, which helps you to stay focused and aware of time. Maintaining concentration for 20 minutes is far harder than it sounds. You will probably find that your mind wanders off. Just accept these ramblings and re-focus your attention on the subject. Do not become annoyed with yourself.

If practised regularly, meditation can bring about mental and emotional calm. If you meditate without the support of an experienced teacher, worries and fears may surface that can increase stress levels. If this happens, don't dismiss meditation but find a teacher you feel comfortable with. Many adult education centres now run relaxation and meditation courses. Courses can be expensive, but some teachers will accept donations that you feel you can afford – check before you enrol.

Transcendental Meditation (TM)* is taught across the UK. However, while TM has the highest profile, it is not the only approach. The Buddhist Society* can put you in touch with teachers of traditional Buddhist and Zen meditation. Various Christian meditation groups also exist – your local church may have details. People who suffer from schizophrenia or other serious psychological illness are advised to seek medical advice first, as meditation may not be suitable for them.

(4) Relaxation

If meditation does not appeal – and it does not suit everyone – you could try relaxation techniques. Relaxation doesn't mean flopping in front of the TV. It is an 'active' process. Find a quiet room where you can sit in a comfortable chair or lie down. Take the phone off the hook and ensure that the lighting is low. Make yourself comfortable and wear comfortable clothes. The room should not be too hot or cold. You could listen to some gentle music or a guided-relaxation tape.

Think about your breathing. Most of us breathe shallowly, using the upper parts of our lungs. However, to relax, you need to breathe deeply and slowly without gasping. Put one hand on your chest and the other on your abdomen. Breathe normally. You may find – especially if you are tense – that the hand on your chest moves, while the hand on the abdomen remains almost still. The hand on your stomach should rise and fall, while the one on your chest hardly alters.

You can then use one of two approaches: *progressive muscular relaxation* or *tension-relaxation*. Whichever of the techniques you choose, try to schedule a relaxation session every day. You might find that first thing in the morning is the best time; some people find that using these techniques last thing at night sends them to sleep. Do not try them after a meal – when your stomach is full, blood diverts from your muscles to your stomach, and trying to relax tense muscles when blood is diverted from them can cause cramps. Furthermore, relaxation, like meditation, increases your awareness of your body's functions, and a full stomach can prove a distraction.

During progressive muscular relaxation, you aim to relax each part of your body in turn. After a few deep breaths, start at your toes. Say to yourself: 'My toes are tingling … They are becoming numb … they are getting heavier and heavier … the tension is draining away,' and so on. Then repeat this with your calves. Then move to your thighs and gradually work your way up your body. Once you reach your forehead, rest for a few minutes before standing up.

During tension-relaxation, you tense a muscle for around ten seconds before relaxing. You repeat this cycle of tension-relaxation three times. The key is to tense your muscles slowly, gently and gradually. Inhale as you tense each muscle, breathe normally as you keep it tense, and then exhale as you relax. You are trying to relax, not build up your muscles. Then rest for a couple of minutes and then tense and relax the muscle another three times. After another rest, tense and relax the muscle a final three times. In other words, you need to tense and then relax the muscle nine times. Then move on to the next part of the body.

You can try tension-relaxation by putting your hands by your side. Inhale and clench your fist as hard as you can. Hold for ten seconds, while breathing normally. Now exhale and slowly relax. Alternatively, try the shoulder shrug – which is useful if you spend hours using a keyboard. Inhale and shrug your shoulder as high as you can. Hold for ten seconds while breathing normally. Now exhale and slowly let your shoulders drop. Another useful exercise to use at work is to drop your head forward until your chin touches your chest. Hold for ten seconds, and then slowly move the head to one side towards your shoulder while keeping your gaze towards the floor. Hold for ten seconds, and then slowly move your head to the other side. However, do not roll your head or put your head right back. This can damage your spine.

Many people who teach tension-relaxation exercises believe that you should master each muscle before moving to the next. This means that it may take two or three months before you can work around your whole body. It is worth making the effort. After a while, you will come to recognise which muscles are tense. Many of us live for years with considerable muscle tension – we have become so used to the feeling we no longer recognise it as abnormal. However, once you know that a muscle is tense you can target it with an appropriate exercise.

Relaxation is undoubtedly an effective way to unwind, reduce anxiety and bolster your stress defences. Relaxation can optimise blood supply to the muscles, reduce oxygen use and muscle activity as well as slowing the heartbeat and breathing. Some days you will find it easier to relax than others – but do not give up. After a while, relaxation sessions will become part of your everyday life. You should find that you feel less tired and less stressed. People with schizophrenia or other serious psychological illnesses should seek advice before trying relaxation techniques.

Flotation therapy

Flotation therapy is a form of sensory deprivation in which your body and mind are isolated from external stimuli. You lie in a tank filled with salty water about 25cm deep. The water is kept at skin temperature and flotation usually takes place in complete or semi-darkness. Some people find flotation therapy very relaxing, and studies suggest that it can reduce the levels of stress hormones in the body. Flotation tanks are found at health clubs or specially designed float centres. People with a history of psychosis or severe psychological illness should talk to their doctor before trying flotation therapy.

---

(5) Assertiveness training

Feeling in control is one of the strongest stress defences. Nurturing this feeling means being assertive when you need to be. If this doesn't come naturally, assertiveness training helps you stand up for your rights without infringing anyone else's. Perhaps most importantly assertiveness training teaches you to be able to say 'no' without feeling guilty. Always saying yes to every request inevitably causes stress – through lack of time if nothing else.

During assertiveness training you may act out situations where you need to be assertive – an unreasonable, last-minute request from your boss to work late that conflicts with other plans, for example. The trainer then comments on your performance, including your voice and body language. Many adult education centres run assertiveness training. Contact your local library or local adult education centre for details.

(6) Counselling

Despite – or perhaps because of – the continuing erosion of family and community support, many people still need someone to talk to. The Samaritans,★ for instance, receive more than four million calls a year – about one every nine seconds – and the number of calls increased by 30 per cent between the mid-1980s and mid-1990s. Trained counsellors also help support people though stressful times.

Counselling seems to work best when you suffer from a defined problem that benefits from a new perspective. You can also undergo counselling for specific problems, such as anger management, bereavement, disabilities and pre-menstrual tension (PMT). Indeed, counselling can be as effective as drugs for relatively minor psychiatric conditions, such as some cases of anxiety, milder depression (especially when linked to life events such as grief or the menopause) and obsessions.

There are more than 11,000 counsellors currently practising in the UK. This means that almost everyone will be able to find someone they can talk to easily. Remember that the relationship between a client and counsellor can be intimate: trust is essential when you are airing your hopes, fears and anxieties. So you need to find someone you feel comfortable with.

Many GPs either employ or have close links to a local counsellor. You can drop in to your practice and ask at reception whether they can recommend someone. The British Association for Counselling and Psychotherapy★ can also put you in touch with counsellors in your area.

Next, interview the counsellor. Most counsellors hold an initial consultation to ask you about your problems and background. You can use this initial consultation to ensure that you are happy exposing your thoughts and feelings to this person. Ask about the counsellor's experience, qualifications and even interests beyond work; obtain references if you wish. However, counselling is also about empathy, and so it is important that you feel comfortable in the counsellor's company.

Alternatively, support groups – such as Cruse★ (bereavement), The Compassionate Friends★ (bereaved parents), Cry-sis★ (sleepless crying babies) and Relate★ (marriage and relationship guidance) can counsel you about specific problems.

Life coaches can offer a new perspective on your problems and how to move forward. Many life coaches advertise locally. You can read about how to apply the principles practised by life coaches in books such as Eileen Mulligan's *Life Coaching* and Fiona Harrold's *Be Your Own Life Coach*.

(7) Cognitive behavioural therapy

Cognitive behavioural therapy (CBT) aims to replace a destructive thought pattern with a more realistic and positive approach by helping clients take responsibility for their behaviour. Essentially, CBT aims to replace unhelpful strategies with behaviour and attitudes that move you towards assertive coping. As such, CBT can help resolve inappropriate coping strategies that contribute to stress.

CBT begins by analysing your unhelpful coping strategies. Typically, clients keep a diary identifying and recording negative thoughts around the problem, such as depression, a phobia etc. This reveals the behaviour that you need to change. The analysis also uncovers the conditions that trigger, maintain and exacerbate the unhelpful coping strategies. So you might learn how these negative thoughts relate to your symptoms of anxiety and depression, for example.

Next the therapist helps you look at the evidence for and against the negative thoughts and explains how to replace them with ideas more firmly rooted in reality. After a while, the person may learn to identify, ignore and, ultimately, change deep-seated negative beliefs. Using a mixture of several techniques, the therapist then encourages positive behaviour and replaces a destructive thought pattern with a more realistic, positive approach to life.

Behavioural approaches tend work more rapidly than psycho-analysis (see opposite) if you suffer from a specific problem. As we've noted throughout this book, behavioural approaches are widely used by psychiatrists to help people suffering from post-traumatic stress disorder, phobias, anxiety, and so on. However, different therapies suit different people. For example, psychotherapy helps people who are unable to adjust to change. It's most successful if the person is articulate, able to see the roots of his or her problems and can cope with delving into painful areas. Behavioural approaches are more appropriate when there is a specific phobia or social skill problem, such as aggression or lack of assertiveness. Psychoanalysis may be more appropriate if you want to understand why you wrote your life script in a particular way.

Contact the United Kingdom Council for Psychotherapy (UKCP)* if you want to find a CBT practitioner. You can also be referred on the NHS.

(8) Psychotherapy and psychoanalysis

There are around 250 varieties of psychotherapy. Some forms of psychotherapy, such as cognitive behavioural therapy (see above), offer practical help for specific problems, without exploring the subconscious. Some – notably psychoanalysis – explore the unconscious causes of the clients' problems and emotions. In this way, psychoanalysis and psychoanalytically based psychotherapy can help clients gain an insight into their problems as well as understanding those past and present relationships that can cause stress.

Psychoanalysis – indeed, psychotherapy generally – is hard work. You need to want to change and believe that therapy will help. In many cases, you will need to make a considerable investment of time and money. Psychoanalysis is often expensive, although some bodies offer reduced fees – the website of the British Confederation of Psychotherapists (BCP)* offers details of lower-cost schemes. While psychoanalysis can ultimately be rewarding and worthwhile, it can also be uncomfortable or distressing. It is inevitably a long process, and might involve several sessions a week for between three and five years.

Psychoanalysts believe that the roots of our psychological distress lie buried in our unconscious. Often these roots are so deeply buried that we are unaware of the causes of our stress or psychological torment. Feeling 'stuck' in life – for example, repeating patterns of relating to other people, or being unable to love or experience joy – is a common reason why people go into psychoanalysis.

Psychoanalysis helps to uncover these roots, which can help the individual to understand his or her problems, subconscious motivations and repressed desires.

You've seen psychoanalysis in the movies. Classically, the analyst sits outside the line of vision, while the client relaxes on a couch. But in modern psychotherapy the analyst sits just to one side and you don't necessarily lie down, you may just sit comfortably. In an analytic session, which lasts 50 minutes, the client is invited to relax and talk about what comes into his or her mind. A thought, a dream or daydream, a memory or a recent event may release a series of other thoughts, memories or feelings. This process is called 'free association'. The client's free associations, unconscious thoughts and feelings become gradually more accessible to consciousness. Through interpretation of the meaning of the client's spoken words (and silences), as well as of their emotional content and the feelings and atmosphere they engender, the analyst seeks to help the patient gain a fuller understanding of his or her unconscious 'internal life', and how this may be influencing current experiences, emotions and relationships.

The main psychoanalytical training bodies are part of the British Confederation of Psychotherapists (BCP).★ There is also a psychoanalytic section of the United Kingdom Council for Psychotherapy (UKCP).★ Children and adolescents who experience problems that might benefit from psychoanalysis can obtain treatment through the NHS and the British Association of Psychotherapists.★ The Association of Child Psychotherapists★ oversees training and standards – contact it to find a local child psychotherapist.

Modern psychoanalysis

There are several different schools of psychoanalysis. Sigmund Freud founded psychoanalysis over 100 years ago. Many of Freud's pioneering ideas on the unconscious remain as important to modern psychoanalysis as ever, but they have been enriched, modified and built upon considerably by succeeding generations of analysts such as Anna Freud, Melanie Klein and the British paediatrician, Donald Winnicott.

Analysts today recognise that Freud's views on children and women reflected the social attitudes of his time and do not necessarily accord with all of modern thinking. Nevertheless, Freud's legacy can provide profound insights into our natures, motivations and 'what makes us tick'.

For example, Freud's theoretical model of the mind describes three components – the id, ego and superego. The id represents our instincts: sexuality, aggression and so on. The ego is our logical, conscious mind. The superego is our internal judge and jury. It is rather like 'conscience', and is an unconscious, 'censoring' agency that often exerts a powerful effect on how we feel. Stress and anxiety, Freudians believe, arise in part when the id's primeval impulses place us in danger or when the superego threatens disapproval or punishment. The ego attempts to deal with the source of the stress. So, for example, the ego drives us to gratify the id's urges. We may explode with anger (or *feel* like doing this) – and then face our superego's retribution. In other words, we feel guilty. But according to Freudians, if the superego is too harsh we may repress the aggression – leaving us passive, uncompetitive and prone to neurotic illness.

Similarly, repression (see pages 37–38) banishes anxiety-provoking thoughts and desires from consciousness. But these repressed thoughts and desires inevitably try to re-surface, causing stress, guilt and anxiety. Alternatively, the repressed thoughts and desires may re-emerge in dreams, when the person is under the influence of drugs or alcohol, or as seemingly irrational thoughts. By exploring the traces of these repressed desires and other unconscious elements, psychoanalysts can form a picture of the internal psychological world of their client, and so help resolve the conflicts, which some clients find alleviates stress and anxiety.

The British Psychoanalytical Society★ represents most psychoanalysts.

Jungian analysts

Carl Jung founded the most important psychoanalytical school to follow in Freud's footsteps. Originally Jung collaborated with Freud. However, Jung came to believe that Freud overemphasised sexuality's role in psychological development and distress. Rather, Jung particularly emphasised the cultural, intellectual and spiritual aspects of our psychological make up. He highlighted the role that society and our environment play in the development of stress, anxiety and other mental problems.

Jung believed that 'neuroses' draw attention to a side of our personality that has been neglected or repressed. Neuroses can signal that the person has been unable to move to a new stage in his or her personal development. Jungian analysts – known as analytical psychologists – help their clients explore their neglected or repressed side or ease them into the next stage of development. This alleviates stress-related symptoms and other neuroses.

For more information contact the Society of Analytical Psychology* or the British Association of Psychotherapists.*

Psychodynamic psychotherapists and brief psychotherapy

Like psychoanalysts, psychodynamic psychotherapists believe that the roots of anxiety and stress lie in the unconscious residues of very early relationships. Psychodynamic psychotherapists work in a similar way to psychoanalysts, although some may tend to take a more active role than traditional analysts. Sessions are usually from one to three times a week, and the analysis extends to the person's work, family and social life. However, the intensity and depth of the work is less than in formal psychoanalysis.

Many psychodynamic psychotherapists use a variation of classical psychoanalysis, called brief psychotherapy. This has more limited – but for many people perhaps more realistic – aims than classical psychoanalysis. Brief psychotherapy doesn't attempt to chart the entire subconscious: rather, it provides an insight into clients' specific problems, conflicts and anxieties in order to resolve symptoms rapidly. For some, this approach is as helpful as traditional analysis, and may be more suitable.

For more information contact the United Kingdom Council for Psychotherapy (UKCP)* and the British Association for Counselling and Psychotherapy (BACP).*

Humanistic psychotherapy

Jung was an optimist. He believed that humanity was essentially positive, idealistic and heroic. This view laid the foundation for humanistic psychotherapy. Humanistic psychotherapists believe that we are driven to fulfil our goals, hopes and ambitions and live peaceful and happy lives. They argue that everyone would grow constructively – if only our circumstances would allow.

Humanistic psychotherapy examines our self-image – which may be radically different to how other people view us. Furthermore, therapists believe children should be raised in environments where they are trusted, respected and loved for who they are – even when they do something that their parents don't approve of. Most parents approve of only certain thoughts and actions. The disapproval surrounding the forbidden thoughts and actions can cause stress and anxiety.

Humanistic psychotherapists alleviate stress by examining and modifying this self-image. First, they help clients understand those feelings and desires they previously denied even to themselves. Secondly, clients explore the cause of their problems. Finally, they learn to act more positively and develop a new, more realistic self-image that adapts to new experiences.

(9) Sort out your finances

Money worries are one of the commonest causes of stress. So sorting out your finances can help markedly reduce your stress levels. However, financial planning is complex and might mean making a considerable investment of time, at least to begin with. Fortunately, several books can help, including *Which? Way to Manage Your Time – and Your Life* and *Be Your Own Financial Adviser* (from Which? Books★). In this section, we'll briefly look at a few simple strategies that can begin to get your finances in order:

- **That's the way the money goes** Remarkably few of us know where our hard-earned money goes. Indeed, according to a 1997 survey by a bank, half of those interviewed did not know their current mortgage payment. A third did not know when they would finally pay off their mortgage. To gain better control of your financial situation, you could keep a diary of how much you spend and on what. This should include everything from the newspaper and cappuccino in the morning to the larger consumer items. Then look at your bank statements to see what you spend on direct debit. Keeping a diary of what you spend can be sobering and, rather like the time audits, takes considerable discipline. Nevertheless, it is a very effective way of tracking your finances when you change your spending habits.
- **Develop a budget** Look at your daily and weekly spending after keeping a money diary for a couple of months and ask

yourself if you are happy about how your money has been spent. Look at the direct debits and see if you can cut back. Break your budget into essential spending (things you genuinely have to spend money on) and desirable purchases you do not strictly need. Consider reducing your essential spending by changing your mortgage lender, switching insurers or gas supplier and so on. Based on this, you can develop a budget that allows you to live within your means and save for the future.

- **Know how much you have in your account** You should keep an eye on your account. Especially if you are making changes to the way that you spend, it is probably worth checking your account more regularly than a monthly statement allows. Fortunately, this is easy now with the Internet, phone banking and statements from cash points. Regularly looking at your balance should help you avoid going overdrawn (or at least limit the size of the debt). But bear in mind that the balance may not be the same as the amount available to spend. Cheques need a few days to clear, although they may appear on your statement before you can access the money. So it is important to keep a running balance and cross-check it regularly with your bank statement. Indeed, if you keep an accurate running balance you will soon gain the confidence to stop checking the state of your account quite so regularly.

- **How much are you worth?** It is also worth keeping an eye on any savings, stocks, shares or ISAs you have. For example, comparing interest rates means you can switch if you spot a better deal. However, with stocks, shares and ISAs you need to take a long-term view and not be too worried by short-term fluctuations in the stock market. For more information, see *The Which? Guide to Shares* (Which? Books★). *Be Your Own Financial Adviser*, also from Which? Books, explains how to organise your finances effectively and choose appropriate investments.

- **Question your direct debits and regular bills** Paying regular bills by direct debit saves time and money: you do not need to write cheques for regular payments and many companies allow a discount for people paying this way. The problem is that it is all too easy to forget about the items you pay by direct debit. Therefore, you need to review your direct debits and regular bills every so often. For example: do you still read the magazines you pay for each year? Are you paying too much on your house or home insurance? You should question each item that you pay for on direct debit and shop around for the best deal. Again, it is the uncontrolled, unconsidered spending habits that you need to address rather than the payment method.

- **Consider consolidating your debts** If you cannot pay them off within a reasonable time, consider pooling your debts into one relatively low-interest loan. Shop around for the best interest rate. A wide variety is now available, especially over the Internet. But this works only if you close your other accounts. Remember that overdrafts, if approved in advance, may be cheaper than credit cards or many other loans. On the other hand, unapproved overdrafts can be more expensive due to the monthly fees charged. Moreover, overdrafts are repayable on demand. So they may not be suitable if you need time to pay off your debts. It all depends on your particular circumstances.

- **Pay back your debts in order of importance** If you are seriously in debt, you should pay your debts in order of importance. For most people, that means the mortgage or rent first; followed by gas, electricity and council tax; then your loans, credit cards and overdrafts. It is essential, if you know that you are beginning to slip into problems, to contact your creditors as soon as possible. This will probably buy you some time, and you may be able to reschedule your payments. Your local Citizens Advice Bureau (look in the phone book) and the National Debtline* offer free debt counselling and may contact creditors on your behalf.

- **Look after the pennies** This somewhat homely piece of advice is a valuable way to help you control your spending. *It does not mean ignoring the big picture*. You need to ensure that you have sorted out the major issues. Nevertheless, looking at the small items allows you to make choices between competing demands on your budget. For instance, a supermarket sandwich, pub lunch or even a cup of coffee on the way to work may not seem like much, but the cost soon adds up into pounds. A car wash costs several pounds. You will probably get a better result – and help yourself stay fit – by washing your own car. Thinking about how much you spend on alcohol and cigarettes can be sobering –

as well as giving you, if you need it, another good reason to quit smoking or control your drinking.

- **Ensure that you take all the tax subsidies you are entitled to** (see *Which? Way to Save Tax* for more information). You may not need to employ an accountant: you can get help and advice for free from the Inland Revenue.★ Be honest – if the Inland Revenue called, could you lay your hands on the paperwork to support your last return? If the answer is 'no', then you need to sort out your paperwork.

(10) Tai chi

Tai chi, the graceful, dance-like exercise performed by millions of people throughout the Far East, is rapidly growing in popularity in the West. It is easy to see why: there is something beautiful and serene in the graceful movements, something far removed from the hectic pace of modern life.

Tai chi looks an undemanding way to unwind – until you try it. Tai chi is mentally, physically and spiritually challenging: mentally, because the forms – the complex series of movements – can involve more than 100 postures; physically, because our unruly bodies are difficult to control; spiritually, because tai chi is a form of moving meditation rooted deep in Eastern philosophy. Indeed, tai chi is a martial art, albeit a non-violent, non-competitive one.

Over 4,000 years ago, Chinese physicians suggested that living in damp, humid conditions stagnates your blood and spirits. They added that you could alleviate this stagnation by performing breathing exercises and a dance that imitated the movements in nature. In common with other forms of traditional Chinese medicine, tai chi aims to balance the flow of Qi (or energy) in the body. Tai chi movements are said to stabilise the two opposing, fluctuating forces of yin and yang, thought to represent the ebb and flow of life. Some other 'soft' martial arts, such as Qi Kung, have a similar philosophy.

The tai chi practised today was developed in the nineteenth century, when Grandmaster Yang Lu-Ch'an founded the Yang style. His grandson and other teachers reorganised the forms into one long, slow series aimed at improving students' health. Since then four other tai chi schools have emerged: Wu, Chen, Woo and Sun. Each differs in the style of the postures and how they link into a form. The Yang style, for example, uses large, open postures. The Chen style typically employs rapid, coiling movements interspersed with slower gentle ones.

Most tai chi styles have two main forms. The short form contains around 30 postures, takes three to ten minutes to perform and can be learnt in about 12 lessons. The longer, more complex form may contain over 100 postures, takes 20 to 40 minutes to perform and a lot longer to learn. Teachers bring their own interpretation to each school. Some concentrate on the spiritual aspects, others emphasise the martial arts side. Nevertheless, all styles integrate three main aspects: meditation, self-defence and healing.

Tai chi undoubtedly helps practitioners relax. The concentration needed to remember even the 30 or so moves of the short forms can distance you from the rat race. Tai chi teachers emphasise the importance of correct breathing – which, again, many people find, helps relieve stress. Older people benefit because the exercise keeps them healthy without making too many demands on their heart. Tai chi also improves flexibility and balance, which helps reduce the risk of falls. It can be adapted for wheelchair users, those recovering from illness or injuries and those with disabilities. However, if you suffer from any medical illness you should consult your doctor before attempting any exercise programme. If your body does not work at its peak, neither does your mind. Tai chi helps develop awareness and a calm mind – again reducing stress. But tai chi is not a quick fix. It takes six months to three years to gain any proficiency. To gain a degree of mastery can take ten years or more.

A number of books and videos are now available that can give you a flavour of tai chi. These should be available from a martial arts shop, or you can try advertisements in a martial arts magazine. However, you should learn the forms from a teacher. Your local library or the Tai Chi Union* can put you in touch with a local teacher.

(11) Yoga

Yoga brings millions of people worldwide some inner peace, relief from stress and improved health. Yoga keeps your mind and body supple. It relaxes and strengthens your stressed-out physique. In other words, yoga is far removed from the image of forcing your body into strange positions in a draughty church hall. Yoga is a complete system that sees every aspect of our lives – consciousness, mind, energy and body – as intertwined. Yoga aims to harmonise these aspects – the Indian root of the word yoga means 'union'.

Yoga is perhaps best known for the postures that improve our control of our bodies. Known as asanas, these postures are more than physical exercises. Correctly performed, asanas involve mental control, correct breathing and using the body with the minimum effort and tension. The postures gently stretch and contract muscles and joints. This allows you to move more freely and improves stamina, flexibility and strength. Practitioners claim asanas train the mind and raise consciousness. A small number of controlled trials also suggest yoga can help health problems including arthritis, diabetes, osteoporosis, high blood pressure and raised cholesterol levels.

Yoga practitioners claim that yoga bolsters your stress defences. For example, many of the events that stress us haven't happened yet – and probably never will. We worry about the future instead of devoting our energy to the present. Yoga, tai chi, meditation and a number of the techniques in this book help practitioners to 'let go' of stress and live in the present.

Yoga also emphasises correct breathing. When you are tense your breaths tend to be shallow and centre on the upper chest. Using breathing exercises that retrain and control the breath, yoga practitioners learn to use the entire lung. Yoga practitioners believe breath control allows them to control their physical and mental processes and helps them attain the ultimate goal of yoga self-enlightenment. Yoga breathing exercises may also bring some more mundane benefits, especially to patients with asthma and other respiratory disorders. However, you should never stop taking your medication or reduce the dose without talking to your doctor first. If you are worried that yoga might be risky for you, consult a doctor or a qualified yoga teacher. Yoga is not recommended during the first 14 weeks of pregnancy, and if you are pregnant you should tell your yoga teacher as you may need to avoid certain positions.

Like meditation, you should aim to perform yoga in a quiet, well-ventilated and warm room. Wear comfortable and light clothes and don't practise on a full stomach. It is best to attend classes run by a professionally trained teacher to learn yoga correctly. Forcing your body into advanced postures before you are ready could lead to injury. Apart from the classes it is a good idea to set aside some time to practise each day – ideally 20 to 30 minutes. The benefits aren't instant. It takes time to learn how to train your body and your mind.

A wide range of books and videos can provide you with a basic understanding of yoga and its benefits. However, you should learn yoga from a teacher. The British Wheel of Yoga★ or the Iyengar Yoga Institute★ can provide further details. Your library or adult education centre may also have details of local courses.

(12) Massage

Massage is one of the oldest stress-relieving techniques. It can relieve muscle tension and promote a sense of well-being and relaxation. As a result, some people find that massage improves stress-related diseases, including tension headaches, fatigue and muscle tension. Several clinical trials have found that massage can reduce levels of anxiety and stress in people who are ill, such as cancer patients, even if it does not alleviate the disease itself. Perhaps most importantly, massage forces you to take time out for yourself – which contributes to its stress-relieving properties.

Depending on the technique, massage may improve blood circulation, stimulate nerves and muscles, and relieve muscle tension and spasm. Using essential oils may enhance the benefits (see 'Aromatherapy', pages 246–47). There are plenty of well-illustrated books available showing various massage techniques for relaxation and health. However, the benefits of do-it-yourself massage are unlikely to be as pronounced as a session with a trained masseur (contact the British Massage Therapy Council★ or the Massage Therapy Institute of Great Britain★). Nevertheless, you can also use the books to explore the erotic possibilities of massage. Certainly, intimate massage can help overcome some stress-causing sexual problems in both men and women.

Japanese massage – shiatsu – is increasingly popular. Shiatsu shares its origins with acupuncture. However, shiatsu is a relatively new technique fusing traditional Japanese massage and osteopathy. Shiatsu masseurs use fingers, elbows, knees and feet to massage various key points around the body. Shiatsu practitioners believe that this helps to rebalance your 'energy'. However, you don't need to believe this to appreciate the physical benefits of the massage. A shiatsu session takes about an hour and each point is pressurised for around seven seconds. You may feel a certain amount of discomfort at first, but it usually disappears after a few sessions. Moreover, most shiatsu practitioners point out that the massage should form part of an overall review of your lifestyle – including diet and mental attitudes. The Shiatsu Society★ is an umbrella organisation for UK practitioners.

You should seek medical advice before having a massage if you have a history of blood clot (thrombosis), varicose veins or inflammation of the veins (phlebitis), a fever, acute arthritis, a severe back problem, a skin infection, cancer, HIV or AIDS, epilepsy or a serious psychiatric illness. Avoid massage of the abdomen, legs or feet during the first three months of pregnancy and consult your doctor during other times of pregnancy.

(13) Autogenic therapy and visualisation

Try to will your saliva to flow. You probably can't. Now imagine your favourite meal. Your saliva probably pours out. Visualisation and autogenic therapy rely on the same principle to retrain your body and they can 'down-regulate' the stress response.

Autogenic therapy comes from humble origins. Towards the end of the last century, a French chemist, Emile Coué, became interested in placebos (inactive drugs that seem to exert a biological effect). He attributed their effectiveness to autosuggestion. In other words, patients benefited because they willed themselves well. Coué decided to cut out the placebo and directly tap the power of the mind. Coué asked his patients to repeat the saying 'every day, in every way, I'm getting better and better' several times a day as a general health tonic. The phrase could vary depending on your complaint. 'Every day, I'm feeling more and more relaxed,' for example.

Couéism became a worldwide craze. By the First World War, Coué was training 40,000 people a year. People chanted in the bath, on trains and over breakfast. However, the medical establishment viewed Couéism as a simplistic joke during the 1930s. Like all crazes, Couéism gradually faded away.

However, around the same time as Couéism was in decline, the German physician Johannes Schultz took autosuggestion a step further. Schultz trained patients to alter their blood flow so that by reciting to themselves 'my hands are warm' they became warm. His technique, autogenic therapy, allows practitioners to exert some control over their autonomic nervous systems. As the autonomic nervous system drives the fight-or-flight reflex (see pages 19–21), autogenic therapy can be used to reduce stress, fatigue and tension.

Autogenic therapy is most effective when taught by approved trainers. The basic techniques are taught on a one-to-one basis or in a small group over eight to ten weekly sessions, each lasting 90 minutes. However, you can try autogenic therapy at home. You need to relax completely. So lie or sit comfortably in a quiet, dark room. Close your eyes. Then, as in progressive muscle relaxation (see pages 228–29), you focus your attention on one part of your body at a time. For example, you could say 'My left leg is warm'. Repeat this a few times and then move to another part of your body. Alternatively, repeat: 'My breathing is calm and regular,' until you relax. Autogenic therapy is harder than it sounds. Ideally, you should practise for 10 to 15 minutes three times a day. Contact the British Autogenic Society★ for details of approved practitioners. Autogenic therapy is not suitable for people with severe mental problems such as psychosis and personality disorders, or those with severe learning disabilities. If it is being used to help treat a medical condition, autogenic therapy should only be undertaken alongside conventional treatment, and your doctor should monitor your progress.

Once you have mastered the basic training you can 'implant' suggestions to meet your specific needs by visualising them in as much detail as possible. So, if your golf handicap is a source of frustration, try to visualise every stroke on the course. Visualise the ball missing the bunker you always hit. Visualise yourself making the putt you always miss.

You can also use visualisation to counter stress. Some people build a place of their own in their minds. They may walk along a favourite river bank surrounded by the early morning mist. They may sit by a cool mountain lake surrounded by the scent of pine trees or lie on a quiet, hot tropical beach. At times of stress, they can close their eyes and take a mental vacation in their favourite spot.

However, visualisation helps you make a more direct assault on stress. Say, for example, that you're feeling stressed because you plan to ask your boss for a rise. You can use visualisation to imagine that your meeting is successful. Visualising success increases the likelihood of it becoming reality – a fact well known, and widely used, by sportspeople.

(14) Biofeedback

Biofeedback is another way to exert some control over autonomic nervous system activity, which, unlike the voluntary nervous system, is not normally under conscious control. A biofeedback machine may make a sound or flash a light that varies according to the level of activity in your autonomic nervous system. By listening to the clicks or watching the display, practitioners train themselves to regulate the signals. This allows them to exert some control over their autonomic functions.

Some biofeedback machines respond to heartbeat, blood pressure, respiration rate or muscle tension. Others – for example those used to aid general relaxation – respond to skin changes. As you become more stressed, you tend to sweat more. As a result, your skin conducts electricity more easily. The machine converts these changes in conductance into a noise that increases in pitch as you become more aroused. More sophisticated biofeedback machines respond to brainwave patterns that seem to relate to mental states – relaxation, for example.

Biofeedback, introduced in the late 1960s, alleviates a variety of stress-related disorders including migraine, insomnia, high blood pressure and chronic pain – in some patients at least. However, biofeedback is not universally effective. It can take considerable perseverance and persistence to learn correctly and patients' responses vary. Feelings of dizziness, disorientation, anxiety and floating sensations have been reported. People with severe personality disorders or psychosis should only use biofeedback under medical supervision. You should tell the practitioner or your doctor if you are on any medication. Moreover, biofeedback is not widely available beyond research centres. You can get more information from the Biofeedback Foundation of Europe.*

(15) Aromatherapy

Aromatherapy uses aromatic essential oils distilled from plants, leaves, petals, barks and roots to promote mental, physical and emotional health. Plants produce essential oils to encourage pollination, prevent invasion by bacteria and fungi, and to attract insects. The 400 essential oils in widespread use have a rich heritage. Ancient priests anointed their followers with oil. Lovers have long used essential oils as aphrodisiacs. Nowadays we spend millions on perfumes and after-shaves to make ourselves feel good. Aromatherapists claim that essential oils can also alleviate stress-related diseases and tension, and randomised controlled trials suggest aromatherapy has mild but short-lasting anti-anxiety effects.

Aromatherapists use essential oils to alleviate tension, restlessness, anxiety and other stress-related symptoms. For example, try sprinkling lavender oil on a handkerchief and taking a few deep breaths. It is difficult to remain physically and mentally tense if you breathe deeply. Some people find that sprinkling essential oils on their pillows at night helps them sleep. Essential oils blended with almond oil or other fats can be massaged into tense muscles. You can also add a few drops of essential oils into your bath, but you need to soak for at least a quarter of an hour.

However, aromatherapy isn't totally free from side effects. For example, bergamot and lemon can make the skin more sensitive to ultraviolet light – in other words, you sunburn more easily; and pregnant women should avoid certain essential oils, such as parsley and camphor, which can trigger miscarriages. However, some women find pregnancy a stressful experience and mothers-to-be – and perhaps their partners – may benefit from using certain oils under the supervision of a qualified aromatherapist. Check with your doctor or a pharmacist before using an essential oil if you are taking a prescription or over-the-counter medicine.

The rapidly growing interest in aromatherapy means that 'aromatherapy oils' are turning up in health shops, chemists and supermarkets. However, the quality varies dramatically between suppliers. Environmental factors, such as soil, climate and the season, can alter the subtle balance of active chemicals in the essential oil. You should ensure that you buy the essential oils from a reputable source. The Aromatherapy Trade Council★ can help, and the Aromatherapy Organisations Council★ can supply lists of approved practitioners.

(16) Exercise

You know that exercise is good for your health. You know that exercise helps you look and feel better. You know that exercise reduces stress. Yet we are a nation of couch potatoes. Only 33 per cent of men and 21 per cent of women currently meet the guidelines for physical activity. It is hard to be motivated by the prospect of good health in 20 years' time if it means getting up an hour earlier on a damp February morning. But it's now clear that you can easily fit sufficient exercise into your life to stay fit.

Traditionally, for example, doctors advised exercising vigorously for 20 minutes three times a week. If that proves difficult, they now suggest five periods of 30 minutes of moderate exercise. You can spread this 30 minutes out over the course of the day – take three ten-minute walks, for example. Walking fast without exertion is one example of moderate exercise.

Remember that exercise, despite what it often felt like at school, can be fun. First, if you are in any doubt about your health consult your GP. Then it's trial and error. With a bit of imagination, everyone can find an exercise they enjoy. It may be performing step aerobics to loud dance music; or you may prefer taking the dog for a long walk; or yoga. Your local library holds lists of local sports clubs – you will probably be surprised at the choice.

If your mobility is restricted – with arthritis, for example – try swimming and aqua-aerobics. Your local swimming pool probably runs classes. You could also ask your GP to refer you to a physiotherapist who will devise an individual exercise programme. After a few training sessions you will be able to exercise at home or in the gym.

Many people gain most psychological benefit from exercise outside the house, however. Your body may not care whether you work out on a ski machine or in the fresh air, but your mind might.

The social side of exercise in a group helps beat stress in its own right. And, of course, it's harder to quit if a friend is waiting for you at the gym. Exercising with a friend also offers some practical benefits – for example, helping you assess whether you are pushing yourself too hard. If you're too out of breath to hold a conversation, you're overdoing it.

The best way to exercise safely is to aim to stay within your target heart rate zone. This varies according to your age (see table opposite). Count your pulse rate over 15 seconds and then multiply by four (double and double again). It should be in the 50 to 75 per cent range. If you're just beginning to exercise stay around the 50 per cent end. As you become fitter, move towards the 75 per cent end. However, don't exceed the maximum rate. It could be dangerous.

Target heart rate zones for various ages

Age (years)	Target heart rate zone (50 to 75 per cent) beats per minute	Average maximum heart rate (100 per cent) beats per minute
20-30	98-146	195
31-40	93-138	185
41-50	88-131	175
51-60	83-123	165
61+	78-116	155

Not having the time to exercise is a common excuse for remaining unfit. But be honest: is lack of time really your problem, or is it just easier to slump in front of the TV than work out? Most of us can find the time if we try (for example, use the time management techniques on pages 219–25). If you feel too tired at night, try getting up 45 minutes earlier. Many swimming pools and gyms run lunchtime sessions. You could ask your partner to cook a meal while you go to aerobics.

When planning your schedule, remember that just three 20-minute sessions of moderate exercise a week keep you fit. Even allowing for showering and changing, that's around 45 minutes each time you work out. There are 168 hours in the week. You need to devote just two-and-a-quarter hours to stay fit.

(17) Music

Music's power to relieve mental torment was recognised in Biblical times: David's harp-playing soothed Saul's madness. Later the Greek philosopher Pythagoras, who lived around 500BC, used music to alleviate mental disorders. During the Middle Ages, music was used to treat fever, alleviate mania, prevent the plague and restore harmony between mind and body. Since the nineteenth century, when German health resorts used music to cure stress-related illnesses, music therapy has found a role in mainstream medicine to treat mental handicap and illness. Music also provides a welcome distraction from the torment of chronic pain, and every day, people play or listen to music to relieve stress.

But musical tastes vary widely. Your teenage son's musical tastes may sound like a cacophony to you – and he probably can't stand your Bach concertos. Moreover, musical tastes vary with mood. Cheerful music is grating if you've got the blues, and you don't want to listen to a fugue at a party. Nevertheless, don't underestimate music's abilities to lift your spirits and alleviate stress. Many studies have shown that music relaxes people and improves their mood. Switch the light off. Put on the headphones, and let your favourite music wash over you. Music also provides a soothing background to relaxation and other stress-relieving techniques.

The Association of Professional Music Therapists★ and the British Society for Music Therapy★ both have details of qualified music therapists.

(18) Hypnotherapy

In hypnotherapy, the therapist induces a hypnotic state, during which a person remains conscious but accepts suggestions more readily than usual, and acts on them more profoundly. Franz Anton Mesmer, a physician from Vienna, is generally regarded as being the founder of hypnotherapy as we know it today. He successfully treated large numbers of people in the late eighteenth century. Towards the end of the nineteenth century a French physician, Ambrose-August Liébeault, used hypnosis to suggest that the headaches, stomach pains or aches and pains of his peasant volunteers would resolve. His success rate was high enough for his fame to spread. Later, another French doctor, Jean-Martin Charcot, found that patients with 'hysteria' could, under hypnosis, mimic symptoms of other illnesses. Before the introduction of chloroform, major operations – including amputations and removing large scrotal tumours – were performed under hypnosis, apparently without patients experiencing pain. A Manchester-based Scottish surgeon, James Braid, helped popularise hypnotism in the UK in the late nineteenth century and it was he who coined the term hypnotism (from the Greek word *hypnos*, meaning 'sleep'). However, the medical profession refused to take hypnosis seriously, although it was more widely accepted among their European colleagues. The tide changed in the 1950s, when the *British Medical Journal* reported that hypnosis cured ichthyosis, a disfiguring disease where the skin appears rough and horny. A young boy was put into a hypnotic state and told which areas of his skin would clear. These areas became almost normal.

The aim of hypnotherapy is to enable a person to gain self-control over behaviour, emotions or biological processes. The best subjects tend to be people who immerse themselves in imaginary worlds – books, films and plays – and strongly identify with imaginary characters. Hypnotherapists suggest that about 90 per cent of the population can be hypnotised, and 10 per cent can be taken into a hypnotic state so deep they can tolerate minor operations without anaesthesia. No one really understands how hypnosis works. One theory is that the left, analytical side of the brain switches off during a hypnotic state, giving the right, creative side free rein. There is debate as to whether the hypnotic state is simply a state of deep relaxation or whether it resembles an altered state of consciousness. Most people feel tired, lethargic and drowsy during hypnosis, but while the brain's electrical activity changes during hypnotherapy, it does not resemble sleep. Indeed, the brain's electrical activity suggests that the subject is fully awake during hypnosis. According to one theory, the brain shuts off nerves supplying sensory information. This leaves subjects susceptible to certain suggestions. Certainly, during hypnosis subjects become very relaxed and compliant, which is why stage hypnotists can make people act as dogs or chickens.

However, hypnotherapy is far removed from the antics of stage hypnotists. Hypnosis is very relaxing, which benefits patients in its own right, but a growing number of studies show that hypnosis also alleviates a wide range of stress-related ailments and forms of behaviour including addictions, irritable bowel syndrome, high blood pressure, insomnia and some social problems. It can also help people recover stress-promoting repressed memories. In fact, hypnotherapy is supported by more scientific evidence than almost any other complementary therapy.

If carried out by a trained practitioner, hypnotherapy should be safe. However, recovering repressed memories can be painful. Some doctors believe there is a risk that hypnosis might trigger underlying psychosis, epileptic attacks or post-traumatic stress disorder. You should always consult a qualified hypnotherapist and discuss any concerns that arise during treatment. For lists of qualified practitioners contact the Central Register of Advanced Hypnotherapists★ or the National Register of Hypnotherapists and Psychotherapists.★

(19) Herbalism

It doesn't matter whether you live in the tropical or concrete jungle, you are still likely to suffer from anxiety, depression and stress-related symptoms. So cultures the world over have developed home-grown stress treatments. Worldwide, some four billion people rely on plants as their main source of medicines. Meanwhile, herbalism is growing in popularity in the UK as a treatment for a range of stress-related problems.

No one seriously disputes that herbalism can be effective for some conditions. After all, many conventional medicines – from aspirin to potent new cancer treatments – have their roots in chemicals derived from plants. But some doctors dispute the safety of certain herbs. They point out that some herbs contain potent, even toxic, chemicals. After all, heroin, cocaine and cannabis are derived from plants. Also, some herbs may interact with conventional medicines prescribed by your doctor.

So if you suffer from a serious illness, are taking conventional drugs or are unsure about what you are doing, consult your GP, a pharmacist or qualified herbalist before taking herbs. As with most drugs, it is probably prudent to avoid taking herbs during pregnancy. The National Institute of Medical Herbalists★ can help you find a local practitioner.

Herbalism takes two approaches to treating disease. The first is pharmacological: you take sufficient quantities of the herb to produce a drug-like effect. For example, a tablespoonful of valerian can help overcome stress-induced insomnia. However, valerian can produce paradoxical effects whereby some users become tense, anxious and agitated. The second approach uses herbs as tonics. For example, taking a smaller quantity of valerian produces a much milder effect which may support your natural sleep cycle. However, if your problem is a broken marriage, neither herbs nor drugs will tackle the problem underlying your insomnia. Whether you take conventional medicines or herbs, you need to identify and deal with the stress-causing problem.

Herbalism's critics argue that few herbs undergo the same rigorous long-term efficacy and safety testing as drugs. Herbalists counter that they draw on a rich heritage. Herbalists know through experience which herbs are dangerous – and which are safe – and they treat all herbs with respect. In moderation, herbalism may be a safe and effective treatment for a variety of stress-related disorders, especially if you consult a qualified herbalist. However, the bottom line is that just because it's natural it doesn't necessarily mean it's safe.

(20) Think about home help

Housework can be a major cause of stress and arguments, especially if your time is pressurised. As a result, many of us employ home helps. About four million people work in domestic service. Indeed, Britain now has more cleaners, gardeners and nannies than accountants.

Home help certainly allows them to buy back your time and can help reduce stress. However, hiring home help can be expensive. So, you need to weigh up the cost against the benefit of hiring someone to do the housework. Perhaps, if you work for yourself, you may decide you would rather do the domestic chores yourself. On the other hand, you can make a trade-off between the cost of employing someone else and maybe sharing the chores around the family.

(21) Prepare for the next day the night before

Getting everyone ready in the morning can be a considerable cause of stress. So prepare for the whole family's departure (to school, work and so on) the night before. Put coats, briefcases and bags by the door, and ensure that they are packed with everything you and your children need. Also, agree on one place to keep the car keys. And put your loose change into a pot in the hall or kitchen. That way you will not waste time finding change for charity, the bus, lunches or for parking. As this suggests, simplifying your life can help reduce your stress levels. *Which? Way to Manage Your Time – and Your Life* offers numerous other tips to simply your life and reduce your stress levels.

(22) Accept that you can't have (or do) it all

Many people seem to want to be perfect homekeepers, as well as a success in their career and in their personal life. Of course, this is difficult, if not impossible. And they inevitably suffer stress as a result. There simply are not enough hours in the day to do everything to perfection. How important is it to have an immaculate house, rather than one that is neat most of the time and sanitary all the time? Accept a few toys lying around or an unmade bed. Mess really depends on how you look at it. Toys sprinkled around the living room are a sign that your children play a central role in your life.

(23) Do not rely on your holiday being the answer to stress

Many television advertisements and programmes, as well as lifestyle and travel features in magazines and newspapers, seem to suggest that holidays are the antidote to stress. It might be a myth. A mid-1990s Gallup poll found that 53 per cent of those questioned said taking a holiday was for them the most stressful life event over the last year. Rather than relying on a single holiday to relieve tension, it is perhaps better to use stress management techniques throughout the year.

(24) Keep a sense of perspective

In a series of books, such as *Don't Sweat the Small Stuff* and *Don't Worry, Make Money* (see 'Further reading'), Richard Carlson emphasised the importance of keeping a sense of perspective. All of us, at one time or another, become anxious, angry and stressed about things that, in the final analysis, do not really matter. Whether it is waiting in the bank, being cut up on the road or having a row with a co-worker or spouse, we are adept at building mountains from molehills, which inevitably causes stress. But by 'not sweating the small stuff' – by not allowing the small things to take over from what really matters – we will stay on track with our larger plans, be less stressed and make better use of our time. Few things waste as much time or cause as much micro-level stress as unnecessary worrying. One telling technique is to ask yourself if the problem will still matter in a month's or year's time. Many of your stress-causing problems lose their potency when considered over the longer term.

(25) Nurture your creativity

Being creative can offer a great way to unwind and is an important stress defence. At its simplest, creativity means bringing something new into existence. What you do does not matter.

Creativity is about more than being a poet, painter or novelist. The psychologist Abraham Maslow pointed out in *Toward a Psychology of Being* that some people are creative outside the conventionally 'arty' areas. One of his women patients, for example, was 'original, novel, ingenious, unexpected, inventive' in the way that she cooked and furnished her home. He writes: 'I learned from her and others like her that a first-rate soup is more creative than a second-rate painting, and that, generally, cooking or parenthood or making a home could be creative while poetry need not be; it could be uncreative.'

You can unleash your innate creativity in several ways. Many artists find visiting a gallery stimulates ideas that they can use in their work. This is not plagiarism. Rather, looking at another artist's view helps them look at their current work with a new eye. And there is no reason why you cannot unleash your creativity in a similar way. Try visiting an exhibition by an artist you do not know. Or borrow a CD from a library by an artist or composer you do not normally listen to. Attending an evening course in something that appeals can help you unleash your creative potential.

> **You can beat stress!**
>
> The ideas in this chapter are only suggestions. Your life is unique and precious. So you need to use your imagination to develop the techniques and approaches that work for you. Take what is useful from these suggestions and adapt them to your particular circumstances. Don't be afraid to experiment. If a particular technique doesn't work, you can always try a different approach. This book offers some basic principles as well as a number of tried-and-trusted solutions that might work for you. So whatever your personal circumstances, by using the techniques outlined in this book you will be better placed to tackle the trials and tribulations inherent in this age of anxiety without developing physiological or physical stress symptoms.

All these tricks can help unleash your creativity. Moreover, nurturing your creativity in one area often spills over into another. So, if you take up a creative hobby, you may well find yourself being more creative at work and at home.

Further reading

Carlson, R. 1998. *Don't Sweat the Small Stuff*. Hodder Mobius
Carlson, R. 1998. *Don't Worry, Make Money*. Hodder & Stoughton
Harrold, F. 2001. *Be Your Own Life Coach: How to Take Control of Your Life and Achieve Your Wildest Dreams*. Hodder Mobius
Maslow, A. 1998. *Towards a Psychology of Being*. John Wiley & Sons
Mulligan, E. 1999. *Life Coaching: Change Your Life in Seven Days*. Piatkus

ANSWERS TO QUIZ ON PAGES 178–79

DEPRESSION SCORES

1. **I still enjoy the things I used to enjoy:**

Definitely as much	0
Not quite so much	1
Only a little	2
Hardly at all	3

2. **I can laugh and see the funny side of things:**

As much as I always could	0
Not quite so much now	1
Definitely not so much now	2
Not at all	3

3. **I feel cheerful:**

Not at all	3
Not often	2
Sometimes	1
Most of the time	0

4. **I feel as if I am slowed down:**

Nearly all the time	3
Very often	2
Sometimes	1
Not at all	0

5. **I have lost interest in my appearance:**

Definitely	3
I don't take as much care	2
I may not take quite as much care	1
I take just as much care as ever	0

6. **I look forward with enjoyment to things:**

As much as ever I did	0
Rather less than I used to	1
Definitely less than I used to	2
Hardly at all	3

7. **I can enjoy a good book or radio or TV programme:**

Often	0
Sometimes	1
Not often	2
Very seldom	3

ANXIETY SCORES

1. **I feel tense or wound up:**
   Most of the time   3
   A lot of the time   2
   From time to time,
   occasionally   1
   Not at all   0

2. **I get a sort of frightened feeling as if something awful is about to happen:**
   Very definitely and quite badly   3
   Yes, but not too badly   2
   A little, but it doesn't worry me   1
   Not at all   0

3. **Worrying thoughts go through my mind:**
   A great deal of the time   3
   A lot of the time   2
   From time to time, not too often   1
   Only occasionally   0

4. **I can sit at ease and feel relaxed:**
   Definitely   0
   Usually   1
   Not often   2
   Not at all   3

5. **I get a sort of frightened feeling like 'butterflies' in the stomach:**
   Not at all   0
   Occasionally   1
   Quite often   2
   Very often   3

6. **I feel restless as if I have to be on the move:**
   Very much indeed   3
   Quite a lot   2
   Not very much   1
   Not at all   0

7. **I get sudden feelings of panic:**
   Very often indeed   3
   Quite often   2
   Not very often   1
   Not at all   0

Bibliography

Introduction

Phillips, D.P., Liu, G.C., Kwok, K. et al. 2001. The Hound of the Baskervilles effect: natural experiment on the influence of psychological stress on timing of death. *BMJ*, 323, 1,443–1,446

Witte, D.R., Bots, M.L., Hoes, A.W. et al. 2000. Cardiovascular mortality in Dutch men during 1996 European football championship: longtitudinal population study. *BMJ*, 321, 1,552–1,554

Ebrahim, S., Tilling, K., Macleod J. et al. 2002. Admissions for myocardial infarction and World Cup football: database survey. *BMJ*, 325, 1,439–1,442

Goldberg, R.J. December 2001. Depression in the workplace: economics and interventions. *Behavioural Healthcare Tomorrow*, 10–11

Chapter 1 What is stress?

Are You Stressed Out? March 1997. *Family Practice Management*

Dudek, B., Merecz, D. and Makowska, Z. 2001. Sense of personal control and the level of occupational stress and related effects. *Med Pr*, 52, 451–7

Dunant, S. and Porter, R. 1996. *The Age of Anxiety*. Virago Press

Eysenck, M. (ed). 1998. *Psychology: an Integrated Approach*. Prentice Hall

Felton, J.S. 1998. Burnout as a clinical entity – its importance in health care workers. *Occupational Medicine*, 48, 237–250

Jain, V.K., Lall, R., McLaughlin, D.G. et al. 1996. Effects of locus of control, occupational stress, and psychological distress on job satisfaction among nurses. *Psychol Rep*, 78, 1,256–8

Kahana, B. 1992. Late-life adaptation in the aftermath of extreme stress *in* Wykle, M., Kahana, E., Kowal, J. et al (eds). *Stress & Health Among the Elderly*. Springer

Kalia, M. 2002. Assessing the economic impact of stress – the modern-day hidden epidemic. *Metabolism*, 51 (6 Suppl 1), 49–53

Lazarus, R.S., Speisman, J.C., Mordkoff, A.M. et al. 1962. A laboratory study of psychological stress produced by a motion picture film. *Psychological Monographs*, 76, 553

Lazarus, R.S. and Folkman, S. 1984. *Stress Appraisal and Coping*. Springer (New York)

Selye, H. 1956. *The Stress of Life*. McGraw Hill (New York)

Tearle, P. 2002. Work-related stress. *Commun Dis Public Health*, 5, 174–6

Wykle, M., Kahana, E. and Kowal, J. et al. 1992. *Stress & Health Among the Elderly*. Springer

Chapter 2 How we respond to stress

Catipovic-Veselica, K., Glavas B., Kristek, J. et al. 2001. Components of type A behaviour and two-year prognosis of patients with acute coronary syndrome. *Psychol Rep*, 89, 467–75

Chiriboga, D.A. 1992. Paradise lost: stress in the modern age *in* Wykle, M., Kahana, E., Kowal, J. et al (eds). *Stress & Health Among the Elderly*. Springer

Cole, S.R., Kawachi, I., Liu, S. et al. 2001. Time urgency and risk of non-fatal myocardial infarction. *Int J Epidemiol*, 30, 363–9

Conroy, R.W. and Smith, K. 1983. Family loss and hospital suicide. *Suicide Life Threat Behav*, 13, 179–194

Eysenck, M. (ed). 1998. *Psychology: an Integrated Approach*. Prentice Hall

Leger, D. 2000. Public health and insomnia: Economic impact. *Sleep*, 23 (suppl 3), S69–S76

Lillberg, K., Verkasalo, P.K., Kaprio, J. et al. 2002. Personality characteristics and the risk of breast cancer: a prospective cohort study. *Int J Cancer*, 100, 361–6

Myrtek, M. 2001. Meta-analyses of prospective studies on coronary heart disease, type A personality, and hostility. *Int J Cardiol*, 79, 245–51

Natural selection. August 2002. *Independent Community Pharmacist*, 28–30

Overmier, J.B. and Seligman, M.E.P. 1967. Effects of inescapable shock upon subsequent escape and avoidance learning. *Journal of Comparative and Physiological Psychology*, 63, 28–33

Rosenman, R.H. and Friedman, M. 1974. Neurogenic factors in pathogenesis of coronary heart disease. *Medical Clinics of North America*, 58, 269–79

Yoshimasu, K. 2001. Relation of type A behaviour pattern and job-related psychosocial factors to nonfatal myocardial infarction: a case-control study of Japanese male workers and women. *Psychosom Med*, 63, 797–804

Chapter 3 Towards assertive coping

Andersen, S. and Keller, C. 2002. Examination of the transtheoretical model in current smokers. *West J Nurs Res*, 24, 282–94

Chiriboga, D.A. 1992. Paradise lost: stress in the modern age *in* Wykle, M., Kahana, E., Kowal, J. et al (eds). *Stress & Health Among the Elderly*. Springer

Clegg, B. 2000. How to have time for your life. *Professional Manager*, Jan, 18–20

Littell, J.H. and Girvin, H. 2002. Stages of change. A critique. *Behav Modif*, 26, 223–73

Mauck, K.F., Cuddihy, M.T., Trousdale, R.T. et al. 2002. The decision to accept treatment for osteoporosis following hip fracture: exploring the woman's perspective using a stage-of-change model. *Osteoporos Int*, 13, 560–4

Rusch, N. and Corrigan, P.W. 2002. Motivational interviewing to improve insight and treatment adherence in schizophrenia. *Psychiatr Rehabil J*, 26, 23–32

Scarnati, J. 1999. Beyond technical competence: the art of leadership. *Career Development International*: 199, 4,325–35

Scarnati, J. 1999. Beyond technical competence: the fundamentals of flexibility. *Participation & Empowerment: An International Journal*, 7, 194–200

Shepherd, R. and Shepherd, R. 2002. Resistance to changes in diet. *Proc Nutr Soc*, 61, 267–72

Suminski, R.R. and Petosa, R. 2002. Stages of change among ethnically diverse college students. *J Am Coll Health*, 51, 26–31

Taylor, S.E. 1995. *Health Psychology*. McGraw Hill

Zimmerman, G.L., Olsen, C.G. and Bosworth, M.F. 2000. A 'stages of change' approach to helping patients change behaviour. *Am Fam Physician*, 61, 1,409–16

Chapter 4 The three ages of stress

Aldwin, C.M. 1992. Ageing, coping and efficacy: theoretical framework for examing coping in life-span developmental context *in*

Wykle, M., Kahana, E., Kowal, J. et al (eds). *Stress & Health Among the Elderly*. Springer

Avery, A.J., Betts, D.S., Whittington, A. et al. 1998. The mental and physical health of miners following the 1992 national pit closure programme: a cross-sectional survey using General Health Questionnaire GHQ-12 and Short Form SF-36. *Public Health*, 112, 169–73

Blake, H. and Lincoln, N.B. 2000. Factors associated with strain in co-resident spouses of patients following stroke. *Clin Rehabil*, 14, 307–14

Bond, L., Carlin, J.B., Thomas, L. et al. 2001. Does bullying cause emotional problems? A prospective study of young teenagers. *BMJ*, 323, 480–4

Burke, R.J. and MacDermid, G. 1999. Are workaholics job satisfied and successful in their careers? *Career Development International*, 4, 277–82

Cacioppo, J.T., Hawkley, L.C., Crawford, L.E. et al. 2002. Loneliness and health: potential mechanisms. *Psychosom Med*, 64, 407–17

Claussen, B., Bjorndal, A. and Hjort, P.F. 1993. Health and re-employment in a two-year follow up of long-term unemployed. *J Epidemiol Community Health*, 47, 14–8

Coleman, M.P., Babb, P., Sloggett, A. et al. 2001. Socioeconomic inequalities in cancer survival in England and Wales. *Cancer*, 91 (1 Suppl), 208–16

Cooper, P.J. and Goodyer, I. 1993. A community study of depression in adolescent girls. I: Estimates of symptom and syndrome prevalence. *Br J Psychiatry*, 163, 369–74 and 379–80

Cropley, M., Steptoe, A. and Joekes, K. 1999. Job strain and psychiatric morbidity. *Psychol Med*, 29, 1,411–6

Gilmour, J., Skuse, D. and Pembrey, M. 2001. Hyperphagic short stature and Prader–Willi syndrome: a comparison of behavioural phenotypes, genotypes and indices of stress. *Br J Psychiatry*, 179, 129–37

Gohlke, B.C., Frazer, F.L. and Stanhope, R. 2002. Body mass index and segmental proportion in children with different subtypes of psychosocial short stature. *Eur J Pediatr*, 161, 250–4

Hawton, K., Fagg, J., Simkin, S. et al. 2000. Deliberate self-harm in adolescents in Oxford, 1985–1995. *J Adolesc*, 23, 47–55

Hodge, G.M., McCormick, J. and Elliott, R. 1997. Examination-induced distress in a public examination at the completion of secondary schooling. *Br J Educ Psychol*, 67, 185–97

Houston, K., Hawton, K. and Shepperd, R. 2001. Suicide in young people aged 15–24: a psychological autopsy study. *J Affect Disord*, 63, 159–70

Jakobovits, A.A. and Szekeres, L. 2002. Interactions of stress and reproduction – a personal view. *Zentralbl Gynakol*, 124, 189–93

Kakimoto, Y., Nakamura, A., Tarui, H. et al. 1988. Crew workload in JASDF C-1 transport flights: I. Change in heart rate and salivary cortisol. *Aviat Space Environ Med*, 59, 511–16

Keller, M.B., Lavori, P.W., Wunder, J. et al. 1992. Chronic course of anxiety disorders in children and adolescents. *J Am Acad Child Adolesc Psychiatry*, 31, 595–9

Kendler, K.S., Bulik, C.M., Silberg, J. et al. 2000. Childhood sexual abuse and adult psychiatric and substance use disorders in women: an epidemiological and cotwin control analysis. *Arch Gen Psychiatry*, 57, 953–9

Kirby, J.B. 2002. The influence of parental separation on smoking initiation in adolescents. *J Health Soc Behav*, 43, 56–71

Kumpulainen, K. and Roine, S. 2002. Depressive symptoms at the age of 12 years and future heavy alcohol use. *Addict Behav*, 27, 425–36

Layton, A.M. 2001. Optimal management of acne to prevent scarring and psychological sequelae. *Am J Clin Dermatol*, 2, 135–41

Levy, B.R., Slade, M.D., Kunkel, S.R. et al. 2002. Longevity increased by positive self-perceptions of ageing. *J Pers Soc Psychol*, 83, 261–70

Mack, K.Y. 2001. Childhood family disruptions and adult well-being: the differential effects of divorce and parental death. *Death Stud*, 25, 419–43

Mallon, E., Newton, J.N., Klassen, A. et al. 1999. The quality of life in acne: a comparison with general medical conditions using generic questionnaires. *Br J Dermatol*, 140, 672–6

Mavin, S. 2000. Approaches to careers in management: why UK organisations should consider gender. *Career Development International*, 5, 13–20

Miller, P. and Plant, M. 1999. Truancy and perceived school performance: an alcohol and drug study of UK teenagers. *Alcohol Alcohol*, 34, 886–93

Mizuno, E., Hosak, T., Ogihara, R. et al. 1999. Effectiveness of a stress management program for family caregivers of the elderly at home. *J Med Dent Sci*, 46, 145–53

O'Connor, T.G., Heron, J., Golding, J. et al. 2002. Maternal antenatal anxiety and children's behavioural/emotional problems at four years. Report from the Avon Longitudinal Study of parents and children. *Br J Psychiatry*, 180, 502–8

Power, C. and Manor, O. 1995. Asthma, enuresis, and chronic illness: long-term impact on height. *Arch Dis Child*, 73, 298–304

Schwefel, D. 1986. Unemployment, health and health services in German-speaking countries. *Soc Sci Med*, 22, 409–30

Serovich, J.M., Kimberly, J.A., Mosack, K.E. et al. 2001. The role of family and friend social support in reducing emotional distress among HIV-positive women. *AIDS Care*, 13, 335–41

Smithard, A., Glazebrook, C. and Williams, H.C. 2001. Acne prevalence, knowledge about acne and psychological morbidity in mid-adolescence: a community-based study. *Br J Dermatol*, 145, 274–9

Tennant, C. 2001. Work-related stress and depressive disorders. *Journal of Psychosomatic Research*, 51, 697–704

Thernlund, G.M., Dahlquist, G., Hansson, K. et al. 1995. Psychological stress and the onset of IDDM in children. *Diabetes Care*, 18, 1,323–9

Wade, T.J. and Cairney, J. 2000. Major depressive disorder and marital transition among mothers: results from a national panel study. *J Nerv Ment Dis*, 188, 741–50

Webster, G.F. 2002. Acne vulgaris. *BMJ*, 325, 475–479

Wethington, E. 2000. Expecting Stress: Americans and the 'Midlife Crisis'. *Motivation and Emotion*, 24, 85–103

Whitlatch, C.J., Schur, D., Noelker, L.S. et al. 2001. The stress process of family caregiving in institutional settings. *Gerontologist*, 41, 462–73

Wolke, D., Woods, S., Bloomfield, L., et al. 2001. Bullying involvement in primary school and common health problems. *Arch Dis Child*, 85, 197–201

Wolke, D., Woods, S., Stanford, K. et al. 2001. Bullying and victimisation of primary school children in England and Germany: prevalence and school factors. *Br J Psychol*, 92, 673–96

Chapter 5 Overcoming alcohol and nicotine abuse

Blondal, T., Gudmundsson, L.J., Olafsdottir, I. et al. 1999. Nicotine nasal spray with nicotine patch for smoking cessation: randomised trial with six year follow up. *BMJ*, 318, 285–8

Bradvik, L. and Berglund, M. 2002. Seasonal distribution of suicide in alcoholism. *Acta Psychiatr Scand*, 106, 299–302

Burns, L. and Teesson, M. 2002. Alcohol use disorders comorbid with anxiety, depression and drug use disorders. Findings from the Australian National Survey of Mental Health and Wellbeing. *Drug Alcohol Depend*, 68, 299

Dick, D.M., Nurnberger, J. Jr, Edenberg, H.J. et al. 2002. Suggestive linkage on chromosome 1 for a quantitative alcohol-related phenotype. *Alcohol Clin Exp Res*, 26, 1,453–60

Feeney, G.F., Young, R.M., Connor, J.P. et al. 2002. Cognitive behavioural therapy combined with the relapse-prevention medication acamprosate: are short-term treatment outcomes for alcohol dependence improved? *Aust N Z J Psychiatry*, 36, 622–8

Flood, A., Caprario, L., Chaterjee, N. et al. 2002. Folate, methionine, alcohol, and colorectal cancer in a prospective study of women in the United States. *Cancer Causes Control*, 13, 551–61

Horn-Ross, P.L., Hoggatt, K.J., West, D.W. et al. 2002. Recent diet and breast cancer risk: the California Teachers Study (USA). *Cancer Causes Control*, 13, 407–15

Hughes, J.R. 2000. New treatments for smoking cessation. *CA Cancer J Clin*, 50, 143–51

Kropp, S. and Chang-Claude, J. 2002. Active and passive smoking and risk of breast cancer by age 50 years among German women. *Am J Epidemiol*, 156, 616–26

Lindstrom, M. and Isacsson, S.O. 2002. The Malmo Shoulder-Neck Study Group Smoking cessation among daily smokers, aged 45–69 years: a longitudinal study in Malmo, Sweden. *Addiction*, 297, 205–15

Macleod, J., Smith, G.D., Heslop, P. et al. 2001. Are the effects of psychosocial exposures attributable to confounding? Evidence from a prospective observational study on psychological stress and mortality. *J Epidemiol Community Health*, 55, 878–84

Olive, M.F., Koenig, H.N., Nannini, M.A. et al. 2001. Stimulation of endorphin neurotransmission in the nucleus accumbens by ethanol, cocaine, and amphetamine. *J Neurosci*, 21, RC184

Panagiotakos, D.B., Chrysohoou, C., Pitsavos, C. et al. 2002. The association between secondhand smoke and the risk of developing acute coronary syndromes among non-smokers, under the presence of several cardiovascular risk factors: The CARDIO2000 case-control study. *BMC Public Health*, 2, 9

Peters, M.J. and Morgan, L.C. 2002. The pharmacotherapy of smoking cessation. *The Medical Journal of Australia*, 176, 486–490

Radon, K., Busching, K., Heinrich, J. et al. 2002. Passive smoking exposure: a risk factor for chronic bronchitis and asthma in adults? *Chest*, 122, 1,086–90

Chapter 6 Stress and physical diseases

Alfredsson, L., Hammar, N., Fransson, E. et al. 2002. Job strain and major risk factors for coronary heart disease among employed males and females in a Swedish study on work, lipids and fibrinogen. *Scand J Work Environ Health*, 28, 238–48

Altwein, J.E. and Keuler, F.U. 2001. Oral treatment of erectile dysfunction with apomorphine SL. *Urol Int*, 67, 257–63

Antoni, M.H., Lehman, J.M., Kilbourn, K.M. et al. 2001. Cognitive-behavioral stress management intervention decreases the prevalence of depression and enhances benefit finding among women under treatment for early-stage breast cancer. *Health Psychol*, 20, 20–32

Blumenthal, J.A., Babyak, M., Wei, J. et al. 2002. Usefulness of psychosocial treatment of mental stress-induced myocardial ischemia in men. *Am J Cardiol*, 89, 164–8

Buston, K.M. and Wood, S.F. 2000. Non-compliance among adolescents with asthma: listening to what they tell us about self-management. *Fam Pract*, 17, 134–8

Callahan, M.J. 2002. Irritable bowel syndrome neuropharmacology. A review of approved and investigational compounds. *J Clin Gastroenterol*, 35 (1 Suppl), 58–67

Campbell, D.A., Yellowlees, P.M., McLennan, G. et al. 1995. Psychiatric and medical features of near fatal asthma. *Thorax*, 50, 254–9

Chang, S.S., Ng, C.F. and Wong, S.N. 2002. Behavioural problems in children and parenting stress associated with primary nocturnal enuresis in Hong Kong. *Acta Paediatr*, 91, 475–9

Cohen, S., Hamrick, N., Rodriguez, M.S. et al. 2002. Reactivity and vulnerability to stress-associated risk for upper respiratory illness. *Psychosom Med*, 64, 302–10

Daud, L.R., Garralda, M.E. and David, T.J. 1993. Psychosocial adjustment in preschool children with atopic eczema. *Arch Dis Child*, 69, 670–6

Dhabhar, F.S. 2000. Acute stress enhances while chronic stress suppresses skin immunity. The role of stress hormones and leukocyte trafficking. *Ann N Y Acad Sci*, 917, 876–93

Dittmann, R.W. and Wolter, S. 1996. Primary nocturnal enuresis and desmopressin treatment: do psychosocial factors affect outcome? *Eur Child Adolesc Psychiatry*, 5, 101–9

Ehlers, A., Stangier, U. and Gieler, U. 1995. Treatment of atopic dermatitis: a comparison of psychological and dermatological approaches to relapse prevention. *J Consult Clin Psychol*, 63, 624–35

Eidlitz-Markus, T., Shuper, A. and Amir, J. 2000. Secondary enuresis: post-traumatic stress disorder in children after car accidents. *Isr Med Assoc J*, 2, 135–7

Fawzy, F.I., Fawzy, N.W., Hyun, C.S. et al. 1993. Malignant melanoma: Effects of an early structured psychiatric intervention, coping, and affective state on recurrence and survival 6 years later. *Archives of General Psychiatry*, 50, 681–689

Gillaspy, S.R., Hoff, A.L., Mullins, L.L. et al. 2002. Psychological distress in high-risk youths with asthma. *J Pediatr Psychol*, 27, 363–71

Glaser, R., Kiecolt-Glaser, J.K., Bonneau, R.H. et al. 1992. Stress-induced modulation of the immune response to recombinant hepatitis B vaccine. *Psychosomatic Medicine*, 54, 22–29

Holtmann, G. 2001. Reflux disease: the disorder of the third millennium. *Eur J Gastroenterol Hepatol*, (13 Suppl), 1, S5–11

Jacobs, J.R. and Bovasso, G.B. 2000. Early and chronic stress and their relation to breast cancer. *Psychol Med*, 30, 669–78

Jarvelin, M.R., Moilanen, I., Vikevainen-Tervonen, L. et al. 1990. Life changes and protective capacities in enuretic and non-enuretic children. *J Child Psychol Psychiatry*, 31, 763–74

Kemp, A.S. 1999. Atopic eczema: its social and financial costs. *J Paediatr Child Health*, 35, 229–31

Khan, M.A., Raistrick, M., Mikhailidis, D.P. et al. 2002. MUSE: clinical experience. *Curr Med Res Opin*,18, 64–7

Khan, S., Hyman, P.E., Cocjin, J. et al. 2000. Rumination syndrome in adolescents. *J Pediatr*, 13, 528–31

Kiecolt-Glaser, J.K., McGuire, L., Robles, T.F. et al. 2002. Psychoneuroimmunology: Psychological influences on immune function and health. *Journal of Consulting and Clinical Psychology*, 70, 537–547

Kiecolt-Glaser, J.K., Glaser, R., Gravenstein, S. et al. 1996. Chronic stress alters the immune response to influenza virus vaccine in older adults. *Proceedings of the National Academy of Sciences USA*, 93, 3,043–47

Koopman, C., Angell, K., Turner-Cobb, J.M. et al. 2001. Distress, coping, and social support among rural women recently diagnosed with primary breast cancer. *Breast J*, 7, 25–33

Koopman, C., Butler, L.D., Classen, C. et al. 2002. Traumatic stress symptoms among women with recently diagnosed primary breast cancer. *J Trauma Stress*, 15, 277–87

Lake, A.E. 2001. Behavioral and nonpharmacologic treatments of headache. *Med Clin North Am*, 85, 1,055–75

Landmark, B.T. and Wahl, A. 2002. Living with newly diagnosed breast cancer: a qualitative study of 10 women with newly diagnosed breast cancer. *Journal of Advanced Nursing*, 40, 112–121

Li, J., Hansen, D., Mortensen, P.B. et al. 2002. Myocardial infarction in parents who lost a child: a nationwide prospective cohort study in Denmark. *Circulation*, 106, 1,634–9

Lustyk, M.K., Jarrett, M.E., Bennett, J.C. et al. 2001. Does a physically active lifestyle improve symptoms in women with irritable bowel syndrome? *Gastroenterol Nurs*, 24, 129–37

Lydiard, R.B. 2001. Irritable bowel syndrome, anxiety, and depression: what are the links? *J Clin Psychiatry*, 62 (Suppl 8), S38–47

Macleod, J., Davey Smith, G., Heslop, P. et al. 2002. Psychological stress and cardiovascular disease: empirical demonstration of bias in a prospective observational study of Scottish men. *BMJ*, 324, 1,247–51

Malcolm, A., Thumshirn, M.B., Camilleri, M. et al. 1997. Rumination syndrome. *Mayo Clin Proc*, 72, 646–52

Monnikes, H., Tebbe, J.J., Hildebrandt, M. et al. 2001. Role of stress in functional gastrointestinal disorders. Evidence for stress-induced alterations in gastrointestinal motility and sensitivity. *Dig Dis*, 19, 201–11

Morag, M., Morag, A., Reichenberg, A. et al. 1999. Psychological variables as predictors of rubella antibody titers and fatigue – A prospective, double blind study. *Journal of Psychiatric Research*, 33, 389–395

Morrow, M. 2000. The evaluation of common breast problems. *Am Fam Physician*, 61, 2,371–8,2385

Penzien, D.B., Rains, J.C. and Andrasik, F. 2002. Behavioral management of recurrent headache: three decades of experience and empiricism. *Appl Psychophysiol Biofeedback*, 27, 163–81

Pinto, C., Lele, M.V., Joglekar, A.S. et al. 2000. Stressful life-events, anxiety, depression and coping in patients of irritable bowel syndrome. *J Assoc Physicians India*, 48, 589–93

Potter, D.C., Wogoman, H.A. and Nietch, P. 1999. Understanding nocturnal enuresis and its treatments. *J Pract Nurs*, 49, 16–21

Poynard, T., Regimbeau, C., Benhamou, Y. 2001. Meta-analysis of smooth muscle relaxants in the treatment of irritable bowel syndrome. *Aliment Pharmacol Ther*, 15, 355–61

Primatesta, P., Brookes, M. and Poulter, N.R. 2001. Improved hypertension management and control: results from the health survey for England 1998. *Hypertension*, 38, 827–32

Roberts, F.D., Newcomb, P.A., Trentham-Dietz, A. et al. 1996. Self-reported stress and risk of breast cancer. *Cancer*, 77, 1,089–93

Sairam, K., Kulinskaya, E., Hanbury, D. et al. 2002. Oral sildenafil (Viagra) in male erectile dysfunction: use, efficacy and safety profile in an unselected cohort presenting to a British district general hospital. *BMC Urol*, 2, 4

Sandin, B., Chorot, P., Valiente, R.M. et al. 2002. Adverse psychological effects in women attending a second-stage breast cancer screening. *J Psychosom Res*, 52, 303–9

Schaubroeck, J., Jones, J.R. and Xie, J.J. 2001. Individual differences in utilizing control to cope with job demands: effects on susceptibility to infectious disease. *J Appl Psychol*, 86, 265–78

Schmaling, K.B., McKnight, P.E. and Afari, N. 2002. A prospective study of the relationship of mood and stress to pulmonary function among patients with asthma. *J Asthma*, 39, 501–10

Schwartz, M.D., Taylor, K.L., Willard, K.S. et al. 1999. Distress, personality, and mammography utilisation among women with a family history of breast cancer. *Health Psychol*, 18, 327–32

Self-reported increase in asthma severity after the September 11 attacks on the World Trade Center – Manhattan, New York, 2001. 2002. *MMWR Morb Mortal Wkly Rep*, 51, 781–4

Smith, T.W. and Ruiz, J.M. 2002. Psychosocial influences on the development and course of coronary heart disease: current status and implications for research and practice. *J Consult Clin Psychol*, 70, 548–68

Spierings, E.L., Ranke, A.H. and Honkoop, P.C. 2001. Precipitating and aggravating factors of migraine versus tension-type headache. *Headache*, 41, 554–8

Steiner, H., Higgs, C.M., Fritz, G.K. et al. 1987. Defense style and the perception of asthma. *Psychosom Med*, 49, 35–44

Thommessen, B., Aarsland, D., Braekhus, A. et al. 2002. The psychosocial burden on spouses of the elderly with stroke, dementia and Parkinson's disease. *Int J Geriatr Psychiatry*, 17, 78–84

Tougas, G. 2002. The nature of pain in irritable bowel syndrome. *J Clin Gastroenterol*, 35 (1 Suppl), S26–30

Tsai, Y.S., Lin, J.S. and Lin, Y.M. 2000. Safety and efficacy of alprostadil sterile powder (S. Po., CAVERJECT) in diabetic patients with erectile dysfunction. *Eur Urol*, 38, 177–83

Van Loveren, H., Van Amsterdam, J.G., Vandebriel, R.J. et al. 2001. Vaccine-induced antibody responses as parameters of the influence of endogenous and environmental factors. *Environ Health Perspect*, 109, 757–64

Vedhara, K., Cox, N.K.M., Wilcock, G.K. et al. 1999. Chronic stress in elderly carers of dementia patients and antibody response to influenza vaccination. *Lancet*, 353, 627–631

Villanueva, A., Dominguez-Munoz, J.E. and Mearin, F. 2001. Update in the therapeutic management of irritable bowel syndrome. *Dig Dis*, 19, 244–50

Weigl, B.A. 2000. The significance of stress hormones (glucocorticoids, catecholamines) for eruptions and spontaneous remission phases in psoriasis. *Int J Dermatol*, 39, 678–88

Weisberg, R.B., Bruce, S.E., Machan, J.T. et al. 2002. Nonpsychiatric illness among primary care patients with trauma histories and post traumatic stress disorder. *Psychiatr Serv*, 53, 848–54

Zautra, A.J., Hoffman, J.M., Matt, K.S. et al. 1998. An examination of individual differences in the relationship between interpersonal stress and disease activity among women with rheumatoid arthritis. *Arthritis Care and Research*, 11, 271–279

Zipfel, S., Schneider, A., Wild, B. et al. 2002. Effect of depressive symptoms on survival after heart transplantation. *Psychosom Med*, 64, 740–747

Chapter 7 Treating depression and clinical anxiety

Albucher, R.C. and Liberzon, I. 2002. Psychopharmacological treatment in PTSD: a critical review. *J Psychiatr Res*, 36, 355

Garcia, R. 2002. Stress, synaptic plasticity, and psychopathology. *Rev Neurosci*, 13, 195–208

Goodwin, R.D., Stayner, D.A., Chinman, M.J. et al. 2002. The relationship between anxiety and substance use disorders among individuals with severe affective disorders. *Compr Psychiatry*, 43, 245–52

Gunnell, D., Rasul, F., Stansfeld, S.A. et al. 2002. Gender differences in self-reported minor mental disorder and its association with suicide. A 20-year follow-up of the Renfrew and Paisley cohort. *Soc Psychiatry Psychiatr Epidemiol*. 37, 457–9

Honey, K.L., Bennett, P. and Morgan, M. 2002. A brief psychoeducational group intervention for postnatal depression. *Br J Clin Psychol* 41, 405–9

Khan, A., Leventhal, R.M., Khan, S. et al. 2002. Suicide risk in patients with anxiety disorders: a meta-analysis of the FDA database. *J Affect Disord* 68(2–3), 183–90

Middleton, N., Gunnell, D., Whitley, E. et al. 2001. Secular trends in antidepressant prescribing in the UK, 1975–1998. *J Public Health Med*, 23, 262–7

Nazroo, J.Y. 1997. Ethnicity and mental health. London: Policy Studies Institute

Pezawas, L., Stamenkovic, M., Jagsch, R. et al. 2002. A longitudinal view of triggers and thresholds of suicidal behavior in depression. *J Clin Psychiatry*, 866–73

Piacentini, J., Bergman, R.L., Jacobs, C. et al. 2002. Open trial of cognitive behavior therapy for childhood obsessive-compulsive disorder. *J Anxiety Disord*, 16, 207–19

Schatzberg, A.F., Kremer, C., Rodrigues, H.E. et al. 2002. Double-blind, randomized comparison of mirtazapine and paroxetine in elderly depressed patients. *Am J Geriatr Psychiatry*, 10, 541–50

Skari, H., Skreden, M., Malt, U.F. et al. 2002. Comparative levels of psychological distress, stress symptoms, depression and anxiety after childbirth – a prospective population-based study of mothers and fathers. *BJOG*, 109, 1,154–63

Sonawalla, S.B., Farabaugh, A., Johnson, M.W. et al. 2002. Fluoxetine treatment of depressed patients with comorbid anxiety disorders. *J Psychopharmacol*, 16, 215–9

Thomas, H.V., Crawford, M., Meltzer, H. et al. 2002. Thinking life is not worth living. A population survey of Great Britain. *Soc Psychiatry Psychiatr Epidemiol*, 37, 351–6

Walsh, B.T., Seidman, S.N., Sysko, R. et al. 2002. Placebo Response in Studies of Major Depression Variable, Substantial, and Growing. *JAMA*, 287, 1,840–1,847

Wildes, J.E., Simons, A.D. and Harkness, K.L. 2002. Life events, number of social relationships, and twelve-month naturalistic course of major depression in a community sample of women. *Depress Anxiety*, 16, 104–13

Zhang, Z. and Hayward, M.D. 2001. Childlessness and the psychological well-being of older persons. *J Gerontol B Psychol Sci Soc Sci*, 56, S311–20

Chapter 8 Other psychological disorders linked to stress

Chambers, R. and Wakley, G. 2002. *Obesity and Overweight Matters in Primary Care*. Radcliffe

Dineen, R., Doyle, J., Bench, J. et al. 1999. The influence of training on tinnitus perception: an evaluation 12 months after tinnitus management training. *Br J Audiol*, 33, 29–51

Esch, T., Stefano, G.B., Fricchione, G.L. et al. 2002. The role of stress in neurodegenerative diseases and mental disorders. *Neuroendocrinol Lett*, 23, 199–208

Folmer, R.L., Griest, S.E., Meikle, M.B. et al. 1999. Tinnitus severity, loudness, and depression. *Otolaryngol Head Neck Surg*, 121, 48–51

Norman, R.M., Malla, A.K., McLean, T.S. et al. 2002. An evaluation of a stress management program for individuals with schizophrenia. *Schizophr Res*, 58, 293–303

Katzmarzyk, P.T. and Davis, C. 2001. Thinness and body shape of *Playboy* centerfolds from 1978 to 1998. *Int J Obes Relat Metab Disord*, 25, 590–2

Troop, N.A., Holbrey, A. and Treasure, J.L. 1998. Stress, coping, and crisis support in eating disorders. *Int J Eat Disord*, 24, 157–66

Troop, N.A. and Treasure, J.L. 1997. Psychosocial factors in the onset of eating disorders: responses to life-events and difficulties. *Br J Med Psychol*, 70, 373–85

Weber, C., Arck, P., Mazurek, B. et al. 2002. Impact of a relaxation training on psychometric and immunologic parameters in tinnitus sufferers. *J Psychosom Res*, 52, 29–33

Wiseman, G. 2002. *Nutrition & Health.* Taylor & Francis

Chapter 9 Beating insomnia and fatigue

Elsenbruch, S., Thompson, J.J., Hamish, M.J. et al. 2002. Behavioral and physiological sleep characteristics in women with irritable bowel syndrome. *Am J Gastroenterol*, 97, 2,306–14

Galea, S., Resnick, H., Ahern, J. et al. 2002. Post-traumatic stress disorder in Manhattan, New York City, after the September 11th terrorist attacks. *J Urban Health*, 79, 340–53

Hall, M., Buysse, D.J., Nowell, P.D. et al. 2000. Symptoms of Stress and Depression as Correlates of Sleep in Primary Insomnia. *Psychosomatic Medicine*, 62, 227–230

Jones, C.R. and Czajkowski, L. 2000. Evaluation and management of insomnia in menopause. *Clin Obstet Gynecol*, 43, 184–97

Leger, D. 2000. Public health and insomnia: Economic impact. *Sleep*, 23 (suppl 3), S69–S76

Owens, J.F. and Matthews, K.A. 1998. Sleep disturbance in healthy middle-aged women. *Maturitas*, 30, 41–50

Rogers, H.L. and Reilly, S.M. 2000. Health problems associated with international business travel. A critical review of the literature. *AAOHN J*, 48, 376–84

Wheatley, D. 2001. Stress-induced insomnia treated with kava and valerian: singly and in combination. *Hum Psychopharmacol*, 16, 353–356

Addresses

Action on Smoking and Health (ASH)
102 Clifton Street
London EC2A 4HW
Email: enquiries@ash.org.uk
Website: www.ash.org.uk

Age Concern Cymru
1 Cathedral Road
Cardiff CF11 9SD
Tel: 029-2037 1566
Fax: 029-2039 9562
Email:
enquiries@accymru.org.uk
Website: www.accymru.org.uk

Age Concern England
Astral House
1268 London Road
London SW16 4ER
Information line: (0800) 009966
Website: www.ace.org.uk

Age Concern Northern Ireland
3 Lower Crescent
Belfast BT7 1NR
Tel: 028-9024 5729
Fax: 028-9023 5479
Email: info@ageconcernni.org
Website: www.ageconcernni.org

Age Concern Scotland
Leonard Small House
113 Rose Street
Edinburgh EH2 3DT
Tel: 0131-220 3345
Freephone: (0800) 009966
Fax: 0131-220 2779
Email: enquiries@acscot.org.uk
Website:
www.ageconcernscotland.org.uk

Al-Anon Family Groups
61 Great Dover Street
London SE1 4YF
Helpline: 020-7403 0888
Fax: 020-7378 9910
Email: alanonuk@aol.com
Website: www.hexnet.co.uk/alanon

Al-Anon Information Centre
Mansfield Park Building
Unit 6
22 Mansfield Street
Glasgow G11 5QP
Helpline: 0141-339 8884
Website: www.hexnet.co.uk/alanon

Alcohol Concern
Waterbridge House
32–36 Loman Street
London SE1 0EE
Tel: 020-7928 7377
Fax: 020-7928 4644
Email:
contact@alcoholconcern.org.uk
Website: www.alcoholconcern.
org.uk

Alcoholics Anonymous
General Service Office
PO Box 1
Stonebow House
York YO1 7NJ
National helpline:
(0845) 769 7555
Website: www.alcoholics-
anonymous.org.uk

Amarant Trust
80 Lambeth Road
London SE1 7PW
Helpline: (01293) 413000
Tel: 020-7401 3855
Fax: 020-7928 9134
Email: jburrell@
amarant.fsbusiness.co.uk
Website: www.amarant.org.uk

Aromatherapy Organisations Council
Tel/Fax: (0870) 774 3477
Email: info@aocuk.net
Website: www.aocuk.net

Aromatherapy Trade Council
P.O. Box 387
Ipswich
Suffolk IP2 9AN
Tel/fax: (01473) 603630
Email: info@a-t-c.org.uk
Website: www.a-t-c.org.uk
Send a SAE for a general information booklet

Association of Child Psychotherapists
120 West Heath Road
London NW3 7TU
Tel: 020-8458 1609
Fax: 020-8450 1482
Email: acp@dial.pipex.com

Association of Professional Music Therapists
26 Hamlyn Road
Glastonbury
Somerset BA6 8HT
Tel/Fax: (01458) 834919
Email: APMToffice@aol.com
Website: www.apmt.org.uk

BackCare
16 Elmtree Road
Teddington
Middlesex TW11 8ST
Tel: 020-8977 5474
Fax: 020-8943 5318
Email: info@backcare.org.uk
Website: www.backcare.org.uk

The Berne Institute
Berne House
Kegworth DE74 2EN
Tel/Fax: (01509) 673649
Email: ta@theberne.com
Website: www.theberne.com

Biofeedback Foundation of Europe
PO Box 75416
1070 AK Amsterdam
The Netherlands
Tel: (00 31) 20 44 22 631
Fax: (00 31) 20 44 22 632
Email: info@bfe.org
Website: www.bfe.org

Breast Cancer Care
Kiln House
210 New Kings Road
London SW6 4NZ
Tel: 020-7384 2984
Helpline: (0808) 800 6000
Textphone: (0808) 800 6001
Fax: 020-7384 3387
Email:
info@breastcancercare.org.uk
Website: www.breastcancercare.
org.uk

British Association of Psychotherapists
37 Mapesbury Road
London NW2 4HJ
Tel: 020-8452 9823
Fax: 020-8452 5182
Email: mail@bap-
psychotherapy.org
Website: www.bap-
psychotherapy.org

British Association for Counselling and Psychotherapy
1 Regent Place
Rugby
Warks CV21 2PJ
Tel: (0870) 443 5252
Fax: (0870) 443 5160
Email: bacp@bacp.co.uk
Website: www.bacp.co.uk

British Autogenic Society
The Royal London
Homeopathic Hospital
Greenwell Street
London W1W 5BP
Tel/Fax: 020-7383 5108
Website: www.autogenic-
therapy.org.uk

British Confederation of Psychotherapists (BCP)
37 Mapesbury Road
London NW2 4HJ
Tel: 020-8830 5173
Email: mail@bcp.org.uk
Website: www.bcp.org.uk

British Massage Therapy Council
Email: info@bmtc.co.uk
Website: www.bmtc.co.uk

British Psychoanalytical Society
112A Shirland Road
London W9 2EQ
Tel: 020-7563 5000
Fax: 020-7663 5001
Email:
editors@psychoanalysis.org.uk
Website: www.psychoanalysis.
org.uk

British Snoring and Sleep Apnoea Association
2nd Floor Suite
52 Albert Road North
Reigate
Surrey RH2 9EL
Tel: (01737) 245638
Helpline: (0800) 0851097
Fax: (01737) 248744
Email: info@britishsnoring.
co.uk
Website: www.britishsnoring.
co.uk

British Society for Music Therapy
25 Rosslyn Avenue
East Barnet EN4 8DH
Tel/Fax: 020-8368 8879
Email: info@bsmt.org
Website: www.bsmt.org

British Tinnitus Association
Ground Floor
Unit 5
Acorn Business Park
Woodseats Close
Sheffield S8 0TB
Freephone: (0800) 018 0527
Tel: 0114-250 9933
Fax: 0114-258 7059
Email: info@tinnitus.org.uk
Website: www.tinnitus.org.uk

British Wheel of Yoga
25 Jermyn Street
Sleaford
Lincs NG34 7RU
Tel: (01529) 306851
Fax: (01529) 303233
Email: office@bwy.org.uk
Website: www.bwy.org.uk

The Buddhist Society
58 Eccleston Square
London SW1V 1PH
Tel: 020-7834 5858
Fax: 020-7976 5238
Email: info@thebuddhistsociety.
org.uk
Website:
www.thebuddhistsociety.org.uk

CancerBACUP
3 Bath Place
Rivington Street
London EC2A 3JR
Tel: 020-7739 2280
Freephone: (0808) 8001234
Fax: 020-7696 9002
Email:
jwhelan@cancerbacup.org.uk
Website: www.cancerbacup.
org.uk

Cancerlink
89 Albert Embankment
London SE1 7UQ
Tel: 020-7840 7840
Fax: 020-7840 7841
Website: www.cancerlink.org

Carers UK
20–25 Glasshouse Yard
London EC1A 4JT
Tel: 020-7490 8818
Fax: 020-7490 8824
Email: info@ukcarers.org
Website: www.carersonline.
org.uk

**Central Register of Advanced
Hypnotherapists**
PO Box 14526
London N4 2WG
Tel: 020-7354 9938
Website: www.n-shap-
ericksonian.co.uk/crah.htm

Childline
Studd Street
London N1 0QW
Helpline: (0800) 1111
Textphone: (0800) 400 222
Tel: 020-7239 1000
Fax: 020-7239 1001
Email: info@childline.org.uk
Website: www.childline.org.uk

The Compassionate Friends
53 North Street
Bristol BS3 1EN
Helpline: 0117-953 9639
Tel: 0117-966 5202
Fax: 0117-914 4368
Email: info@tcf.org.uk
Website: www.tcf.org.uk

Cruse
Cruse House
126 Sheen Road
Richmond
Surrey TW9 1UR
Tel: 020-8939 9530
Helpline: (0870) 167 1677
Fax: 020-8940 7368
Email: info@
crusebereavementcare.org.uk
Website: www.
crusebereavementcare.org.uk

Cry-sis
B.M. Cry-sis
London WC1N 3XX
Helpline: 020-7404 5011

Depression Alliance
35 Westminster Bridge Road
London SE1 7JB
Tel: 020-7633 0557
Fax: 020-7633 0559
Email: information@
depressionalliance.org
Website: www.
depressionalliance.org

Digestive Disorders Foundation
3 St Andrew's Place
London NW1 4LB
Tel: 020-7486 0341
Fax: 020-7224 2012
Email:
ddf@digestivedisorders.org.uk
Website:
www.digestivedisorders.org.uk

Eating Disorders Association
103 Prince of Wales Road
Norwich NR1 1JW
Adult helpline: (0845) 634 1414
Youthline: (0845) 634 7650
Administration: (0870) 770 3256
Fax: (0160) 366 4915
Email: info@edauk.com
Website: www.edauk.com

**Enuresis Resource and
Information Centre**
34 Old School House
Britannia Road
Kingswood
Bristol BS15 8DB
Helpline: 0117-960 3060
Fax: 0117-960 0401
Email: info@eric.org.uk
Website: www.eric.org.uk

Families Need Fathers
134 Curtain Road
London EC2A 3AR
Tel: 020-7613 5060
Email: fnf@fnf.org.uk
Website: www.fnf.org.uk

**Friends of the Earth England,
Wales and Northern Ireland**
26–28 Underwood Street
London N1 7JQ
Tel: 020-7490 1555
Fax: 020-7490 0881
Email: info@foe.co.uk
Website: www.foe.co.uk

Friends of the Earth Scotland
Information Department
72 Newhaven Road
Edinburgh EH6 5QG
Tel: 0131-554 9977
Fax: 0131-554 8656
Email: info@foe-scotland.org.uk
Website: www.foe-scotland.org.
uk

Gingerbread
7 Sovereign Close
Sovereign Court
London E1W 3HW
Tel: 020-7488 9300
Fax: 020-7488 9333
Email:
office@gingerbread.org.uk
Website: www.gingerbread.
org.uk

Greenpeace
Canonbury Villas
London N1 2PN
Tel: 020-7865 8100
Fax: 020-7865 8200
Email: info@ukgreenpeace.org
Website: www.greenpeace.
org.uk

Help the Aged England
207–221 Pentonville Road
London N1 9UZ
Tel: 020-7278 1114
Fax: 020-7278 1116
Email:
info@helptheaged.org.uk
Website: www.helptheaged.
org.uk

Help the Aged Northern Ireland
Ascot House
24–30 Shaftesbury Avenue
Belfast BT2 7DB
Tel: 028-9023 0666
Fax: 028-9024 8183
Email:
infoni@helptheaged.org.uk
Website: www.helptheaged.
org.uk

Help the Aged Scotland
11 Granton Square
Edinburgh EH5 1HX
Tel: 0131-551 6331
Fax: 0131-551 5415
Email:
infoscot@helptheaged.org.uk
Website: www.helptheaged.
org.uk

Help the Aged Wales
CSV House
Williams Way
Cardiff CF10 5DY
Tel: 029-2041 5711
Fax: 029-2041 5712
Email:
infocymru@helptheaged.org.uk
Website: www.helptheaged.
org.uk

IBS Network
Northern General Hospital
Sheffield
S5 7AU
Helpline: (01543) 492192
Website: www.ibsnetwork.
org.uk

Inland Revenue
Look in the phone book for
your local Inland Revenue
Enquiry Centre
Helpline: 020-7667 4001
Website: www.inlandrevenue.
gov.uk

Iyengar Yoga Institute
223a Randolph Avenue
London W9 1NL
Tel: 020-7624 3080
Fax: 020-7372 2726
Email: office@iyi.org.uk
Website: www.iyi.org.uk

Kidscape
2 Grosvenor Gardens
London SW1W 0DH
Tel: 020-7730 3300
Fax: 020-7730 7081
Email: info@kidscape.org.uk
Website: www.kidscape.org.uk

Leukaemia Care Society
2 Shrubbery Avenue
Worcester WR1 1QH
Helpline: (0800) 169 6680
Tel: (01905) 330003
Fax: (01905) 330090
Email:
enquiries@leukaemiacare.org.uk
Website: www.leukaemiacare.
org.uk

Lymphoma Association
PO Box 386
Aylesbury
Bucks HP20 2GA
Helpline: (0808) 808 5555
Tel: (01296) 619400
Fax: (01296) 619414
Email:
support@lymphoma.org.uk
Website: www.lymphoma.
org.uk

Manic Depression Fellowship
21 St George's Road
London SE1 6ES
Tel: 020-7793 2600
Fax: 020-7793 2639
Email: mdf@mdf.org.uk
Website: www.mdf.org.uk

Massage Therapy Institute of Great Britain
PO Box 2726
London NW2 4NR
Tel/Fax: 020-7724 4105

Migraine Action Association
Unit 6
Oakley Hay Lodge Business Park
Great Folds Road
Great Oakley
Northants NN18 9AS
Tel: (01536) 461333
Fax: (01536) 461444
Email: info@migraine.org.uk
Website: www.migraine.org.uk

Migraine Trust
45 Great Ormond Street
London WC1N 3HZ
Tel: 020-7831 4818
Fax: 020-7831 5174
Email: info@migrainetrust.org
Website: www.migrainetrust.
org

MIND
15–19 Broadway
London E15 4BQ
Tel: 020-8519 2122
Fax: 020-8522 1725
Email: contact@mind.org.uk
Website: www.mind. org.uk

MIND Cymru
3rd Floor
Quebec House
Castlebridge
5–19 Cowbridge Road East
Cardiff CF11 9AB
Tel: 029-2039 5123
Fax: 029-2022 1189
Website: www.mind.org.uk/
mindcymru/index.asp

National Association for Premenstrual Syndrome
41 Old Road
East Peckham
Kent TN12 5AP
Helpline: (0870) 7772177
Tel/Fax: (0870) 7772178
Email: contact@pms.org.uk
Website: www.pms.org.uk

National Asthma Campaign
Providence House
Providence Place
London N1 0NT
Helpline: (0845) 7010203
Tel: 020-7226 2260
Fax: 020-7704 0740
Website: www.asthma.org.uk

National Childbirth Trust
Alexandra House
Oldham Terrace
Acton
London W3 6NH
Enquiry line: (0870) 444 8707
Tel: (0870) 770 3236
Breastfeeding line:
(0870) 444 8708
Fax: 020-8992 5929
Email: enquiries@national-
childbirth-trust.co.uk
Website: www.nctpregnancyand
babycare.com

National Debtline
The Arch
48–52 Floodgate Street
Birmingham B5 5SL
Tel: (0808) 808 4000
Fax: 0121-703 6940
Email:
advice@nationaldebtline.co.uk
Website: www.nationaldebtline.
co.uk

National Eczema Society
Hill House
Highgate Hill
London N19 5NA
Helpline: (0870) 241 3604
Tel: 020-7281 3553
Fax: 020-7281 6395
Email: info@eczema.org
Website: www.eczema.org

National Federation of Solo Clubs
PO Box 2278
Nuneaton
Warwickshire CV11 5PA
Tel: 024-7673 6499
Website: www.federation-solo-
clubs.co.uk

National Institute of Medical Herbalists
56 Longbrook Street
Exeter EX4 6AH
Tel: (01392) 426022
Fax: (01392) 498963
Email:
nimh@ukexeter.freeserve.co.uk
Website: www.nimh.org.uk

National Phobics Society
Zion Community Resource
Centre
339 Stretford Road
Hulme
Manchester M15 4ZY
Helpline: (0870) 7700 456
Fax: 0161-227 9862
Email: natphob.soc@good.co.uk
Website: www.phobics-
society.org.uk

National Register of Hypnotherapists and Psychotherapists
Suite B
12 Cross Street
Nelson BB9 7EN
Helpline: (0800) 161 3823
Tel: (01282) 716839
Fax: (01282) 698633
Email: nrhp@btconnect.com
Website: www.nrhp.co.uk

NHS Direct
Tel: (0845) 4647
Website: www.nhsdirect.nhs.uk

Open University
PO Box 724
Milton Keynes
MK7 6ZS
Tel: (01908) 653231
Fax: (01908) 654806
Email: general-enquiries@open.ac.uk
Website: www3.open.ac.uk

Parentline Plus
Unit 520 Highgate Studios
53–57 Highgate Road
London NW5 1TL
Tel: (0808) 800 2222
Textphone: (0800) 783 6783
Email: headoffice@parentlineplus.org.uk
Website: www.parentlineplus.org.uk

Quitline
Ground Floor
211 Old Street
London EC1V 9NR
Advice line: (0800) 002200
Tel: 020-7251 1551
Fax: 020-7251 1661
Email: info@quit.org.uk
For smokers:
stopsmoking@quit.org.uk
Website: www.quit.org.uk

Registered Nursing Homes Association
15 Highfield Road
Edgbaston
Birmingham B15 3DU
Freephone: (0800) 0740194
Tel: 0121-454 2511
Fax: 0121-454 0932
Email: info@rnha.co.uk
Website: www.rnha.co.uk

Relate
Herbert Gray College
Little Church Street
Rugby
Warwickshire CV21 3AP
Tel: (0845) 456 1310
Fax: (01788) 535007
Email: enquiries@relate.org.uk
Website: www.relate.org.uk

Rethink
30 Tabernacle Street
London EC2A 4DD
Frontline: (0845) 456 0455
Advice line: 020-8974 6814
Fax: 020-7330 9102
Email: info@rethink.org
Website: www.rethink.org

Royal College of Psychiatrists
17 Belgrave Square
London SW1X 8PG
Tel: 020-7235 2351
Fax: 020-7245 1231
Email: rcpsych@rcpsych.ac.uk
Website: www.rcpsych.ac.uk

Royal National Institute for Deaf People
19–23 Featherstone Street
London EC1Y 8SL
Information line:
(0808) 808 0123
Tel: 020-7296 8000
Textphone: (0808) 808 9000
Fax: 020-7296 8199
Email: informationline@
rnid.org.uk
Website: www.rnid.org.uk

Samaritans
The Upper Mill
Kingston Road
Ewell
Surrey KT17 2AF
Helpline: (08457) 909090
Tel: 020-8394 8300
Fax: 020-8394 8301
Email: jo@samaritans.org
Website: www.samaritans.
org.uk

SANE
1st Floor
Cityside House
40 Adler Street
London E1 1EE
Saneline: (0845) 767 8000
Fax: 020-7375 2162
Email: sanelineadmin@sane.
org.uk
Website: www.sane.org.uk

Seasonal Affective Disorder Association
PO Box 989
Steyning
BN44 3HG
Website: www.sada.org.uk

Seniorline
Freephone: (0808) 800 6565
Tel: 020-7278 1114
Fax: 020-7278 1116
Email: info@helptheaged.
org.uk
Website: www.helptheaged.
org.uk

Shiatsu Society
Eastlands Court
St Peter's Road
Rugby
Warwick CV21 3QP
Tel: (0845) 130 4560 *(local rate)*
Fax: (01788) 555052
Email: admin@shiatsu.org
Website: www.shiatsu.org

Society of Analytical Psychology
1 Daleham Gardens
London
NW3 5BY
Tel: 020-7435 7696
Fax: 020-7431 1495
Email: sap@jungian-analysis.org
Website: www.jungian-analysis.
org

Stroke Association
Stroke House
240 City Road
London EC1V 2PR
Tel: 020-7566 0330
Fax: 020-7490 2686
Helpline: (0845) 303 3100
Email: info@stroke.org.uk
Website: www.stroke.org.uk

Tai Chi Union
1 Littlemill Drive
Crookston
Glasgow G53 7GE
Tel: 0141-810 3482
Email:
secretary@taichiunion.com
Website: www.taichiunion.com
Send a SAE for further information

Tenovus
43 The Parade
Cardiff CF24 3AB
Tel: 029-2048 2000
Fax: 029-2048 4199
Email: post@tenovus.com
Website: www.tenovus.com

Transcendental Meditation (TM)
Freepost
London SW1P 4YY
Tel: (0870) 514 3733
Email: info@t-m.org.uk
Website: www.transcendental-
meditation.org.uk

Triumph Over Phobia
PO Box 1831
Bath BA2 4YW
Tel: (01225) 330353
Fax: (01225) 469212
Email: triumphoverphobia@
compuserve.com
Website:
www.triumphoverphobia.com

**United Kingdom Council for
Psychotherapy (UKCP)**
167–169 Great Portland Street
London W1W 5PF
Tel: 020-7436 3002
Fax: 020-7436 3013
Email: ukcp@psychotherapy.
org.uk
Website: www.psychotherapy.
org.uk

Weight Watchers
Weight Watchers House
St Peters Road
Maidenhead
Berkshire SL6 7QZ
Tel: (0845) 3451500
Fax: (01628) 513048
Email: customerservice@
weight-watchers.co.uk
Website: www.weightwatchers.
co.uk

WellBeing
27 Sussex Place
Regents Park
London NW1 4SP
Tel: 020-7772 6400
Fax: 020-7724 7725
Email: wellbeing@rcog.org.uk
Website: www.wellbeing.org.uk

Which? Books
PO Box 44
Hertford SG14 1SH
Tel: (0800) 252100
Email: books@which.net
Website: www.which.net

Which? Magazine
PO Box 44
Hertford SG14 1SH
Tel: (0800) 252100
Email: which@which.net
Website: www.which.co.uk

Women's Health Concern
PO Box 2126
Marlow
Buckinghamshire SL7 2RY
Advice line: (01628) 483612
Fax: (01628) 474042
Email: info@womens-health-concern.org
Website: www.womens-health-concern.org

Index

WHICH? BOOKS

The following titles were available as this book went to press.

General reference (legal, financial, practical, etc.)

Be Your Own Financial Adviser	448pp	£10.99
420 Legal Problems Solved	352pp	£9.99
160 Letters that Get Results	352pp	£10.99
Rip-off Britain – and how to beat it	256pp	£5.99
What to Do When Someone Dies	192pp	£9.99
The Which? Computer Troubleshooter	192pp	£12.99
The Which? Guide to Baby Products	240pp	£9.99
The Which? Guide to Changing Careers	352pp	£10.99
The Which? Guide to Choosing a Career	336pp	£9.99
The Which? Guide to Choosing a School	336pp	£10.99
The Which? Guide to Computers	352pp	£10.99
The Which? Guide to Computers for Small Businesses	352pp	£10.99
The Which? Guide to Divorce	368pp	£10.99
The Which? Guide to Doing Your Own Conveyancing	208pp	£9.99
The Which? Guide to Employment	336pp	£11.99
The Which? Guide to Help in the Home	208pp	£9.99
The Which? Guide to Gambling	288pp	£9.99
The Which? Guide to Getting Married	256pp	£10.99
The Which? Guide to Giving and Inheriting	256pp	£9.99
The Which? Guide to Going Digital	272pp	£10.99
The Which? Guide to Insurance	320pp	£10.99
The Which? Guide to the Internet	320pp	£10.99
The Which? Guide to Living Together	192pp	£9.99
The Which? Guide to Money	448pp	£9.99
The Which? Guide to Money in Retirement	288pp	£10.99
The Which? Guide to Money on the Internet	256pp	£9.99
The Which? Guide to Planning Your Pension	368pp	£10.99

The Which? Guide to		
Renting and Letting	352pp	£11.99
The Which? Guide to Shares	288pp	£9.99
The Which? Guide to		
Working from Home	256pp	£9.99
Which? Way to		
Buy, Own and Sell a Flat	352pp	£10.99
Which? Way to		
Buy, Sell and Move House	320pp	£10.99
Which? Way to Clean It	256pp	£10.99
Which? Way to		
Drive Your Small Business	240pp	£10.99
Which? Way to		
Manage Your Time – and Your Life	208pp	£9.99
Which? Way to Save and Invest	336pp	£14.99
Which? Way to Save Tax	242pp	£14.99
Wills and Probate	192pp	£10.99
Make Your Own Will	28pp	£10.99

Action Pack (A5 wallet with forms and 28-page book inside)

Take Control of Your Pension	48pp	£10.99

Action Pack (A5 wallet with calculation sheets and 48-page book inside)

Health

The Which? Guide to Children's Health	288pp	£9.99
The Which? Guide to		
Complementary Therapies	256pp	£10.99
The Which? Guide to		
Managing Asthma	256pp	£9.99
The Which? Guide to		
Managing Back Trouble	160pp	£9.99
The Which? Guide to Managing Stress	252pp	£10.99
The Which? Guide to Men's Health	336pp	£9.99
The Which? Guide to Personal Health	320pp	£10.99
The Which? Guide to		
Women's Health	448pp	£9.99
Which? Medicine	544pp	£12.99

Gardening

The Gardening Which? Guide to Growing		
Your Own Vegetables (hardback)	224pp	£18.99
(paperback)	224pp	£12.99

The Gardening Which? Guide to		
Patio and Container Plants	224pp	£17.99
The Gardening Which? Guide to		
Small Gardens	224pp	£12.99
The Gardening Which? Guide to		
Successful Perennials	224pp	£12.99
The Gardening Which? Guide to		
Successful Propagation	160pp	£12.99
The Gardening Which? Guide to		
Successful Pruning	240pp	£12.99
The Gardening Which? Guide to		
Successful Shrubs	224pp	£12.99

Do-it-yourself

The Which? Book of		
Plumbing and Central Heating	160pp	£13.99
The Which? Book of Wiring and Lighting	160pp	£16.99
Which? Way to Fix It	208pp	£12.99

Travel/leisure

The Good Bed and Breakfast Guide 2002	624pp	£14.99
The Good Food Guide	768pp	£15.99
The Good		
Skiing and Snowboarding Guide	384pp	£15.99
The Good Walks Guide	320pp	£13.99
The Which? Guide to Country Pubs	576pp	£14.99
The Which? Guide to Pub Walks	256pp	£9.99
The Which? Guide to Scotland	528pp	£12.99
The Which? Guide to Tourist Attractions	544pp	£12.99
The Which? Guide to		
Weekend Breaks in Britain	528pp	£13.99
The Which? Hotel Guide	704pp	£15.99
The Which? Wine Guide	544pp	£14.99
Which? Holiday Destination	624pp	£12.99

Available from bookshops, and by post from:
Which?, Dept BKLIST, Castlemead,
Gascoyne Way, Hertford X, SG14 1LH
or phone FREE on (0800) 252100
quoting Dept BKLIST and your credit card details

The Which? Guide to Personal Health

From time to time, we all come up against personal health problems that we're reluctant to mention to anyone – even our doctors. They might be embarrassing, owing to where they occur in the body; they could be trivial, or mainly cosmetic, but are none the less troubling; or the symptoms could be so deeply disturbing that we hesitate to bring them to the attention of a medical professional for fear of what they may indicate.

If you are experiencing sexual difficulties or genito-urinary problems; are bothered about rashes, unwanted hair, body odours, wind or snoring; or are worried about a lump or a growth, or unexplained bleeding, let *The Which? Guide to Personal Health* be your medically-qualified confidant. In question-and-answer form, the book provides reassurance and advice that is easy to understand and to act upon. It gives you the key facts relating to your condition and the confidence to decide whether you need to seek help.

The author, Dr Ann Robinson, has over ten years' experience as a GP and a medical columnist. She offers possible solutions to real concerns – the ones that she knows, from her own patients and her many readers, that people worry about most. Her book deals with health matters at all stages of life, and covers both physical and psychological issues. *The Which? Guide to Personal Health* discusses treatment options and preventive measures, and lists useful organisations and support groups.

Paperback   216 x 135mm   320 pages   £10.99